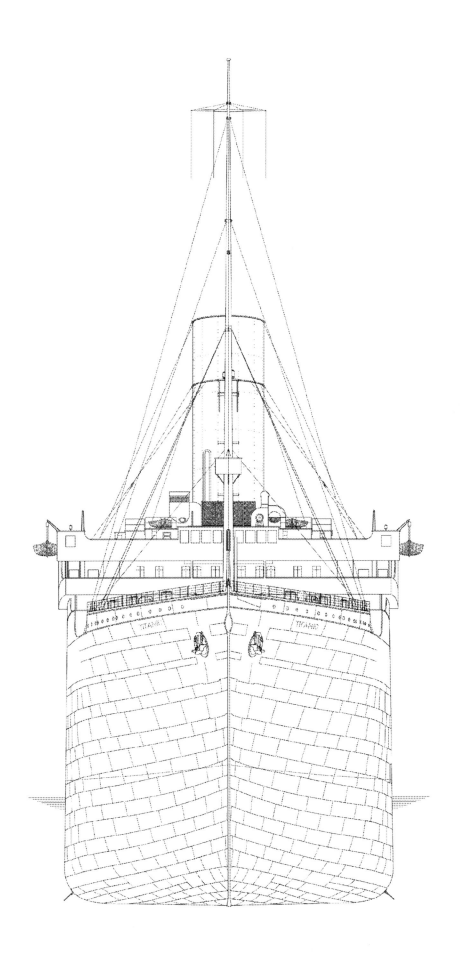

TITANIC & OLYMPIC

The Truth Behind the Conspiracy

Steve Hall lives in the small coastal town of Ballina in northern New South Wales. He has been active in the Titanic research field for some 15 years specializing in the photographic history of the ship. During these years he was amassed one of the largest privately held collections of Titanic photographs including many which continued to remain unpublished. Throughout this period he has held numerous Titanic photographic exhibitions, spoken extensively on the subject and had numerous articles published. He retired from the Information Technology industry several years ago and is presently writing a series of children's novels.

Bruce Beveridge is an Honorary Lifetime Member of the British Titanic Society, a member of The Titanic Historical Society, and the Irish Titanic Historical Society. He has written articles and columns for many publications based on the Olympic class liners. He is a founding member, and Trustee, of the Titanic Research and Modeling Association. He was the technical advisor of the Hahn Titanic Plans. He is considered a leader in the field when it comes to the exterior and general working arrangements of the Titanic.

TITANIC & OLYMPIC

The Truth Behind the Conspiracy

STEVE HALL AND BRUCE BEVERIDGE

ISBN 0-7414-1949-1

Published by:

PUBLISHING.COM

519 West Lancaster Avenue
Haverford, PA 19041-1413
Info@buybooksontheweb.com
www.buybooksontheweb.com
Toll-free (877) BUY BOOK
Local Phone (610) 520-2500
Fax (610) 519-0261

Printed in the United States of America
Printed on Recycled Paper
Published January 2004

Bruce Beveridge would like to dedicate this book to:
My wife Lisa, my children Sarah, Scott and Bill, and my father Karl, who have been the most effected
by the personal sacrifice brought on by co-writing this book.

Edited by: Kathy Savadel
Additional Editing. Karen Andrews
Cover Design by: Robert Barnes
Additional Text: Scott Andrews
Illustrations: Bruce Beveridge
Research Assistant: Robert Compton

C O N T E N T S

PREFACE

"The *Titanic* is unsinkable." This phrase, which rings a chord in the mind of any *Titanic* enthusiast, is re-iterated in nearly every *Titanic* book printed. Recently the phrase has taken on a new meaning in the ever-growing number of enthusiasts who keep her memory alive. Since 1912 the *Titanic* story has spawned research into everything from her passengers to her offerings of food.

Inaccurate stories are not new. Immediately after the sinking, there were even reports of Capt. Smith being seen on the streets of New York City. Some researchers, however, have used elements from the information available on the *Titanic* to form "conspiracy theories".

While researching this book, the authors uncovered stories that were farfetched, completely ridiculous, or both. The "Jesuit Conspiracy Theory", while offensive to many, is mentioned here as an example of the ridiculous.

The "Jesuit Conspiracy" evolved from individuals critical of J. P. Morgan, other bankers of the early 20th century and the Jesuit religious order of the Catholic Church. There are many variations of the conspiracy which is based on the belief that the Jesuits have been controlling world events behind the scenes for hundreds of years. One is as follows.

As the United States was without a national bank in the 1900s, the Jesuits of that era were seeking a means to fund their schemes and wars. In 1910, a clandestine meeting supposedly occurred on J.P. Morgan's "Jekyll Island" off the coast of Georgia, attended by Nelson Aldrich and Frank Vanderlip of the Rockefeller financial empire; Henry Davidson, Charles Norton and Benjamin Strong representing J.P. Morgan (a member of the Jesuit order); and Paul Warburg of the Rothschild banking dynasty of Europe (reportedly the banking agent for the Jesuits). Their sole common interest was the elimination of outside competition in the banking world. In order to control the growth of smaller American banks, they supported the creation of a central bank backed by the United States Government to be known later as the "Federal Reserve". This scheme however, was not supported by certain influential businessmen such as Benjamin Guggenheim, Isador Strauss and John Jacob Astor, arguably the wealthiest man in the world at the time. In order to eliminate these barriers, the Jesuits ordered Morgan to arrange for these three powerful "enemies" to board the *Titanic*, which was then building in the Protestant hot seat of Belfast, for a pre-arranged fatal maiden voyage.

The theory claims that Capt. Smith was a "Jesuit tempore co-adjator" (not a priest, but a Jesuit of the short robe who served the order through his profession). Therefore, an "accidental sinking" could be arranged by having his "Jesuit master" (reportedly, Father Francis Browne) board the liner for the short trip between Southampton and Cherbourg and order Smith, a veteran sea captain, to run his ship at full speed through an ice field on a moonless night, ignoring any ice warnings including those from the lookouts, with the purpose of hitting an iceberg severely enough to cause the ship to founder and these three men to drown. In other words, the ship was to be built and her crew and passengers were to be sacrificed to eliminate these three men. As their evidence, these theorists point out that after the sinking, all opposition to the Federal Reserve disappeared. In December of 1913, the Federal Reserve was brought to life in the United States, and eight months later the Jesuits had sufficient funding to launch a European war. This theory however, has never addressed why conspirators in 1910 would feel sinking a ship was an economical way to eliminate "enemies" or how they would arrange for all three victims to board a specific ship on a specific voyage two years later.

Until 1985, the wreck of the *Titanic* was a much sought after prize many considered equal to the quest for the Holy Grail. Over 50 books had been published covering the disaster from every conceivable angle. In the years following the discovery of the wreck, an estimated 120 new books were published, generally re-telling the same old story, albeit with a wealth of new technical data and photographs acquired during the numerous return expeditions to the wreck site. While answering many long-standing questions, the wreck has presented us with questions never considered prior to her discovery. Thus the "switch theory", the most publicized conspiracy, was born.

Simply put, the "switch theory" suggests that the wreck lying over 12,000 feet below the surface IS NOT the *Titanic*. The theory holds that severe, crippling damage to the *Olympic* caused by her collision with the *Hawke* was concealed because she was too costly to repair. The court hearing in the matter of the incident produced a judgment that both parties were to pay their own expenses, but the *Olympic* was found responsible of improper navigation. The White Star Line could not recover the cost of the repairs and lost income that was not covered by insurance. Therefore, the *Olympic* was "switched" with her new sister, the *Titanic*, and deliberately sunk AS the *Titanic*, for whom insurance claims would be paid.

Support for this theory is partially based on the following points:

- photographs taken of the *Titanic* on April 10th in Southampton show hull plates which appeared to be as faded and discolored as those of a ship which had been at sea for over 12 months, not those of a ship that had been recently painted.
- there were remnants of white paint found on hull of the wreck -- a color painted only on the *Olympic*, never on her younger sister, the *Titanic*.
- the fact that the *Titanic*, the world's newest and largest ship, was never opened for public inspection while she was at Southampton as was customary. (The theory holds that such public inspection may have revealed that the ship was, in actuality, the *Olympic*.)
- During the American investigation into the loss of the ship, Senator Smith persistently tried to establish whether the ship's lifeboats were new since almost none of the lifeboats had lanterns as required by the Board of Trade and some started leaking once lowered into the water. (The older lifeboats of the *Olympic* being susceptible to leakage unlike new boats as would be installed on the *Titanic*.)
- Supposedly, there was a conversation on the MV *Kooliga*, an Australian vessel, in 1971, in which a person claiming to be a surviving *Titanic* crewman stated that when he joined the ship at Belfast, he heard rumors that the two ships had been switched and that the true reason for the sinking of the ship had been covered up.
- Was it at all possible to have successfully switched the ships?
  There was one opportunity – possibly the greatest April fools day lark of all time.

This theory does not address how the White Star Line could successfully and *secretly* switch these two huge ships despite the presence of thousands of Harland & Wolff employees and, as with most conspiracies, does not hold up to technical scrutiny. It seems, in fact, that "switch theorists" have never researched basic principles of ship construction nor have they taken the time to carefully analyze photographs.

There is no question that the wreck can only be one of two ships; either it is the *Titanic* or her nearly identical sister, the *Olympic*. Those agreeing that the wreck is the *Titanic* point to the fact that the number 401 was sighted on the thrust side of one of the wreck's propeller blades. However, the switch theorists believe the propeller blade was merely one borrowed from the *Titanic* when the *Olympic* was laid up for the *Hawke* collision repairs.

Claims that the *Titanic* sported nameplates, as opposed to engraved letters, at the *bow* are also surrounded by controversy. Is the name and port of registry on the stern missing from the wreck because the letters were not attached properly during construction or because the *Titanic's* name plates had been hastily relocated to the *Olympic* during the "switch" prior to departing Belfast?

Over the course of time, theory and fact have a way of becoming intertwined. It is the intent of this book to examine this "switch theory" and some of the mysteries surrounding the *Titanic* and her nearly identical sister, the *Olympic*. The wreck that today sits over 12,000 feet below the waters of the icy North Atlantic is nothing more than a crumpled and dismembered steel hulk. Is the ship really Titanic?

C H A P T E R   1

Ismay's Titans

The *Olympic*-class liners—namely, the *Olympic,* the *Titanic,* and the *Britannic*—represented a 50% increase in size over the Cunard vessels *Lusitania* and *Mauretania,* which were the largest and fastest liners in the world at that time. Although the *Olympic*-class liners would not be as fast as the two Cunard greyhounds, White Star's policy was to emphasize passenger accommodations rather than speed.

To facilitate the construction of these three colossal vessels, Harland & Wolff would be required to make major modifications to its shipyard construction facilities. Two new slips were constructed, covering an area that was originally used to construct three ships. The William Arrol Company Ltd. was contracted to construct these new huge gantries. When completed, they covered an area of approximately 840 ft - 270 ft.

Although the *Olympic*-class liners were originally conceived by Bruce Ismay Managing Director of the White Star Line, and Lord Pirrie, Managing Director of Harland & Wolff, they were planned and designed by the shipyard's principal architect, Alexander Carlisle. Thomas Andrews was head of the yard's design department and oversaw the creation of the class prototype's plans, but Carlisle took charge of the details. Carlisle resigned from Harland & Wolff in 1911 and took a position with the Welin Davit Company, which manufactured and supplied the lifeboat davits for the *Olympic* and the *Titanic.* Throughout all of the stages of design and planning, all drawings and specifications were submitted to Ismay for his approval. Any modifications or suggestions he believed necessary were without doubt carried out. History tells us that all his later suggestions were aesthetically based.

The *Olympic* and the *Titanic* were built first, within close temporal proximity of each other, whereas the *Britannic* was not added to the fleet until the summer of 1914. When completed, the three ships registered in at approximately 45,500 gross tons each (the *Britannic* would later register at about 50,000 tons) and measured 882 ft, 9 in. long and 92 ft, 6 in. wide at the maximum breadth of the ship. As a comparison to later ships, the German-registered *Imperator* (1913) was 909 ft. long, and the *Queen Mary* (1936), was just over 1,000 ft.

The *Olympic*-class ships were driven by a triple-screw arrangement. Two giant reciprocating engines drove her port and starboard wing propellers, while a low-pressure turbine drove the centerline shaft. The port and starboard propellers were each three bladed; had a diameter of 23 ft, 6 in.; and weighed a massive 38 tons each. They were of "built-up" construction, having manganese bronze blades bolted onto a cast steel hub. The center propeller had a diameter of 16 ft, 6 in. and weighed 22 tons. It had four blades and was cast as a single piece in manganese bronze. Because the turbine was not equipped to move in "reverse", the center propeller operated only in the "ahead" direction.

The reciprocating engines were of the four-cylinder, triple-expansion, direct-acting inverted type configuration with a high, an intermediate, and two low-pressure cylinder bores of 54-in., 84-in., and 97-in. diameter, respectively, all with a 75-in. stroke. Each of these engines developed 15,000 IHP (indicated horsepower) at 75 rpm. The low-pressure turbine developed around 16,000 SHP (shaft horsepower) at 165 rpm. The exhaust steam drove this center turbine from the two reciprocating engines. Harland & Wolff manufactured all three of the sister's turbines which were basically the same in general design and in that they operated only in the "ahead" direction. However, the *Britannic's* turbine could deliver 18,000 horsepower and was the largest marine turbine ever constructed, although it certainly was not the most powerful. This impressive array of machinery was capable of generating up to 51,000 horsepower combined, giving the ships a service speed of 21—21½ knots. The maximum speed of each ship was believed to be 24 knots. The steam required to power all this machinery was provided by 29 huge boilers that comprised 159 furnaces. These furnaces had a heating surface of approximately 144,142 square ft. There were 24 double-ended boilers and 5 single-ended boilers. These boilers provided a maximum steam pressure of 215 psi. To feed these massive boilers, the ship's coal bunkers had a combined capacity of 6,611 tons and, operating at 21—22 knots, could consume 620—640 tons of coal per day, all hand fed by shovel. A further 1,092 tons of coal could be shipped in the reserve bunker hold forward of boiler room number 6.

The frames of the *Olympic*-class ships were constructed from 10-in. steel channels, which were spaced 36 in. apart amidships, which was gradually reduced to 24 in. forward and 27 in. aft. Attached to these ribs were the hull, or shell, plates. The shell plates were fastened with rivets that were applied both by hand hammering and hydraulic press. It is a common misunderstanding that all of the rivets were hydraulically applied. This is not true. The hydraulic riveting machine had limitations—for example, its jaws could not be worked around more than moderate bends in the plates or get into confined areas. More than half a million rivets were used on the double bottoms of these ships, and the weight of these rivets alone was estimated to be 270 tons. When completed, each ship had about 3 million rivets with an estimated weight of over 1,200 tons.

On average, the shell plates used on these ships were 6 ft wide and 30 ft long and weighed between 2½ and 3 tons each. The largest shell plating used was 36 ft long and weighed 4¼ tons. The thickness of the plates averaged 1 in. amidships and thinned toward the ends but was thicker in other areas depending on the need for extra strength. Each ship was fitted with a cellular double bottom, 5ft, 3in. deep throughout the ship's length, which increased to 6ft, 3 in. in the reciprocating-engine room. This double-bottom structure was divided into 75 separate compartments. These compartments were used for the storage of fresh water, for makeup boiler feed water, for domestic use, and to hold water ballast for trimming the ship.

The hulls were divided into 16 watertight compartments. The forward, or "collision" bulkhead was carried to C deck, whereas those from the forward end of the reciprocating engines and aft were carried to D deck. The remainder of these bulkheads terminated at E deck, with the top of the lowest of these—the bulkhead between boiler rooms 1 and 2—being 10 ft, 9 in. above the maximum-load waterline. This arrangement allowed the *Olympic* and *Titanic* to easily withstand a breach of two adjacent compartments amidships, typical of the damage sustained through a collision with other ships. Furthermore, each ship was capable of remaining afloat with all of the first four compartments flooded, providing ample protection if the ship rammed a floating body in her path.

After the sinking of the *Titanic*, the *Olympic* and *Britannic* were fitted with an extra bulkhead in the electric engine room, resulting in a total of 17 watertight compartments. Along with this, five of the bulkheads were extended some 40 ft above the waterline as far up as the bridge deck.

Access through each of these transverse bulkheads was gained by means of watertight doors, which were held in the open position by a friction clutch. The doors could be released by means of a powerful electromagnet that was controlled by a switch on the bridge. These doors could also be closed on site by a releasing lever in the event of a switch failure, or from the deck above. The doors were also coupled to a float-activated switch; in the event that the compartment flooded and the water reached a predetermined level, the doors would close automatically.

The ships had four huge funnels rising 72 ft above the boat deck. Elliptical in section, they measured 24 ft, 6 in. - 19 ft and had a rake of 2 in./ft. The funnels were painted black at the top to mask the accumulation residue caused by the smoke. The fourth funnel was a dummy; however, many artists at the time took some artistic license and often showed smoke pouring from all four funnels. In actuality, the ship's fourth funnel was used for ventilation of the turbine engine room, galleys, and fumes emitted from the turbine engine. It was thought at the time that it would be more aesthetic to have four funnels for such a large ship. This gave the illusion of power and stability, which the public bought into, and also followed the four-funnel arrangement seen on some of the German liners as well as the Cunard liners *Lusitania* and *Mauretania*.

Each ship was fitted with two masts, which towered at a height of 205 ft and, like the funnels, had a rake of 2 in/ft. The foremast was fitted with a derrick for lifting heavy items, such as automobiles, into the foreholds. The ladder to the crows nest also was located inside the foremast, and was accessed on C deck.

The *Olympic*-class liners were each fitted with a cast steel rudder, which weighed 101¼ tons and had an overall length of 78 ft, 8 in. and a width of 15 ft., 3 in. The rudders of these liners were unbalanced and were later believed by some to be too small. It is commonly believed that the size of the rudder was one of the critical flaws that contributed to the *Titanic* disaster, although this notion was effectively disputed in the discussions following publication of the article "*Titanic*, The Anatomy of a Disaster: A Report From the Marine Forensic Panel (SD-7)" by William H. Garzke, Jr., et al. In their commentary on page 50 of the article, naval architects Chris Hackett and John Bedford stated that "It must also be remembered that, although the rudder area was lower than we would adopt nowadays, *Olympic's* turning circles compare favorably with today's standards." Their conclusion was arrived at and based on hard data rather than the speculation and conjecture on which statements to the contrary have been based.

Mounted on both sides of each ship, at the very bottom curve of the hull, was a pair of 300-ft long bilge keels. They were located about amidships and were 25 in. in depth. The bilge keels were used to reduce the rolling motion of the ship in heavy seas. The *Olympic*-class ships were each fitted with five anchors. The center anchor, called the bower anchor, weighed 15 ¼ long tons and could be lowered by a wire rope through the extra hawse pipe in the ship's stem. This center anchor was stowed in a recessed well immediately abaft the ship's stem at the forepeak. A crane for lowering the anchor over the side was fitted at the centerline of the fo´c'sle deck. Both the port and starboard side anchors weighed approximately 8 long tons each and were connected to 330 fathoms of chain, which had an accumulated weight of approximately 98 long tons. Each anchor had the manufacturer's name molded (raised) on it, as well as a serial ID number and the weight. On *Olympic*, the anchors were numbered: center 644, starboard 644s and port 644x. For *Titanic*: center 617, starboard 617s and port 617x. The numbers on the port and starboard anchors were located inboard as fitted, in other words, not visible once attached to the ship. However, on the center 15 ¼ ton anchor, the ID number & manufacturer's name were cast on the same side.

The main whistles were located only on the first and second funnels. They were manufactured by Smith Brothers and Co., Nottingham, England. The whistles seen on the third and fourth funnels were dummies, installed for appearance only. Each whistle comprised three separate bells mounted on a common branch piece, the starboard diameter being 9 in., the center diameter 15 in., and the port diameter 12 in. These whistles were electrically operated on the Willett—Bruce system from the ship's bridge. They could be operated either manually or by engaging an electric timer, which would automatically blow the whistles for approximately 10 seconds every minute. This practice was required during fog or inclement weather. Some witnesses said at the time that the whistles were so loud they could be heard 10 miles away when sounded at Southampton when the atmospheric conditions were right.

The ships had eight full steel decks, the uppermost being the ship's boat deck. The deck below the boat deck was designated A deck, and then the decks progressively descended alphabetically down to the ship's lowest level, G deck. Directly below G deck were the final three levels, these being the orlop decks fore and aft, a lower orlop deck forward, and finally, the tank top.

The boat decks of the *Olympic* and the *Titanic* were where 18 of the lifeboats were fitted: Sixteen wooden lifeboats were hung beneath Welin double-acting davits, and 2 Engelhardt collapsibles, designated C and D, were secured to the deck itself. There were 2 more Engelhardt collapsible lifeboats, designated A and B, secured to the roof of the officers' quarters forward. The ships were originally planned by Carlisle to carry 64 lifeboats; the double-acting Welin davits were specially designed to launch up to 3 or 4 lifeboats from one location. The number was then decreased to 32. However, sometime between March 9 and March 16, 1910, the number was reduced to 16—the minimum number required by the Board of Trade. By fitting these extra 4 Engelhardt collapsibles, White Star exceeded the Board of Trade requirements for vessels over 10,000 tons by 17%. The required lifeboat capacity, expressed in cubic capacity, set by the Board of Trade for these massive 45,000-ton ships was 9,625 cubic feet; however, the first two *Olympic*-class liners carried lifeboats with a capacity of 11,327 cubic feet.

The *Titanic* carried the arrangement of 14 standard (30-ft) lifeboats, 2 emergency cutters (25 ft 2 in), and the 4 Engelhardt collapsibles (27 ft 5 in). These Engelhardt lifeboats were called *collapsibles* because they had adjustable canvas sides that could be pulled up and snapped taut.

The 14 standard lifeboats and the 2 emergency cutters were all permanently suspended beneath the 16 Welin double-acting davits. The total lifeboat capacity was 1,178 people. The ships carried 48 life buoys and 3,560 life jackets.

The ships were designed with an extensive array of electrically operated equipment. Each liner had more than 200 miles of cable installed to operate the large assortment of machinery: winches and cranes, electric heaters, electrically operated kitchen appliances, a 50-line telephone switchboard, a wireless telegraph set, fans, and ventilators, plus dozens of other electrically operated appliances. Electric passenger elevators—three in first class and one in second class—were installed in the passenger reception areas. In addition, four electric service lifts were provided, one with its terminus in the officers' pantry and another whose terminus was in the restaurant pantry. The service lifts were used between D deck and the bridge deck, to move provisions from the storerooms to the galleys, and for lowering and raising mailbags, stores and supplies. Also fitted to the ships were more than 1,500 electric bell pushes, or service buttons, mostly mounted on wall plates attached conveniently close to the normal lighting switches. Forty-eight clocks were in use, which could all be adjusted simultaneously by two master clocks located in the chart room. All clocks were electrically linked for quick and uniform adjustment.

There were literally hundreds of miles of electrical cable and plumbing pipes running all over these massive ships; the lighting alone was provided by way of approximately 10,000 incandescent lamps. The electrical supply required to operate these "floating cities" was supplied by way of four 400-kilowatt, 100-volt DC steam-operated generators. As a reserve, there were two 30-kilowatt emergency generators, which were situated on the ship's D deck.

The Marconi room, with its 5-kilowatt radio transmitter, was located on the ship's boat deck, adjoining the officers' cabins. The transmitting apparatus for this powerful radio transmitter was connected to four parallel aerial wires, extended between the ship's towering masts. These wires were attached to the very top of the masts by way of light spans that acted as spreaders to keep the wires from touching. From these aerial wires, cables led directly to the radio equipment in the wireless room. The radios consisted of two complete sets of apparatus: one for transmitting and the other for receiving transmissions. The transmitters had a guaranteed minimum range of 400 miles; however, at night or during certain atmospheric conditions, the range of this equipment extended to more than 2,000 miles.

In addition, the ships were fitted with two large electrically operated Morse lamps, which were positioned on the roofs of both the port and starboard side bridge wing cabs and were equipped with a large array of various pyrotechnic signaling rockets

Each ship had four Lord Kelvin standard compasses. One of these was located on the captain's bridge, with a second one located immediately aft inside the wheelhouse. The third one was located on the stern docking bridge. The fourth compass was installed on a large brass work platform located between the second and third funnels. This elevated platform rose 12 ft above the boat deck so it would be located well above any surrounding ironwork. This allowed accurate compass readings, as the compass was free of any metallic interference.

The luxurious accommodations for the passengers were augmented by the addition of a well-equipped gymnasium that was 45ft, 6in. long and 17ft, 3in. wide, with an impressive 9ft, 6in. high ceiling. The gymnasium was situated on the Boat deck, immediately abaft the forward grand entrance and staircase. It was lighted by the usual electric lighting; however, this was also supplemented by eight large pebbled windows that provided natural light. It boasted such equipment as an electrically driven mechanical horse and camel, two fixed cycling bikes, a weight lifting press, and even a boat rowing machine.

Turkish baths were located on F deck and included such facilities as steaming, shampooing, and cooling rooms as well as an electric bath that was available for women between 10:00 a.m. and 1:00 p.m. and for men between 2:00 p.m. and 6:00 p.m.

There was a heated, 6-ft deep, tiled saltwater swimming pool, with changing-room facilities, 30 ft long and 20 ft wide, located on the starboard side of F deck. The *Olympic* and the *Titanic* were not the first ships to have a swimming pool. Other ships had small pools, called *plunge baths*, but the *Olympic*-class ships were the first to have large swimming pools.

A squash court, measuring 30 ft long and 20 ft wide, located on G deck, was provided for athletically inclined passengers. The facility also boasted an elevated spectator gallery, located at the after end of the court.

For passengers inclined to take in the sun, deck chairs covered in a steamer blanket could be checked out for the cost of $1. The ships published a daily newspaper called the *Atlantic Daily Bulletin,* which carried articles such as the daily menus, horse racing results, advertisements for on-board activities, and society gossip.

The passenger capacity for the *Olympic*-class liners was generally as follows: 735 first class; 674 second class; and 1,026 third, or steerage. The crew numbered approximately 900, 500 of whom—such as cooks, stewards, store and laundry attendants—looked directly after the passengers. There were 320 crewmen actively employed in the mechanical workings of the ship, such as fireman, trimmers, engineers, and electricians.

In addition, there were 65 crewmen who belonged to the navigating department; they comprised lookouts, quartermasters, and able seamen. The captain and his seven deck officers were responsible for the safe navigation and management of the ship. The ships' staff also included two radio operators who were contracted through (i.e., employed by) the Marconi Company and numerous privately employed restaurant personnel and musicians. The ships would eventually be certified safe for the transportation of 3,547 people.

C H A P T E R   2

Olympic and Titanic

Work on the construction of the *Olympic*, keel number 400, commenced on December 16, 1908. By January 1, 1909, the *Olympic*'s hydraulically riveted keel had been completed. By this time the workforce at Harland & Wolff had grown to well over 10,000 workers. In less than 3 months, when the keel of her sister ship *Titanic* was laid on the adjacent slip; the workforce had increased to approximately 14,000. At this stage it should be noted that not all of these workers were actively engaged in the construction of these two ships. Harland & Wolff had other contractual arrangements with other shipping companies, and work on other contracts proceeded in other parts of the yard. Approximately 6,000 men were involved with the building of the *Olympic* and *Titanic*, about one-sixth of whom were on nightshift.

While work on the *Olympic* and *Titanic* was in progress, construction was underway on the new White Star Line tenders *Nomadic* and *Traffic*. These tenders were specially constructed to service all White Star Line steamers calling at Cherbourg. The shipyard was also constructing the George Thompson & Co. Liner *Demosthenes* and the Union Castle liner *Galway Castle*, as well as other smaller projects.

After the keel of the *Olympic* was laid, work proceeded at a brisk pace. Photographs reveal that by late November 1909 all but the last of the ship's frames had been raised into position. By late April 1910 the hull of the *Olympic* was completed. As with the ship's keel, hydraulic riveting had been adopted whenever possible. The seams of the *Olympic*'s bottom hull plating were double riveted, whereas the top side hull plating had been triple and quadruple riveted for extra strength.

For the last 6 months, work had been continuing within the hull of the *Olympic* with the laying of deck plating, transverse bulkheads, plumbing, electrical work, and the fitting of auxiliary equipment. The ship's heavy machinery, such as boilers and engines, would be lowered into the hull after the ship had been launched. Looking at the launch photographs, one can notice two very obvious details. First, the ship's funnels had not been fitted. The reason for this is so the aforementioned boilers and other heavy machinery could be lowered into the hull through the funnel casing openings. The second item of interest is that the ship's hull had been painted a very light gray, with a red ochre paint applied below the ship's intended waterline.

Olympic *at time of her launch October 20, 1910*

Titanic *prior to launch on May 31ˢᵗ 1911*

Lord Pirrie directed the white to be painted on the hull of the *Olympic* to add a dramatic visual appearance while she slid down the slipway into the River Lagan. The light paint would give the hull an overwhelming appearance of size, providing excellent photographic opportunities for the press to capture what was to be the world's largest ship*. Pirrie's decision to paint the ship's hull light gray to grab maximum press coverage would later pay handsome dividends as the photographs were seen worldwide. Following the *Olympic*'s launch, her hull would be painted with the traditional dark gray undercoat. The practice of painting the ship's hull light gray appeared to be the one and only time this would be done concerning the later sisters, as the *Titanic* and, later, the *Britannic*, would be painted in the traditional dark gray right from the beginning.

It is believed that on October 20, 1910, well over 100,000 people witnessed the launching of the *Olympic,* with the normal press, dignitaries, and senior management of Harland & Wolff and the White Star Line present. The *Olympic*'s launch weight, excluding the launch cradle, was 24,600 tons, and the bearing surface pressure would be 2.6 tons per square ft. To lubricate the slipway and reduce the friction on the ways, some 15 tons of tallow and 3 tons of train oil mixed with 3 tons of soft soap were used. Just before 12:15 p.m. the last of the supporting shores had been removed, leaving the *Olympic* resting solely on the fore and aft poppets and the sliding ways. Only 62 seconds after the launch triggers had been released the ship slid gracefully stern first into Belfast's River Lagan. The 24,600-ton hull reached a maximum speed of 12½ knots before being brought to a standstill by 6 anchors and 80 tons of drag cable and chain.

At 12.15 p.m. on 20th October 1910 the Olympic *was successfully launched.*

May 31st 1911, seven months after Olympic's *launch, the* Titanic *slides stern first into the River Lagan.*

Following her launch, the *Olympic* was taken in tow by tugs and was moored at the new deep-water wharf, which was owned and operated by the Belfast Harbor Authority. To bring all the heavy machinery from the workshops to the outfitting wharf, Harland & Wolff operated a steam tram with small rail trucks, which could carry all the necessary equipment, such as boilers, funnels, engine bedplates, turbines, condensers, and other peripheral equipment. An extensive network of rail lines ran throughout the yard and terminated at the outfitting wharf.

To facilitate the raising and lowering of all the heavy equipment from the dockside onto the ship, Harland & Wolff purchased a 200-ton floating crane with a maximum lifting weight of 150 tons, a lifting height of 150 ft, and a loading radius of 100 ft. The crane also had a smaller cable-operated hook, capable of lifting 50 tons. By the last week of March 1911, the ship's four funnels and two towering masts had been fitted. All of the heavy machinery, such as boilers, reciprocating engines, turbine engine, and so on, had been lowered and secured to their bedplates.

On April 1, 1911, the *Olympic* was docked in the new, Belfast harbor commissioner's Thompson dry dock. This dock had been specifically constructed for this new generation of super liner and was

---

*The Olympic's hull was actually painted in light gray while the sheer strakes were painted white. This was by no means the first and last time a ship would be painted white at the time of launch. It was common practice for the first of a class or a special ship to be painted a light color, and this was true for the *Mauretania*, *Oceanic*, and *Queen Mary* to name only a few well known liners.

quite impressive in its dimensions. The length of the dry dock floor was 850 ft, with a width of 100 ft. This length could be extended to 886 ft, 7½ in. if a caisson were placed against the outer facing quoins. The dock floor depth at the center, below the level of high water of ordinary spring tides, was 37 ft, 3 in. The distance from the top of the dry dock coping level to the base of the dry dock measured 43 ft, 6 in.

In the months following the *Olympic's* dry docking, most members of the workforce that had been actively engaged in the ship's construction were now completing the interiors. This consisted of painting, laying carpet and tile, installing plumbing and electrical fixtures, and so on. By this stage the ship was receiving her final coat of black paint, and the ship's three massive propellers were being fitted onto the shafts. During the last week of April 1911, the dry dock was flooded, and the *Olympic* was removed and berthed in the deep water outfitting basin. On May 2, 1911, the *Olympic* underwent her basin trials, during which the engines were turned for the first time.

Before departing on her sea trials on the morning of May 29, 1911, the world's newest and largest liner was opened for public inspection. A small admission fee was charged, and thousands of people took the opportunity to see the new liner. All of the money collected was donated to various Belfast hospitals.

On May 29 the *Olympic* steamed through the Belfast Lough and the Victoria Channel for her sea and acceptance trials. She was under the command of the White Star Line's most senior and experienced captain, E.J. Smith. Having been loaded with over 3,000 tons of Welsh coal a few days prior, her sea trials extended over a period of two days. The trials proved that the ship was slightly faster and more maneuverable than had been originally expected by the builders. At the completion of her trials, Mr. Francis Carruthers, the Board of Trade Surveyor, issued a seaworthiness certificate valid for one year. Carruthers is believed to have inspected the *Olympic* on no less than 2,000 occasions during her construction. Following the completion of her sea trials, the *Olympic* returned to Belfast Lough to be present for the launching of her younger, and soon to be larger sister, the *Titanic*.

Olympic *sporting 14 portholes along her fo´c'sle on October 20ᵗʰ 1910*

Titanic *on May 31ˢᵗ 1911. Notice the 14 portholes along her fo´c'sle*

The *Olympic* sailed on her maiden voyage at 4:30 p.m. on May 31ˢᵗ 1911, stopping first for a courtesy call to her official port of registry, Liverpool. It was at this time that the *Olympic* was officially handed over from the builders to her new owners, the White Star Line, who now had the world's largest and most luxurious liner afloat. On her arrival at Liverpool on June 1, 1911, the *Olympic* was moored in the Mersey and was opened for public inspection. Just before midnight that same evening, the *Olympic* weighed anchor and steamed for Southampton.

The *Olympic* was berthed at the White Star Dock in the early hours of June 3, 1911, on arriving at Southampton. The ship was provisioned, last-minute mechanical adjustments were made, and some furniture and fittings were installed that had been waiting at Harland & Wolff's facility in Southampton. The *Olympic* was ready to leave on her maiden voyage and was scheduled to depart at midday on June 14, 1911.

The *Olympic* departed Southampton with 1,316 passengers and 850 crew on board; her first port of call was Cherbourg, France. After collecting passengers in Cherbourg, the *Olympic* proceeded to Queenstown (now Cobh), Ireland. From there, she made her first transatlantic crossing to New York. The *Olympic* arrived in New York on June 21, 1911—5 days, 16 hours, and 42 minutes after departing Queenstown, having traveled an average speed of 21.7 knots. The *Olympic* was maneuvered into the White Star Line's temporarily lengthened Pier 59, but not without incident. She damaged one of the assisting tugs, the *O.L. Hallenbeck*, which was caught up in the suction created by the liner's propellers and dragged under her counter. On the *Olympic*'s return voyage from New York to Queenstown on June 28, 1911, she averaged nearly 22.7 knots, arriving at Southampton on July 5, 1911—an excellent time when one considers that not all of the boilers had been fired to conserve fuel.

Olympic *at the outfitting wharf*

A similar view of Titanic *at the outfitting wharf. August 1911*

The *Olympic* was never intended to be a contender for the Blue Riband, and her return average speed of 22.7 knots proved she would not be a greyhound like the Cunard liners *Lusitania* and *Mauretania*. She did prove, however, that she could easily maintain the White Star Line's weekly service operating out of New York and Southampton. The Cunarders were not quick enough to operate a two-ship weekly return service from New York, so the additional 4- or 5-knot advantage that the Cunard ships had over White Star was to prove to no great advantage. Although many passengers enjoyed traveling on the fastest ships, White Star had an unassailable position in size, luxury, and safety over their Cunard competitors.

Before the *Olympic* entered service, the White Star Line was already operating a weekly

Olympic *tied up waiting for the dry-dock to be cleared. As can be seen, these ships are almost identical. March 2ⁿᵈ 1912*

Titanic *secured to the outfitting wharf after being removed from dry-dock. March 2ⁿᵈ 1912*

transatlantic service between Southampton and New York, with the 21-knot *Oceanic* (17,274 gross register tonnage), the 17-knot *Adriatic* (gross register tonnage 24,541) and the two 20-knot liners *Teutonic* (gross register tonnage 9,685) and *Majestic* (gross register tonnage 9,861). It was planned that when the *Olympic* entered service she would replace the *Adriatic* and that when the *Titanic* entered service she would replace the *Majestic*. The *Oceanic* would operate with the *Olympic* and *Titanic* until being replaced by the third *Olympic*-class liner, the *Britannic*. When the *Britannic* was completed, the *Oceanic* would then be relegated as a reserve liner and would be returned back to transatlantic service when an overhaul of any of the *Olympic*-class liners was deemed necessary.

Construction of the *Titanic* commenced with the laying of keel number 401 on March 31, 1909. The *Titanic* was constructed from the same building plans as the *Olympic* and mirrored her construction schedule, albeit 7 months behind.

It is recorded that by May 15, 1909, the *Titanic* had been framed to the height of her double bottom, and by April 6, 1910, the ship had been fully framed. Work proceeded at a comfortable pace after the experience gained 3 months prior with the *Olympic*. The *Titanic* had been fully plated by October 19, 1910. Because of a certain perceived lack of interest in the building of the *Titanic*, her construction details are somewhat sketchy. To this day, much of the media information and construction documentation are not readily available.

A brilliant show of timing took place on May 31, 1911, when the *Titanic* was launched, coinciding with the *Olympic's* departure from Belfast. J. Bruce Ismay, J.P. Morgan, and other distinguished guests traveled in the chartered ferry *Duke of Argyll* to Belfast. Dressed in holiday attire, the dignitaries and their guests were present for more then just the two celebrations: It was also Lord and Lady Pirrie's birthday. The *Titanic* towered overhead in the gantry as more than 100,000 people turned out to see the spectacular event. At 12:15 p.m. the *Titanic* was afloat and clear of the gantry.

Following her successful launch, the yard workers proceeded to detach the metal hawsers from the river anchors and drag chains, which had been used to arrest the massive hull to an eventual standstill. She was taken in tow by five tugs, which escorted her to the deep water outfitting wharf.

After seeing the launch of the *Titanic*, the dignitary's guests dined at the Grand Central Hotel in Belfast, while Lord Pirrie's party stayed at Queen's Island. Other attendants and the press were allowed to dine after the main party had finished. Later, the dignitaries and their guests departed aboard the tender *Nomadic* to be taken to the location of the *Olympic*, where at 4:15 p.m. she departed for Liverpool.

The *Titanic's* launch attracted a visibly smaller crowd than had been in attendance to witness the launch of the *Olympic* 7 months earlier. This may have much to do with the fact that there were two events occurring on the same day, compared to the day the *Olympic* was launched from her construction berth. Even though approximately 100,000 people were present, it is said that most of them were busy marveling over the *Olympic* at where she was docked and paid less attention to the *Titanic*.

It was reported in the media that large crowds witnessed the launching of the world's largest manmade movable object. When one considers that the hulls of these two ships were built from the same set of plans, how could the *Titanic* be larger then the *Olympic*? The retrofitting later specified by Ismay, making the *Titanic* larger, had not yet been undertaken.

Olympic *nearing completion. A few weeks later the ship is opened up for public inspection.*
April 1911

Titanic *with all heavy machinery in place and funnels fitted. A week later she would be dry-docked.*
September 1911

People may argue that the *Titanic* was heavier at the time of her launch than the *Olympic*. The 24,600-ton weight of the empty hulls should not be confused with the 45,000-gross register tonnage, which in reality indicated the inside volume of the revenue-producing portions of the completed ships rather than actual weight. The undeniable fact is that close examinations of photographs of both the *Titanic* and *Olympic* immediately after launch reveal that the *Olympic* had settled lower into the water then the *Titanic*. This alone indicates that the *Olympic* was heavier at the time of her launch than the *Titanic*. The advertisements that stated the *Titanic* was "larger" than the *Olympic* would in reality be indicating the *Titanic*'s gross tonnage.

Olympic *departing Belfast on sea trials.*   Titanic *departing Belfast on sea trials.*

In the beginning, the *Titanic* was to be nearly an identical replica of the *Olympic*. Photographs taken when the *Titanic* was launched in 1911 show how similar the two actually were. The only obvious difference was the color of the hull. If one closely examines the photographs one will notice that, externally, the only differences were in the porthole arrangements in the plating around and below the poop deck (the area painted in white at the stern) and the porthole arrangement along the sides of the hull. Looking in the area painted in white about amidships, one can see a difference in sizes of some of the portholes.

In the weeks following the *Titanic*'s launch, and following observations noted during the *Olympic*'s maiden voyage, Ismay decided that certain modifications were to be made to the *Titanic* to increase the luxury of her first-class accommodations. Ismay believed that the *Olympic's* B deck promenade was an extravagant waste of valuable space. By removing this promenade, the *Titanic's* first-class suites on B deck could be extended into even more luxurious suites, and from the remaining space a private promenade deck could be carved out for each of the two B-deck parlour suites. The Café Parisien was added onto the aft portion of her starboard B deck, and on the port side the à la carte restaurant was extended out to the ship's side. This gave a balanced and consistent appearance in this area, and also removed the 2nd class promenade that was right outside the windows of the exclusive 1st class restaurant. The alterations to B deck required the removal of almost all the original external windows and framing. The result was a distinctly less uniform pattern than that on the *Olympic*. The other obvious external alteration was the enclosing of the forward part of the A deck promenade with steel-framed screens to protect passengers from sea spray.

A photograph taken in September 1911 shows the *Titanic* with all four funnels fitted. This indicates that all her heavy machinery, such as the boilers and engines, had been lowered into place and that she was ready to be placed into the dry dock for the installation of her three massive propellers and the repainting of her lower hull. As stated earlier, detailed construction timetables and information about ship movements are rather sketchy. *Titanic* entered dry-dock on September 18th which was than captured on film in a short 2 minute newsreel. This newsreel is to this day, the only known film of the ship.

After colliding with the 7,350-ton cruiser HMS *Hawke* on September 20, 1911, the *Olympic* was required to return to Belfast for extensive repairs. Programmed work on the *Titanic* was therefore suspended as she was removed from the dry dock on October 4 to allow the necessary inspections and repairs to be carried out on her sister. The *Olympic* departed Belfast following the completion of repairs on November 3, 1911.

As a result of the forced return of the *Olympic*, the *Titanic*'s construction program had been delayed, as workers needed to be diverted to repair the damaged sister. Because 6 weeks were required to repair the *Olympic,* the White Star Line management was forced to reschedule the *Titanic*'s planned maiden voyage to April 10, 1912, from the originally planned date of March 20.

On February 24, 1912, the *Olympic* was once again forced to return to Belfast after shedding one of her propeller blades on her port side. It is alleged that she had passed over a submerged wreck some 750 miles off Newfoundland. Because of the *Olympic*'s return, the *Titanic* was once again removed from the dry dock, on February 29, to allow a replacement blade to be fitted to the *Olympic.* This work was completed on March 3, and she departed for Southampton on March 7.

When the *Olympic* left the graving dock, she had to be turned to accommodate her outward departure. The *Titanic* was again put back into the dry dock to allow for sufficient turning room in the narrow confines of the channel. It is believed that the *Titanic*'s placement back in the dry dock was not required for any other reason. It would be reasonable to believe that the dry dock was therefore not drained, because the *Titanic*'s propellers would have been fitted and the hull plates below the waterline would have already had the red antifouling paint applied. It is unknown when, after the departure of the *Olympic*, the *Titanic* was removed from the dry dock, but the next time she was seen, 1 week later, she was moored at the outfitting wharf.

Olympic *seen here departing Belfast for the first of two days of sea trials. May 29th 1911*

Titanic *departing Belfast on her sea trials. April 2nd 1911*

The *Titanic*'s sea trials had been planned for Monday. April 1. The required tugs, owned by the Alexander Towing Co. had been dispatched from Liverpool to Belfast on March 31. Some of the same tugs that escorted the *Olympic* on May 29, 1911, were now called on for the job of escorting the younger sister. The weather was bitter and cold, with a strong northwesterly wind, turning the normally calm Victoria Channel into rather treacherous seas. Although the *Titanic* was due to depart Belfast at about 10:00 a.m., it was decided that the conditions in the channel presented a potential risk for the safe navigation of the ship. To avoid the risk of damaging the *Titanic*'s hull, the trials were suspended until the following day.

On Monday, April 2, 1912, the weather conditions had improved considerably, and a clear sky and calm waters were a sight for which all concerned were grateful. By 6:00 a.m. the *Titanic* had been taken in tow and was escorted up the River Lagan, the Victoria Channel, and Belfast Lough by the tugs *Herculaneum, Hornby, Hercules, Herald,* and *Huskisson.*

While at sea, the *Titanic's* compasses were calibrated. This operation was carried out only while the ship was totally free of any land-based magnetic distractions. Of interest, and to clear up a frequently asked question, Captain Smith was in command of the *Titanic* during her sea trials. He had handed the command of the *Olympic* over to Captain Herbert James Haddock a short time earlier.

During these sea trials, the *Titanic's* two radio operators John (Jack) Phillips and Harold Bride were tuning and testing the ship's new Marconi wireless system. The equipment was in constant use as messages about the details of the sea trials were transmitted to Ismay. Other Marconi-equipped vessels were also being contacted to test the vessel's equipment. At this time Phillips and Bride experienced freak atmospheric conditions and established communications with Port Said, some 3,000 miles distant.

Titanic returned to Belfast at 6:30 p.m. that evening and was obliged to lower both starboard and port anchors as a final directive by the Board of Trades representative. Carruthers, being satisfied with the ships performance throughout the trials, signed the certificate of seaworthiness, valid for one year. With this document in hand, the directors of the White Star Line would have seen the obligations of the contract finalized thereby acknowledging the official transfer of the vessel from builder to owner.

With the formalities dispensed with, and the departure ashore of the officials, the ship than weighed anchor on or about 8:00 p.m. On leaving Belfast Lough, she briefly tracked eastward into the Irish Sea and made course for Southampton. During the 570-mile trip from Belfast to Southampton, the opportunity was taken to perform additional engine and maneuvering trials. Making an average of 18 knots, it was expected that the *Titanic* would conveniently arrive at Southampton upon the high tide. Although the ship had the misfortune of encountering fog six hours into the voyage, the unfavorable conditions cleared just after 6:00 a.m.

One notable highlight of the trip south was that Smith directed the engineers to make a short all out push. The new ship did not disappoint, producing a brief but impressive 23.5 knots. Unfortunately as history was to later reveal, this was to be the quickest the ship obtained throughout her brief career.

The *Olympic* departed Southampton just after noon on that same day. Although some speculation suggests that she may have departed closer to 4:00 p.m. This delay could however substantiate the Hampshire Independent's article printed the following day that the two sisters had passed each other 'a short distance somewhere off Portland'. Although this article appears to have been adopted as fact, the Southampton harbormaster's log appears to end any speculation with the following entry: P 205; 3rd April 1912 - "Noon" - *Olympic* - Haddock - New York - W.Star 20,894 - 45,324.

At approximately 10:00 p.m. that evening, *Titanic* progressed past the Isle of White into Spithead, past the Nab lightship and made the obligatory stop for the embarkation of the Southampton pilot. With the pilot now on her bridge, she proceeded cautiously at half ahead passing Cowes, rounded the notorious Brambles sandbank and eventually into Southampton water. A short period later, 5 Red Star tugs, *Ajax, Hector, Hercules, Neptune* and *Vulcan* assisted the ship into the calm, and darkened waters of the River Test. The time was just after 11:30 p.m. With the bow facing downstream, it was than necessary to bring the ship through a 90° turn to port to align the vessel up parallel with the dock. Using a push pull action, the tugs maneuvered the huge hull slowly astern. It was just after midnight when the ship was finally secured alongside Berth 44 - stern first.

The *Titanic* was never opened up for public inspection like the *Olympic*. This, no doubt, was caused by the lost time incurred by the forced return of the *Olympic* on two separate occasions. As it turned out, work was still commencing on the ship during her trails, as well as on her trip to Southampton. This is further evidenced by the fact that the *Titanic* was unable to make a courtesy call at Liverpool like the *Olympic.* In fact, the *Titanic* was never officially opened up to the general public at any time.

Although when fully completed the *Titanic* was the largest man made movable object, the difference in gross tonnage between her and the *Olympic* would be only some 1,500 tons. It is interesting to note that the title of "the world's largest ship" belonged to the *Titanic* for only a little over

2 weeks. After the ship sank on April 15th 1912, the title of "world's largest ship" returned to the *Olympic*.

During the *Olympic*'s construction more than 150 photographs were taken of her at Harland & Wolff. Compared to the 45 odd photographs taken of the *Titanic* during a similar period of time. It is quite apparent that the *Titanic* attracted less photographic and media attention during her beginnings than her sister the *Olympic* did. The lack of progressive construction photographs has been disappointing and frustrating over the years for liner enthusiasts, historians and researchers. For that period, we are simply left with two minutes of moving pictures taken during the ship's dry-docking in September 1911, and several dozen photographs.

Both the *Olympic* and *Titanic* were constructed from the same set of plans. When launched, their hulls, machinery and deck arrangements were almost exactly identical. Even when completed, they were almost indistinguishable, even from a short distance. Apart from the different window spacing on the *Titanic*'s B deck and her enclosed forward promenades on A deck-modifications made only after her launch-the casual observer would have been hard-pressed to tell them apart.

C H A P T E R   3

Seeds of the Conspiracy

At 11:25 a.m. on September 20, 1911, the *Olympic* had departed Southampton's White Star Dock to begin her fifth voyage across the Atlantic. Aboard were 1,313 passengers and 885 crew. As with the four previous voyages, *Olympic* was under the command of Capt. E.J. Smith. To reach the open sea from Southampton water, the *Olympic* would have to make the usual reverse *S* maneuver that led the ship into Spithead. To assist in the navigation of the ship as far as the Nab lighthouse, the *Olympic* required the attendance on the bridge of the Southampton pilot, Capt. George Bowyer. From the Calshot Spit buoy, Bowyer would take the ship through a series of maneuvers that would lead the ship safely through the channel and into the Solent.

Capt. Bowyer approached the Thorn Knoll buoy, which marked the most complicated part of the *Olympic's* turn. To safely perform this task, the ship's rudder would need assistance, so the port engine was ordered full astern, then slow ahead. When the ship was about two thirds of the way from the Thorn Knoll buoy to the West Brambles buoy the helm was put hard-a-starboard, and the port engine was stopped and then reversed. The captain sounded two blasts on the ship's whistles, which signaled that the liner was to make a port turn. By 12:43 p.m. the turn had been successfully completed, and the course was altered to south 59 degrees east, with her engines then put full ahead. The *Olympic* progressively increased her speed from 12 to 16 knots.

At about the time the *Olympic* signaled her turn to port, the HMS *Hawke*, a Royal Navy armored cruiser, was rounding Egypt Point approximately 4 miles distant from the *Olympic's* present course. At the time the *Olympic* had sounded her two blasts on the whistle in preparation for a port turn around the notorious Brambles shoal, the *Hawke* was only about 2 miles from the *Olympic* and closing in quickly. By the time the *Olympic* had completed her turn around the West Brambles buoy the gap between the two ships had closed to 1¼ miles. It was now obvious that the ships were on a converging course into the same channel and, recognizing this, the *Hawke's* captain altered his course by 5 degrees to starboard, to allow additional navigating space for the *Olympic* as she proceeded into Spithead.

The *Hawke* came up on the *Olympic's* starboard quarter at an estimated speed of 16 knots. At this time the *Olympic* was traveling at approximately 14 knots. Slowly the *Hawke* started to overtake the *Olympic* on the starboard side. How far the *Hawke* overtook the *Olympic* is open to debate. Statements on how far the *Hawke* reached forward on the *Olympic's* starboard side at this stage have varied. Capt. Smith estimated that the *Hawke's* bow reached as far forward as the ship's compass tower between the second and third funnels before she started to pull away because of the *Olympic's* increasing speed. Bowyer estimated that the *Hawke's* bow progressed as far forward as the *Olympic's* bridge, whereas Chief Officer Wilde believed the *Hawke* reached an area around the *Olympic's* forward funnel. Whichever estimate one accepts, it is clear that the *Hawke's* bow did not proceed forward of the *Olympic's* bridge-or did it?

As the *Olympic* finally matched, and then surpassed, the speed of the *Hawke*, she began drawing away from the cruiser until the *Hawke* suddenly began to swing to port, toward the *Olympic's* towering hull in the area of the liner's third funnel. On the bridge of the *Olympic*, Smith and Bowyer noticed that the *Hawke* was being drawn close to the *Olympic's* side. Smith anxiously stated, "I don't believe she will get under our stern, Bowyer." Bowyer replied, "If she is going to strike, sir, let me know in time so I can put the helm hard over to port." "Yes, she is going to strike us in the stern" was the reply.

Unknown to those on the bridge of the *Olympic*, Capt. Blunt, on the bridge of the *Hawke,* ordered his helmsman to turn the cruiser to starboard to open up a suitable margin between the two ships; however, the cruiser swung 4 or 5 points in the opposite direction. Instead of turning away from the *Olympic*, she now headed toward her. No doubt believing the helmsman had turned the wheel the wrong way, Blunt, seeing the seriousness of the situation exploded, "What are you doing? Port, hard a port, stop port engine, full astern starboard!" The quartermaster on the wheel called up, "The helm's jammed!" With the helm jammed at 15 degrees to the port, the *Hawke* was being pulled into the *Olympic's* starboard quarter. With the *Hawke* now powerless to maneuver, a collision between the 7,350-ton cruiser and the 45,000-ton liner seemed unavoidable. Capt. Blunt quickly descended the ladder from the bridge to the wheelhouse and used the engine room telegraphs to order "full astern both." On the *Olympic*, Bowyer ordered the ship's helm hard a port in a vain and now-futile effort to swing the liner's stern clear of the rapidly closing *Hawke*; however, a collision was a certainty.

The *Olympic's* bow had swung 7 degrees to starboard when the cruiser's cement-reinforced bow rammed against her hull 86 ft from her stern post. The collision almost capsized the aging cruiser. Fortunately for the *Hawke*, the *Olympic's* forward momentum resulted in the cruiser being sheared away to one side, and she quickly returned back to an even keel. At the time of the collision, Capt. Smith had ordered the closing of the watertight doors and disengaged the ship's engines. The *Olympic* continued for a short distance before coming to an eventual stop, well clear of the *Hawke*. One could safely assume that the *Olympic's* two bow anchors were then lowered.

SOUTHAMPTON WATER AND THE COURSES OF THE OLYMPIC AND THE HAWKE

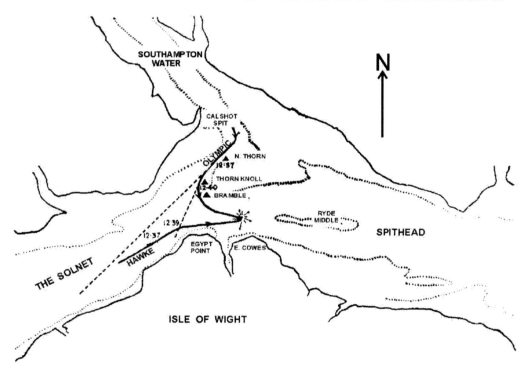

The damage to the *Olympic* was quickly assessed, although a full evaluation of the damage was not possible. An inspection by the ship's carpenter, chief engineer, and Capt. Smith found that the ship had been rendered unseaworthy, and the voyage was subsequently canceled. Unable to return to Southampton because of the tide, the *Olympic* was anchored in Osborne Bay off Cowes, Isle of Wight, where some of her passengers and nonessential crew disembarked. The *Hawke* managed to cautiously steam back to Portsmouth at a reduced speed.

Although the *Olympic's* two aftermost compartments had been breached and flooded, the ship was in no danger of sinking, and the following day she was towed back to Southampton by tugs for a full damage evaluation at Harland & Wolff's maintenance facility.

An assessment of the damage revealed that all three starboard manganese-bronze propeller blades were severely chipped and would require replacing, and 18 ft of the starboard propeller boss arm plating was deranged, twisted, and fractured. The starboard propeller shaft had been bent out of alignment and rendered inoperable. Eleven hull plates had been damaged above the waterline; 8 of these were beyond repair and had to be replaced. A hull breach of 7 ft with a 12-ft - 14-ft pear-shaped hole rose from the waterline to D deck, and a gash approximately 40 ft wide was incurred below the waterline. Many of the ship's frames had been bent and twisted, and thousands of her hydraulically fitted rivets were no longer watertight.

The repair work for the *Olympic* was beyond the capabilities of the limited resources of the Harland & Wolff maintenance facility at Southampton. She required a layup, and the only facility available for the dry docking of a ship of the *Olympic's* size was at Belfast. To allow the *Olympic* to safely return to Ireland, the workforce at the maintenance facility attached steel plates to the breached hull plating below the waterline and timber above the waterline. Although the patches were believed to stop the stern compartments from flooding, on the voyage back to Belfast they were only marginally successful, for on her arrival at Belfast it was revealed that the stern compartments were again flooded. It would appear there may well have been other unknown breaches in the hull, and only a full inspection in dry dock would locate the suspect areas.

The images above illustrate the Olympic *after the* Hawke *collision, and being towed into Southampton. Her stern is noticeably down in the water.*

The temporary repairs at Southampton required about 2 weeks to complete. Some theorists believe that the damage may have been more extensive than what was disclosed at the time; however, the *Olympic* was required to empty all her cargo, surplus coal (she was carrying sufficient coal for a Southampton—New York passage) perishable food stores, etc., from the canceled voyage, as well as to have all the necessary repairs completed. Therefore, 2 weeks would not have been a totally unexpected period of time to complete the temporary repairs. Harland & Wolff would have undoubtedly required a little lead time to make the necessary arrangements for her arrival.

"S.S. Olympic" at Southampton. Docks
after. Collision 20.9.1911

DAMAGE TO WHITE STAR R.M.S. OLYMPIC after collision with H.M.S. HAWK
SEPT. 20 1911.

On Wednesday, October 4, the crippled *Olympic* departed Southampton for the 570-mile run to Belfast. Because the starboard engine, shaft, and propellers had been rendered unserviceable, she steamed the distance to Belfast on only her port engine. With her speed reduced to 8—10 knots, *Olympic* arrived at Belfast just before midday on the Friday, October 6.

The *Olympic* *in the Thompson Graving Dock – Harland & Wolff.*
The damage to the manganese bronze propeller blades is evident.

To clarify the number of hull plates that had been either damaged or replaced after the *Hawke* collision, the authors obtained a drawing of the *Olympic* from Harland & Wolff's technical services department. The schematic indicated the areas where plating either had been removed to expedite internal repairs or had been replaced because of collision damage. The schematic was divided into two sections.

Knowing that the damage was concentrated about 86 ft from the ship's stern post, and in light of the fact that the *Hawke's* bow had allegedly reached only as far forward as the *Olympic's* bridge, the damaged area revealed on the drawing held no real surprises. The drawing indicated that hull plating had been replaced in five of the aft compartments. The two aft stern compartments indicated where the damaged hull plating had been replaced after being directly breached by the bow of the *Hawke*. The forward three compartments indicated where plating had been obviously removed as the single plates could range anywhere in the area of 30 ft in length. Some of the damaged areas indicated on the drawing may also be the result of frame, or internal ironwork damage. However, a bow schematic sent from Harland & Wolff revealed that the *Olympic* had sustained hull damage in the area of the waterline as far forward as the ship's second watertight compartment from the bow. It indicated that hull plating between watertight compartments 2, 3, and 4 had possibly been either damaged or breached. If this occurred in the *Hawke* collision, why is it not mentioned in any of the reference materials available? On the basis of this new information, we must ask if the *Olympic* was more extensively damaged than had ever been known outside Harland & Wolff and the White Star Line. This new information would seem to indicate that the *Hawke* first collided with the *Olympic* 100 ft forward of the bridge, causing damage to about 115 ft of the *Olympic*'s hull plating below, or in the area of, the waterline. If this were the case, then the casual observer would not have seen any visual damage to the *Olympic* beside the breached hull plating on her stern. These damaged plates would have been visible only when the ship had been placed in dry dock. It would appear that the White Star Line managers were going to receive a few costly surprises when the dry dock was drained. Were they aware of this fact all along?

Although the hull plating may well not have been damaged to the point that the ship was taking on water in the affected areas, 115 ft of the ship's hull plating had been sufficiently damaged to require replacement or repair. If the plating had been damaged, there would be a possibility that the 10-in. steel channel rib frames supporting the affected hull plating had also been damaged and required replacement. Her structural integrity must have been compromised over this area of the hull.

Even with the hull plating repaired, the damaged area would never be as structurally sound as it originally was unless all the damaged 10-in. steel channel ribs were fully replaced. These ribs extended over multiple decks; therefore, replacement would require the removal of all the attached hull plating. Replacement of the rib frames would have been extremely expensive, labor intensive, and time consuming.

The White Star Line management no doubt wanted their flagship repaired and returned to service as quickly as possible. The longer *Olympic* stayed at Belfast—diverting the workers who were normally engaged in the construction of the *Titanic*—the longer it would take to complete the *Titanic*. Therefore, the *Olympic*'s hull plating may have been simply replaced and the channel steel rib frames bent back into place and reinforced. This was not a dangerous comprise, considering the ship could remain afloat even with the first four compartments opened to the sea. However, if this had been the case, *Olympic* now had an Achilles heel on her starboard side, below the waterline between watertight compartments 2—4.

The repairs to the *Olympic* were completed by Harland & Wolff by November 20, after 6½ weeks, and she returned back to commercial service. The total cost in lost revenue and repairs amounted to some $750,000.* The White Star Line had other ships, and although the company would have lost money due to cancellations by people who especially wanted to travel on *Olympic,* the fact remains that other passengers would have simply sailed on the *Olympic*'s replacement while she was out of service. As a double blow, the forced diversion of workers from the construction of the *Titanic* had set back her planned maiden voyage from March 20, 1912, to April 10, 1912. If the *Olympic* had not collided with the *Hawke*, the *Titanic* would have departed Southampton 3 weeks earlier than she did, and history may have changed. This may well have been the case; however, the *Titanic* was to work on a 2-week turnaround out of Southampton, so she still would have departed on April 10, although on her second transatlantic crossing, not her maiden voyage. In this case, Capt. Smith supposedly would not have been the captain, and Bruce Ismay would not have been on board, but the ice field and bergs would have still been in the same area of the North Atlantic. Would the same circumstances have arisen that led to *Titanic's* demise on April 14 if the voyage had been her second crossing?

No benefit would be gained from a protracted description of the resulting court cases that attempted to ascertain who was at fault in the *Hawke* collision. The British Admiralty claimed the *Olympic* had crowded the *Hawke* out of the channel by sailing too far south and that the huge wake of the 45,000-ton *Olympic* had caused, by way of her forward movement, a huge displacement of water in the restricted space between the liner and the 7,350-ton *Hawke*, the resulting suction causing the

---

* The full amount of the repairs combined with lost revenue is questionable. The figure of £250,000 has been given in some references. According to the New York Times, the International Mercantile Marine, who controlled the White Star Line, claimed damages of $750,000, which was their insurance deductible. At a general exchange rate of $4.85 USD to £1 this would give a price of £154,639.

Hawke to be drawn into the liner's side. Therefore, the court passed down a verdict in favor of the Admiralty based on negligent navigation of the *Olympic*, stating that the captain had led the liner too far south and crowded the *Hawke* out of the channel.

The White Star Line, not happy with the court's decision, appealed the verdict, claiming that the *Hawke* had at that time been overtaking the *Olympic*. To back this up officials for the White Star Line set out to locate the location of the *Hawke's* sheared-off bow ram to pinpoint the exact position of the collision; the court, however, dismissed this on the basis that the *Hawke's* ram had fallen from the ship some time after the collision. If the *Olympic* had sustained impact damage by the *Hawke* 100 ft forward of the bridge, then why did the White Star Line choose not to cite this damage as evidence that would prove conclusively that the *Hawke* had indeed been in the process of overtaking the *Olympic* when she was drawn into the liner's side? A quick inspection of the *Olympic* would conclusively prove that the ship had indeed been damaged this far forward. The officers of the White Star Line would have the proof they needed. The appeal was heard in January 1913, 8 months after the *Titanic* had sunk. Is it possible that White Star Line officials could not produce hard evidence because they no longer had the *Olympic* to put forth?

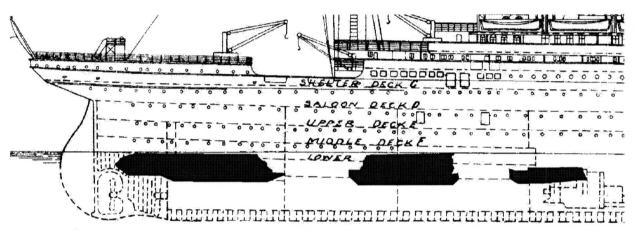

On January 10th 1997, the Administration Manager of Harland & Wolff's Technical Services was asked to specify the area of damaged shell plates on the Olympic, *which were repaired or removed after the* Hawke *collision. The diagram shown above is what was sent from Harland & Wolff via Fax.*

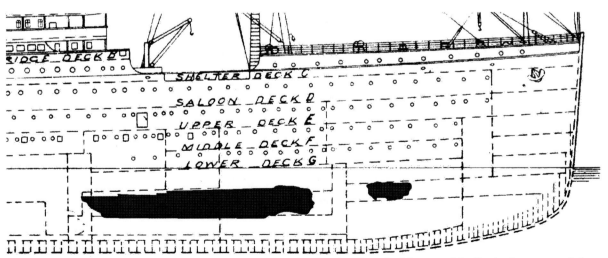

The author's received a Fax in response stating "Thanks for the Fax, but I cannot indicate the area of damaged plating as you did not indicate the bow section in your drawing."

White Star, having lost the case, again appealed, this time to the House of Lords; the case was again lost. In a judgment handed down on November 9, 1914, the House of Lords dismissed the case. Right to the end, the White Star management maintained that they were morally in the right.

Why the White Star Line had played down the damage to the bow of the *Olympic* is in need of explanation, but it leaves one imagining what other damage, if any, the *Olympic* had suffered in the *Hawke* collision. Could the *Olympic* have been deemed an economic liability—not in the short term but perhaps in the longer term? One could hardly advise one's shareholders that one of the company's prime assets was now a technical write off. Having lost the case against the Admiralty, White Star had to accept a loss of the widely accepted sum of £250,000. There is only one possible cause that would make the *Olympic* an economic write off: if the ship's keel had been damaged. Was there any evidence that the keel of the *Olympic* had been damaged in the collision? Sources at Harland & Wolff stated that the *Olympic* sailed from Southampton only on her port engine, the starboard engine having been rendered inoperable. They further stated that the center turbine was not engaged, not because it had been rendered unusable, but by choice. The center turbine and, therefore, the center shaft, is driven by the exhaust steam from the port and starboard main engines. With only the port main engine in operation on her 570-mile run back to Southampton, would there have been sufficient exhaust steam to operate the center shaft, albeit at reduced speed? Could the center turbine, which is located on the centerline of the ship, resting directly over the keel, have been deemed a possible threat by way of vibration to a suspected damaged keel?

It is at this point that a conspiracy theorist could make a case. For argument's sake, we will explore the following theory: If the *Olympic*'s keel had been damaged, this damage would have occurred near the reciprocating-engine room based on the fact that the starboard main engine would have been jolted when the *Hawke*'s bow came into contact with the *Olympic*'s turning starboard propeller. The resulting staggered rotation of the blades would have transferred the shock back up through the starboard shaft and momentarily impeded the engine's free-flowing cycle, placing pressure on the engine's crankshafts. It is believed that this would have occurred regardless of how quickly the engine was disengaged. Something would have had to break, and it did. Part of the starboard propeller's shaft was damaged and needed replacing. Could the resulting shock have transferred through the engine and subsequently to the engine bedplates? Could this severe shock have been transferred from the engine bedplates to the ship's keel? If so, might this have been sufficient to damage her keel? There may have been no external evidence of any damage to the keel, but had the integrity of the metal being used been compromised, the *Olympic* would no longer be as strong in the area of the reciprocating-engine room as she had been prior to the collision. Under normal operating conditions, the keel may have been perfectly sound; however, if placed under excessive pressure, it may well have fractured. To this day there has been much speculation as to why the *Titanic*'s keel snapped into two pieces. Could the answer be simply that it was the *Olympic* that broke in two on the tragic morning of April 15, 1912? Was the break due to a possible pre-existing weakness in the keel located around the area of the reciprocating-engine room? We address the possibility of damage to the keel caused by the *Hawke* collision later in this volume. Since 1911 many theories have been put forth; some have been based on accurate information, some on not-so-accurate information.

If the *Olympic* had been more severely damaged than revealed, there is no doubt that she would certainly not pass the Board of Trade inspection for the renewal of her certificate of seaworthiness, due in May 1912, just a few weeks after *Titanic* sank. The ramifications of this would have been catastrophic. The White Star Line recently had been forced to cancel the *Olympic*'s voyage to New York, and it may also have had to cancel many more voyages in the future. For the *Olympic* to achieve certification renewal, all damaged areas would need to have been repaired. The full cost of all the repairs and the loss of income from canceled voyages would possibly have even been beyond the interest of J. P. Morgan, the ultimate owner of the *Olympic* and the White Star Line.

The *Olympic* was again returned prematurely to Belfast following the loss of one of her port side propeller blades at 4:26 p.m. on February 24, 1912. After departing New York, she was about 750 miles off the coast of Newfoundland (latitude 44° 20' N, longitude 38° 36' W), eastbound, when she was believed to have passed over an underwater obstruction and shed one of her three port side propeller blades. It is most curious that she passed over an obstruction, when one considers that the average depth of the Atlantic at that point is more than 12,000 ft. If the *Olympic* had passed over an obstruction, why was there no evidence of damage done to the hull of the ship? The alleged obstruction would have passed along the whole length beneath the ship before coming into contact with the port side propeller. The only other possible scenario would have been if the *Olympic* nicked an obstruction on the outside of her port wing. Whatever the obstruction was, the fact is that one of the port side blades had been sheared off by some unknown agent. The effect on the ship would prove to be dramatic, as the now hopelessly unbalanced propeller would need to be disengaged. The subsequent stress on the port side propeller shaft and associated machinery would have been substantial. Had the engine continued to drive the unbalanced propeller for a prolonged period, the vibration would have certainly caused damage.

The HMS Hawke's *bow after the collision*

The *Olympic* continued her eastbound crossing to Southampton at a reduced speed, arriving on February 29. After the passengers had disembarked, the unnecessary crew were discharged, and the cargo and mail were unloaded. The *Olympic* departed for Belfast the following day for the dry dock and a replacement blade.

At this point it may be interesting to highlight the fact that Harland & Wolff was believed to have carried only one full set of replacement propeller blades. Added to this is some speculation as to whether the blades to be fitted to the *Titanic* were slightly larger than those on her older sister, the *Olympic*. If Harland & Wolff did not carry any more spare blades, the only alternative may have been to fit the *Olympic* with one of the *Titanic's* spare reserve blades. Replacing only one blade would have left the port side propeller arrangement out of balance, creating a vibration. The only alternative, if one were to accept this hypothesis, would have been to remove the other two, smaller blades and fit all three of *Titanic's* larger blades onto the *Olympic*. Would having slightly larger blades on the portside affect the ship's performance? There is no doubt: The thrust surface area on the port side would have

Two images of Titanic *leaving dry-dock on March 2nd 1912.*

been greater than that on the starboard side. Under normal conditions this would not affect the ship's overall performance; however, it could marginally affect her ability to turn and her response time when required to do so. Also, having two propellers of differing diameter and/or pitch would have caused other problems. To compensate for the difference, it would have been necessary to run the port and starboard engines at substantially different rpms to achieve equal thrust. With both engines running at widely different rpms, serious vibration would tend to result.

There is some controversy over the excessive time the *Olympic* spent at Belfast. The fitting of a replacement blade should have taken only 2 days; however, she was at Belfast for 6 days. It is reported that the weather was so inclement the day prior to her departure that the *Olympic* was put back into the dry dock, this being the only berth available. However, another fact, which is not widely known is that, after the initial repairs had been completed, the first attempt to remove the *Olympic* from the dry dock proved troublesome—the ship bottomed out by striking submerged rocks in the lough. The workmen had to return the *Olympic* to the dry dock to inspect the hull. Apparently there was no significant damage. After the return to the dry dock after the grounding, and the bad weather on March 6, she was removed from the dry dock once again, leaving Belfast on March 7. The *Olympic's* scheduled departure from Southampton to New York on March 6 was therefore canceled.

Olympic's *port side propeller boss missing one blade.*

If, for argument's sake, the *Titanic* and *Olympic* had been switched, and *Olympic* was in fact the ship that collided with an iceberg on the night of April 14, one has to wonder: Could the previous damage sustained by the *Olympic* on September 20, 1911, possibly have played a crucial part in the sinking?

An argument based solely on the similarity of the areas damaged on the *Olympic* (in October—November 1911) and *Titanic* (plating damaged by the iceberg) as positive proof that the latter had sunk because of a pre-existing structural weakness comes up a little short. Coincidence is not proof. The addition of at least a strong second reference would be necessary to give the theory some further and supportive credibility.

Although the fax cover sheet from Harland & Wolff's Technical Services does not state that all of the damaged sections identified on the schematics had been the result of the *Hawke* collision, the damage on the stern is beyond doubt.

CHAPTER 4

Mystery or History

The two stories in this chapter provide an insight into what some people could potentially deem circumstantial evidence. It should be noted that both stories should be viewed more as mystery than as actual history and, not inadvertently, as profiling a stronger case for a conspiracy. They are what they appear to be—a mystery—and, as with any mystery, the mind demands a solution. Although they may not be worthy of the great Baker Street detective himself, they still provided an elusive and consuming challenge.

As we begin our profile of the two main characters in these mysteries, we are first introduced to James Fenton. Fenton alleged that he was a surviving crewman; he claimed that when he joined the *Titanic* at Belfast other crewmen told him that the *Titanic* was in actuality the *Olympic*. Was his bizarre story, as told to a young Dennis Finch back in 1971, simply an isolated incident? Apparently not: Fenton had been telling the same story for more than 40 years to any person interested in hearing it.

Next we look at Constance Evans, a passenger whose husband was allegedly attached to the Harland & Wolff guarantee party. Neither Constance nor her husband appear on any passenger or subsequent survivor lists. At first glance, it would appear they were not on board the *Titanic* at all but, during the Senate inquiry, surviving passenger Daisy Minahan stated that she had seen a couple,

The *Kooliga*

known to her as Mr. and Mrs. Blair, taking tea with the Widener party in the á la carte restaurant. The Blairs, like the Evanses, fail to appear on any list. Could they be the same people?

We address the James Fenton story first. An interesting letter to the editor appeared in *The Northern Star*, an Australian newspaper, on July 31, 1996. The letter was authored by Frank Finch, a retired seaman, who at the time operated a modest but comprehensive maritime museum from a small country town on the far north coast of New South Wales. The letter was later established to have been written in response to a previously published article regarding the alleged *Titanic–Olympic* switch theory.

The letter quoted below was initially handwritten in pencil, then later mailed to the editor by Frank Finch. It was based partially on a lead story that had appeared in *The Northern Star* weeks before. Adding to the information he had read, Finch included what he had learned from a conversation with his eldest son, Dennis, an experienced and still actively employed seaman in the Australian maritime industry. In early July 1996, Dennis had the occasion to visit his parents for a few days while on leave. Over lunch one day, the family discussed the topic of a possible conspiracy surrounding the *Titanic* and *Olympic*.

On this particular occasion, Dennis recalled a conversation he had with an old bo'son named James Fenton while serving on a ship called the *Kooliga* back in 1971. This story becomes even more amazing when one considers that neither Dennis nor his father had read or even heard of a conspiracy to switch the ships. Frank's initial opinion concerning the possibility of the two 46,000-ton ships being switched was less than favorable. In fact, Frank later confided that before having this talk with his son Dennis the whole idea or even the suggestion that these two ships were switched was farcical.

The following is a partial quote from Frank Finch's letter. The body of the letter itself is derived directly from the conversation that Dennis had with James Fenton while they were serving on the *Kooliga* in 1971.

[James] Fenton first went to sea in 1898 as an 8-year-old cabin boy aboard a sailing ship called the "Red Rock." They went missing for 180 days in the Indian Ocean; the vessel was "becalmed." In 1912 Paddy [claimed he] was a 22-year-old ordinary seaman aboard the *Titanic*.

He always maintained that the iceberg alone did not sink the *Titanic*, that it had a fire burning in the coal bunkers for a week and that the Captain and the company knew about it. Paddy also said that when the crew joined the *Titanic* there was [sic] rumors that the company had switched ships at lay up and that an insurance scam was going on.

They sailed in a great hurry from Belfast and said that when they hit the iceberg it did not do serious damage but when the cold water hit the coal fire, it exploded and caused the fatal damage. The Chief Mate put Paddy in charge of a lifeboat, keeping older hands on deck for lowering boats.

When the surviving crew got to port they were all taken aside and met by two men, one in a high position in the company, the other man was in a very high position in the Government. The Government man read the crew the "Official Secrets Act" explaining that if they told of the real reason for the sinking, or the rumors of an insurance scam, they would serve a minimum of 20 years in jail and would never get a job when they got out.

Paddy said that the guilt of keeping quiet all those years had taken a great toll on his health and the sanity of the surviving crew.

To verify the accuracy of Fenton's story some information must first be established. Was there a ship called the *Kooliga*? Yes. She was constructed in 1958 and was operated by a company called Associated Steamship Pty Ltd. Her port of registration was Melbourne, and she was crewed by 38–40 personnel. She operated between Melbourne, Adelaide, and numerous other West Australian ports.

Did Fenton and Finch ever sail together on the *Kooliga*? Again, the answer is yes: Records from the Australian Marine Crews Manager reveal that a James A. Fenton served as a bo'sun on board the *Kooliga* between July 9, 1971, and September 6, 1971. Finch served as an ordinary seaman on board the same vessel between July 6, 1971, and October 5, 1971.

With the elements of Fenton's service validated, we now look into the facts pertaining to the *Titanic* and the identity of this man in greater depth.

Was there a man by the name of James Fenton? Yes; he was born James Anthony Fenton in the small Northern Ireland town of Dundalk County Louth, Eire in 1892. His claim that he was a 22-year-old ordinary seaman on board the *Titanic* is a little off; if he was born in 1892, then he would have

James (Paddy) Fenton - Brisbane 1962

been only 20, not 22, as he claimed. Either age is an acceptable one to hold this post.

Was Fenton's name listed on any of the *Titanic*'s crew lists at either Belfast or Southampton? In short, no. At this stage, one would start to reconsider the veracity of the whole story.

Consider the following example of an alleged crewman who appeared to vanish into thin air. Mrs. H. W. Bishop, who left *Titanic* in Lifeboat 7, made the following observation: "The conduct of the crew, as far as I could see, was absolutely beyond criticism. One of the crew was Jack Edmonds and there was another man, a lookout [Hogg], of whom we all thought a great deal."

One could assume that Edmonds must have been one of the more active crewmen aboard the lifeboat; otherwise, why would Mrs. Bishop ever have cause to recall the name? Given the fact that Mrs. Bishop's statement does acknowledge Edmonds's presence based mainly on his seemingly noteworthy actions that night, would it not be feasible to consider the opposite view? If Fenton had not at any time drawn undue attention to himself, but silently manned the oars like many other crewman that night, it may well have contrived against any acknowledgment of his presence. If one accepts this, Fenton's obscurity was almost guaranteed.

Was Jack Edmonds on board the *Titanic*? Although Mrs. Bishop's statement is striking, one must always allow for the possibility that she may have heard the man's name incorrectly.

There appears to be no definitive answer to this mystery. Edmonds's name, like Fenton's, fails to appear among any crew or passenger lists taken on board the *Carpathia*. Compounding this is that neither name appears on the handwritten crew rosters or even in the crew discharge documents.

George Behe, an advisor of the *Titanic* Historical Society, said that "The fact that the name is missing from the crew documents is very significant, since it means that 'Edmonds' was never paid for his *Titanic* voyage. I think it's unlikely that a crewman would voluntarily abandon money that he had earned in such a trying circumstance, and that's what leads me to believe that Mrs. Bishop misheard the man's name while she was in the lifeboat."

The passenger and crew lists from the *Titanic* are sometimes unreliable. Greaser Thomas G. Ranger and Bathroom Steward S. J. Rule, both of whom testified before the British inquiry, appear only on the ship's handwritten list, and Rule's name fails to appear on the list of survivors taken aboard the *Carpathia*. With this information at hand, one is forced to wonder how many other unlisted crew members were actually aboard the *Titanic* when she went down.

Fenton stated that the *Titanic* sailed in a great hurry from Belfast. The *Titanic*'s sea trials had been scheduled for the morning of April 1; however, because of excessive winds and treacherous conditions in the Victoria Channel the trails had been postponed and later rescheduled until the following morning. This 24-hour delay would have thrown the *Titanic*'s planned 2-day sea trial schedule into disarray. There is no doubt that the *Titanic*'s departure from Belfast had been planned for the evening of April 2, because if she had departed any earlier she would not have berthing facilities at the already-crowded Southampton. It should be noted that, prior to the *Titanic*'s arrival at Southampton, the White Star Line's pier had been occupied by her sister ship *Olympic* until just after midday on April 3.

Although there is no written record to confirm this, it is worth considering that the trials may have been scheduled for completion in only 1 day, not the popularly accepted 2, especially if the ship had originally been scheduled to stop at Liverpool first.

In light of the above, the *Titanic* would not have departed Belfast in "a great hurry." The only apparent rush would have been caused by the fact that the allocated trial date had been set back because of the inclement weather. Therefore, the only burden of pressure would have been among the ship's officers and management to have successfully completed the sea and acceptance trials in the limited time available. As it turned out, the morning of April 2 dawned clear, and the *Titanic* apparently performed faultlessly during the trials. A Board of Trade certificate of seaworthiness was issued that was valid for 12 months, and the ship was then formally handed over from builder to owner.

The *Titanic* would not have departed Belfast in "a great hurry," as stated by Fenton. However, in defense of his claim, the delay may have caused an air of tension aboard ship. The crew would have without doubt realized that if the inclement weather continued the following day it would have likely forced another postponement.

The next part of Fenton's statement requires greater attention. Fenton claimed that when the crew joined the *Titanic* there were rumors that the company had switched the *Titanic* with the *Olympic* at lay-up and that there was an insurance scam going on.

This is without doubt a bold statement. Fenton did not mention at what location these rumors among the crew began circulating. Obviously, it was either Belfast or Southampton. One can reasonably assume that other crewmen with whom Fenton would have mixed, such as other able seamen, would have spread these rumors. Even today there is a hierarchy system on any ship: Officers normally mix only among themselves, stewards mix with other stewards, and so on. There is no doubt that in 1912 the situation would have been the same. One therefore can reasonably assume that Fenton would not have heard this rumor from any of the ship's officers, engineering staff, or other trade qualified personnel. Because most seamen mix only with others of their own ranks, the rumor of the switch most likely came from another able seaman, or possibly one of the ship's quartermasters or lookout men. Although it is impossible to expand on this further, one can rest assured it was not a rumor that would have been openly expressed on board the *Titanic*.

While the *Titanic* was sinking, Chief Officer Wilde put Fenton in charge of a lifeboat, electing to keep the older and more experienced hands on deck for lowering the boats. Wilde was active in the loading and lowering of only three lifeboats: Lifeboat 2, lowered at 1:45 a.m., lifeboat 14, lowered at 1:30 a.m., and Collapsible C, lowered at 1:40 a.m. This does not cancel Fenton's presence out, but he was definitely not in charge of any of these lifeboats. The position of chief officer aboard the *Titanic* was originally assigned to First Officer Murdoch. Wilde replaced him at the eleventh hour at Southampton. Therefore, some of the crew may have been still unaware of this fact even at the time of the disaster. If Fenton had been placed in charge of a lifeboat believing that Murdoch was still the chief officer, any of the lifeboats loaded and lowered under the direction of Murdoch could be a potential candidate for the one Fenton was in. (Murdoch was active in loading and lowering of 6 lifeboats.) Fenton's claim that he was placed in charge of a lifeboat on the pretense that the officer wanted experienced seamen to remain on board would indicate that he likely left in one of the earlier lifeboats. There are simply endless possibilities.

Fenton said, "The iceberg did not do serious damage to the ship." An ordinary seaman would not have been anywhere near the areas that were opened up to the sea, or any area directly affected by the flooding that resulted after the collision. We now know that the damage was indeed minor, but did the resulting damage caused by the iceberg sink the ship?

Fenton also mentioned "the fire in the coal bunker." Like the proverbial bad penny, this keeps popping up. Evidence given at both the American and British Inquiries confirms that the coal bunker fire had been extinguished by Saturday April 13th, and there is no evidence to suggest otherwise. The area on the wreck alleged by some people to have been caused by an explosion is almost directly above the reserve coal bunker.

The managers of the White Star Line probably considered themselves fortunate to scrape together 4,427 tons of coal at Southampton, compliments of other laid-up IMM ships. There was a national coal strike at the time which left many ships stranded at the dock. The *Titanic* left with 5,892 tons, well short of her 6,611-ton total capacity. The ship certainly did not have any spare coal; as such, the reserve coal bunker would have been unquestionably empty. However, the fire had weakened the watertight bulkhead. This fire-damaged bulkhead did later fail at a crucial time, adding to the flooding of Boiler Room 5. Prior to this failure, the ship appeared to be maintaining its precarious trim aided by the pumps. So, to give some support to what Fenton said, the coal bunker fire damaged a bulkhead, a bulkhead that later failed because of the force of the water in the adjoining flooded boiler room, No. 6.

Fenton stated that the crew had been advised that if they told anyone of the real reason of the sinking or about the rumors of an insurance scam they would serve a minimum of 20 years in jail and would never get a job when they got out. Even to this day nobody really knows what went on behind closed doors.

The *Carpathia* arrived in New York at 9:35 p.m. on April 18. Thirty-eight of the surviving crew members, including the 4 officers, were all subpoenaed to appear before the American inquiry panel. The remaining 172 crew members were allowed to return back to England on board the Red Star Line's *Lapland*. The ship arrived back at Plymouth on April 29. After the American inquiry, the 34 crewman detained by Sen. Smith returned to Liverpool on board the *Celtic*. The *Titanic's* surviving officers returned to Liverpool on board the *Adriatic* 4 days later.

Fenton said that when the surviving crew members arrived at the port of Plymouth, they were all taken aside and met by two men, one in a high position in the White Star Line, the other from the government. History does tell us that Harold Sanderson and E. C. Grenfell, both White Star directors, met the crew on board the *Lapland*. Representing the government was Mr. W. Woolven, Receiver of Wrecks. These men would have been without doubt strongly advised that any unfounded rumors or speculations regarding the sinking of the *Titanic* would not be tolerated. Silence would have been by far the safest and wisest option available.

Fenton said that the guilt of keeping quiet all those years had taken a great toll on his health and the sanity of the surviving crew. This part of the statement would appear to confirm that in the years following the disaster he kept in reasonably close contact with many of the surviving crew.

DAILY SKETCH.

No. 979—MONDAY, APRIL 29, 1912.   THE PREMIER PICTURE PAPER.   [Registered as a Newspaper.] ONE HALFPENNY.

FIRST SURVIVORS OF TITANIC TO REACH ENGLAND.

The Lapland, the Red Star liner, arriving in Cawsand Bay, off Plymouth, yesterday morning with the Titanic survivors on board. The crew of the lost liner were not brought ashore against the taffrail of the immediately, but waited on the tender (Sir Richard Grenville) until the mails and passengers were got away from Plymouth. In the lower photograph the Titanic men are seen leaning tender.—Daily Sketch Photographs.

A few months following the article in the newspaper, one of the authors had the opportunity to speak with Dennis Finch. He asked Finch if he could recall any additional information from his conversation with Fenton of years past. Finch said only one additional snippet of relevant information came to mind: "From memory, [Fenton] said that when he joined the ship she had false portholes painted on her side."

Is this additional information relevant? In essence, both the *Titanic* and the *Olympic* shared identical porthole arrangements below C deck. However, the porthole arrangements just above both ship's sheers were distinctly different. On C deck between the third and fourth funnels the arrangements were also slightly different. In fact, only several portholes were different in size, not in number. Finally, the arrangements of portholes in the port side plating of the fo´c'sle were initially different on both ships. These were all obvious differences; however, the arrangement could be circumvented, if one wanted to accept this, by filling some portholes and painting on additional portholes elsewhere.

Before anyone starts entering into the realm of fantasy, examination of photographs of both the ships show no evidence of tampering. The only mystery is the number of portholes on the ship's port side fo´c'sle plating. The *Olympic* supposedly had only 14 until 1914. Harland & Wolff advised that the additional 2 portholes were added in 1914 during her conversion to a troop ship. However, as far back as March 1912, the *Olympic* had 16 as is evidenced in photographs. Giving support to Fenton, if the additional 2 had been painted onto the *Olympic* for aesthetic or other reasons, like making them appear identical in March 1912, than this may well be the answer.

The last word must go to Dennis Finch:

> I remember Fenton well from my earlier days a sea, he was well known among the Australian sea going fraternity. Although I sailed with him on only one ship, I did regularly drink with him ashore, yet I failed to hear the *Titanic / Olympic* story he told many times over. I believe that James passed away peacefully in an aged nursing home in late 1972. He had no direct family.

Fenton told an amazing tale. What is even more amazing is that he had been telling the same story to anyone who chose to listen, for some 60 years. How many others heard his story?

Our second mystery surrounds David Evans and his wife, Constance. It is alleged that David was attached to the Harland & Wolff guarantee party that joined the ship at Belfast. The following recollections come from Peter Quinn, a retired businessman who had the story passed down to him from his late father, Joshua Quinn.

Peter's mother was Gladdis Mullins, who married Peter's father in 1914. His mother had an elder sister named Constance. She had earlier married a young engineer from Harland & Wolff named David Evans in January 1912. By today's standards, the Mullins family would have been deemed upper middle class; therefore it is not surprising that both girls married professional men.

Following the completion of the *Titanic*, Evans and his wife had planned to take a belated honeymoon in New York. Their intent was to book second-class passage aboard one of the White Star Line ships from Queenstown to New York; stay a week, then return. As it turned out, Evans was offered the option to travel on board the *Titanic* from Belfast to New York. If agreeable, he would receive payment for his services while on board. He naturally accepted. Peter's father told him that Harland & Wolff officially sanctioned this arrangement. Because Constance would be accompanying David, the couple received an unexpected bonus: Their passage was elevated to first class.

On the evening of April 14, David and Constance dined with the captain in the á la carte restaurant. Constance stated that also present at the table that evening for a period of time was Thomas Andrews, whom both she and David knew very well.

For the short period that Andrews was in the restaurant, he and Evans discussed the ship's engineering department. It was during this conversation that Andrews acknowledged that there was a vibration problem. Evans confirmed this observation that apparently the starboard engine or drive shaft was increasingly adopting an occasional but severe vibration. Evans's recommendation was short and simple: "Until we can accurately identify the probable cause, we may have to recommend reduced revolutions."

In support of this, first-class passenger Mahala D. Douglas and her husband, who coincidentally both dined that evening in the same restaurant as Andrews and Evans, stated that the vibration, as one passed the stairway in the center of the ship, was very noticeable. This is not a surprising comment—after all, this aft staircase was directly above the reciprocating engines. We can only wonder if the Douglases possibly overheard the discussion between Andrews and Evans.

Although Ismay (who dined separately from the captain and the Evanses) and Capt. Smith were not directly involved in the conversation, Mrs. Evans believed that they were privy to what had been discussed. If they had, Ismay and Smith would have been mortified. It was at the captain's table that evening where the guests heard Smith proudly boast that the *Titanic* was making excellent progress and that she could possibly better the *Olympic's* time.

After the meal, David and Constance Evans made their apologies and left the restaurant. Later that night, David allegedly returned below to the engineering department. Constance never saw him again.

While on board the *Carpathia*, Constance had the occasion to speak to one of the ship's officers. This unidentified officer indicated that on the night of the disaster, Ismay had spoken to the captain on the bridge (prior to the collision). Although he was not privy to what was said, the conversation appears to have been centered on the ship's speed.

In the years following the disaster, Constance spent the remainder of her reclusive life living in the small Welsh town of Rhyl. In 1935–1936 the *British Times* approached her for her story; however, it was never published. Documentation held by Constance's family in Cardiff supports the fact that she received from Harland & Wolff a token pension for the loss of her husband.

Peter Quinn stated that his Aunt Connie lived well into her 90s and that even to the last her mind was as sharp as a bell. She passed away in either 1983 or 1984 and was buried in Rhyl.

It is necessary to examine David Evans a little more. Was there a David or Constance Evans listed on board the *Titanic*? The passenger lists for Southampton, Cherbourg, and Queenstown indicate that there were not. Does Constance Evans appear on either the official White Star Line list of survivors or that compiled on board the *Carpathia*? Again, no on both counts.

At this point the story, like Fenton's, appears doubtful. However, there is an unexpected possible lead.

On day 15 of the American inquiry (May 10) a letter from first-class passenger Daisy Minahan was submitted to the inquiry panel. The letter states that on the evening of April 14 Daisy took tea with her brother, William Edward Minahan, and his wife, Lilian, in the á la carte restaurant. She also identified by name two unknown passengers who dined with the captain that evening. Listed below is part of this interesting document:

> Dear Sir: I have given you my observations and experiences after the disaster, but I want to tell you of what occurred on Sunday night, April 14.
>
> My brother, his wife, and myself went to the café for dinner at about 7.15pm [ship time]. When we entered, there was a dinner party already dining [sic], consisting of perhaps a dozen men and three women. Capt. Smith was a guest, as also were Mr. And Mrs. Widener, Mr. And Mrs. Blair [?], and Major Butt. Captain Smith was continuously with his party from the time we entered until between 9:25 and 9:45, when he bid [sic] the women good night and left. I know this time positively, for at 9:25 my brother suggested my going to bed. We waited for one more piece of the orchestra, and it was between 9:25 and 9:45 (the time we departed), that Capt. Smith left.

What is the significance of the vibration of the starboard engine? As stated in an earlier chapter, the *Titanic's* sister ship, the *Olympic,* had been involved in a collision with the HMS *Hawke.* We briefly recap the subsequent damage to *Olympic's* starboard engine: The *Hawke's* bow had damaged the bossing around the *Olympic's* starboard propeller shaft; all three starboard propeller blades were damaged and required replacing, and the shaft itself had been strained off true [balance].

Although all the necessary repairs had been carried out, some theorists believe that the starboard engine would have been suspect under load. They base this on the thought that the starboard engine's bed plates would have taken a severe jolt as the engine and shafting slaved to turn the propellers as they continually impacted with the *Hawke's* keel.

Is it purely coincidental that the *Titanic* suffered starboard engine or propeller shaft problems during her crossing 7 months later? If the *Olympic's* starboard engine, bed plates, or shafting had been still suspect, even after the repairs were made, perhaps running at maximum revolutions over an extended period may have caused severe vibration. The obvious answer here is that the *Titanic* was indeed the *Olympic*.

Would David Evans have been given a first-class berth? The answer may well be yes. Like Thomas Andrews, William H.M. Parr, assistant manager in the electrical department, and Roderick Chisholm, chief ship's draughtsman, both traveled first class. The other six Harland & Wolff employees—Anthony W. Frost, outside foreman engineer; Robert Knight, leading hand fitter engineer; William Campbell, joiner apprentice; Alfred Fleming Cunningham, fitter apprentice; Francis (Frank) Parkes, plumber apprentice; and Ennis Hastings Watson, electrician apprentice—all traveled second class. All 9 of these men were tragically lost in the disaster: Could Evans make it 10?

Could the Blairs have been the Evanses? They both were in the right place at the right time; there is no mistaking that. Did David Evans work for Harland & Wolff? Harland & Wolff does not give out details of present or previous employees. Unfortunately like Fenton, the trail is indeed cold. There is simply insufficient evidence to put forward a strong case for either. What started out as a mystery remains, in the end – just that.

CHAPTER 5

The Lifeboat Evidence

Provision of sufficient lifeboats became one of the most contentious issues that arose in the wake of the *Titanic* disaster. Much of the blame was leveled at the hopelessly outdated regulations set by the British Board of Trade, which had not been amended since 1894. At the time of the last revision of the Board of Trade lifeboat regulations, the 12,950-ton Cunard vessel *Campania* was the largest ship afloat. In the years following this revision no allowance was made for the dramatic increase in the size and passenger capacity of subsequent ships. At the time the plans were drawn for the construction of the *Olympic*-class ships in 1908, the regulations showed no distinction between the 12,950-ton *Campania* and the 46,000-ton *Olympic* and *Titanic*. Under the regulations in force at that time, all British vessels of more than 10,000 tons were required to carry 16 lifeboats, with a capacity of 5,500 cubic ft. According to this outdated regulation, the White Star Line was under no obligation to provide additional lifeboats.

It is stated that, during the significant planning stages of the *Olympic* and the *Titanic*, between 4 and 5 hours were devoted to discussing the ships' interior fittings and décor, with only 10 minutes given to discussing lifeboat capacity. Harland & Wolff's chief architect, Alexander Carlisle, had grave misgivings about the British Board of Trade's hopelessly outdated lifeboat regulations. Carlisle's original sketch incorporated a provision for 64 lifeboats, which would have been sufficient for all on board; however, as discussions proceeded between Harland & Wolff and the White Star Line, Carlisle was obliged to modify his original plans. The number of lifeboats for the *Olympic* and the *Titanic* was first reduced to 48, then to 32, and then to only 16. There is no doubt that Bruce Ismay, the White Star Line's managing director, believed that the *Olympic*-class ships were practically unsinkable. In the event of an incident, each ship's watertight compartments would be capable of keeping the vessel afloat until rescue ships could arrive on the busy North Atlantic. Clearly, if this theory were correct, 16 lifeboats would have been sufficient to ferry the passengers and crew to any rescue ship when used in conjunction with lifeboats provided from other ships.

In addition to the 16 regular wooden lifeboats, the White Star Line provided an additional 4 Engelhardt collapsible boats with a seating capacity for 188 people. The *Titanic's* 14 standard lifeboats had a capacity of 910, and the 2 emergency cutters had a capacity of 80—a total capacity of 1,178, well in excess of the official requirements.

Sixteen of the lifeboats provided on board the *Olympic* and *Titanic* were fitted under Welin double-acting davits, which had been designed to attach and lower 3 lifeboats in succession. The davits could have been easily adapted to increase this number to 4. Eight pairs of these Welin davits had been fitted on both the port and starboard side of each ship, the foremost pair on each side being permanently swung out while at sea to accommodate quick access in the event of an emergency. It was quite common for these large vessels, steaming in excess of 20 knots, to collide with fishing vessels on the Grand Banks.

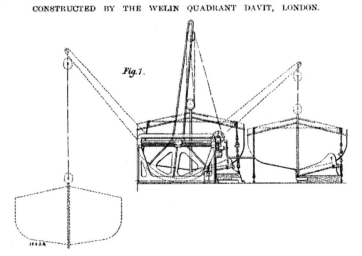

QUADRANT DAVIT FOR DOUBLE-BANKED BOATS.

CONSTRUCTED BY THE WELIN QUADRANT DAVIT, LONDON.

Fig. 1.

The Welin "double quadrant" design, and it's ability to accommodate an inboard row of lifeboats.

Therefore, the two foremost lifeboats were swung out during the voyage to be used in the event of a collision with a smaller vessel as well as an occurrence of a man overboard. Collapsibles A and B were stowed on either side of the roof of the officers' quarters abeam of the first funnel, and Collapsibles C and D were placed on either side at the forward end of the officers' promenade on the boat deck, mounted under the emergency cutters.

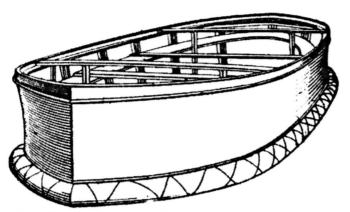

Engelhardt collapsible with canvas bulwark raised.

A great deal of mystery surrounds the *Titanic's* lifeboats, from the time they were fitted to their recovery following the disaster. It is not our intention to pursue what happened on each individual lifeboat. However, our research has identified some suspect facts that could be used to help determine whether the *Olympic* and the *Titanic* were switched.

We begin our discussion with the recovered lifeboats and the mystery surrounding the reason why all of the salvageable lifeboats were not taken aboard the *Carpathia*. We next look into the poorly provisioned lifeboats and draw some possible conclusions based on survivors' accounts. We look at the Board of Trade inspections of the *Titanic's* lifeboats and equipment and establish that, on the basis of the Board of Trade's lifeboat regulations, the *Titanic* should not have been cleared to leave port. We give attention to the possibility that the lifeboats aboard *Titanic* were not new, as would be expected. We also investigate their mysterious disappearance from New York.

Lifeboats 1, 2, and 3 were all unloaded alongside the *Carpathia* and then recovered and returned to New York. Lifeboats 4, 14, and 15 were unloaded alongside the *Carpathia* and then abandoned. These lifeboats were later sighted by the crew of the *Californian* but were not recovered and were never seen again. Lifeboats 5–13 and 16 were recovered and returned to New York. Collapsible A was abandoned during the night when all people aboard transferred to Lifeboat 14. It was later recovered by the *Oceanic* on May 13 and returned to New York. Collapsible B was abandoned just before sunrise, when all of its passengers were transferred to Lifeboat 12. This collapsible was later sighted by the crew of the *Californian* but was not recovered. Collapsible B was again sighted by the *Mackay–Bennett* on April 22, 1912, but was not recovered and was never seen again. Collapsible C was unloaded alongside the *Carpathia* and then abandoned. This collapsible was later sighted by the *Californian* at about 10:00 a.m. the same day but was not recovered and also was never seen again. Collapsible D also was unloaded alongside the *Carpathia* and abandoned.

Lifeboat No. 14 towing collapsible D to the Carpathia

Why Capt. Rostron elected to abandoned Lifeboats 4, 14, and 15 remains a mystery, which is further compounded when one considers that they were all only 5 months old and were in as good a condition as any of the others taken on board. Some of these abandoned lifeboats were partially flooded; however, one would assume that this fact would not have excluded their salvage.

The *Carpathia* arrived in New York on the evening of the April 18, carrying the 13 lifeboats that were recovered on the morning of April 15. Seven of these lifeboats were lowered into the water, and 4 were lowered to the deck of the tug *Champion*. From there, they were towed or carried to the White Star Line's Pier 59. The final 2 lifeboats were unloaded the following morning and then rowed across to join the other 11 lifeboats already secured by rope to the pier. Collapsible A would later be added to the list after being recovered by the *Oceanic*. Some time during the night, souvenir hunters removed and stole many of the lifeboats identification numbers—the small plates bearing the ship's name—and various onboard safety equipment.

Collapsible D approaches the Carpathia

White Star Line ship. However, current research indicates that it is highly probable that the lifeboats were sold and never left the United States. The *Titanic's* lifeboats may have been left to simply rot in a shipyard after being sold off to satisfy the requirements for the "Limitation of Liability" regulations.

We now examine the *Titanic's* lifeboats in more detail to determine if we can identify any clues to support the theory that the *Olympic* and the *Titanic* were switched. One component of the emergency equipment that was supposed to be provided in each of the *Titanic's* lifeboats was an oil lamp. These lamps would have been used to provide light on board the lifeboats should they be required to be launched in the dark. These lamps could have also been used as a pilot lamp to allow other lifeboats to be clearly seen in the area. They could have also been used as a crude Morse lamp. We know that on the night of the disaster, almost all the *Titanic's* lifeboats were hopelessly lost in the dark. These lamps may well have helped identify the locations of various other lifeboats left floating in the water and helped survivors find some debris on which to float on.

It is reasonable to presume that all the *Titanic's* lifeboats and safety equipment had been inspected by Board of Trade representatives and the builders following their installation on the *Titanic*. It would be reasonable to state that all the required safety

From this point, the fate of the *Titanic's* 13 recovered lifeboats remains somewhat of a mystery. It is believed that the lifeboats remained afloat alongside the pier for another 48 hours and then were all hoisted to a second-floor storage loft between the White Star Line's Piers 58 and 59. However, a photograph exists that shows what is later believed to be the *Titanic's* lifeboats tied up and floating at Southampton a few weeks later, with the *Olympic* clearly seen in the background. This would lead us to believe that the lifeboats had been shipped back to England aboard the *Olympic*, reconditioned, and later fitted to another

One of Titanic's *cutters being brought aboard* Carpathia

equipment, including the oil lamps, would have been in place and available for use on the night of the disaster. It has been suggested that the lamps were believed to have been stored in the ship's lamp room when not in use. This does not excuse the fact that most of the lamps had no oil in them. Listed below are some recorded references to the oil lanterns or lack thereof. Unless otherwise noted, all individuals were passengers.

> Lifeboat 3, Elizabeth W. Shutes: "We were told to hunt under seats, any place, anywhere, for a lantern, a light of any kind. Every place was empty. There was no water- stimulant of any kind. Not a biscuit."
> Lifeboat 4, Mrs. E. B. Ryerson: "We had no lights [lantern] or compass."
> Lifeboat 5, H. S Etches, steward: "There was no lamp in number 5."
> Lifeboat 7, J. R. McGough: "There was no light [lantern] in the boat."
> Lifeboat 9, W. M. Wynne, quartermaster: "There was no lamp [lantern] or compass in the boat."
> Lifeboat 12, John Poigndestre, AB (Able Bodied Seaman) "No light. No compass."
> Lifeboat 13, Washington Dodge: "Our lifeboat was found to contain no lantern, as the regulations require."

There is no doubt that Dr. Washington Dodge had been sufficiently disturbed by the lack of a lantern to establish that it should have been there. To have made the comment, he certainly confirmed that, by law, a lantern should have been in the lifeboat.

> Lifeboat 14, Daisy Minahan: "Fifth Officer Lowe had asked us all to try and find a lantern, but none was to be found."
> Lifeboat 15, S. J. Rule, bathroom steward: "No lamp."
> Collapsible D, A. J. Bright, quartermaster: "They had a lantern in the boat but no oil to light it."

For Lifeboats 1, 10, 11, and 16, no lanterns were listed among the equipment on inspection of the on-board equipment in New York. Although these oil lanterns may well have been stolen while they were in storage at New York, there is no reference by any passengers or crew to any of these lanterns having been either found on board or even used during the hours of darkness.

> Lifeboat 2, Mrs. Walter D. Douglas: "The rowing was very difficult, for no one knew how. We tried to steer under Mr. Boxhall's orders, and he put an old lantern, with very little oil in it, on a pole, which he held up for some time."

"An old lantern" on a supposedly brand-new ship?

> Lifeboat 6, Mrs. Helen Churchill Candee: "[Quartermaster Robert Hichens commanded] some of the other ladies to take the light and signal to other lifeboats."
> Lifeboat 8, Mrs. J. Stuart White: "The lamp in the boat was worth absolutely nothing."

During the American inquiry, Sen. Smith put the following questions to J. Bruce Ismay, no doubt to bring into question the condition of the lifeboats fitted to *Titanic*.

> Sen. Smith: Can you tell us anything about the inspection, and the certificate that was made and issued before sailing?
> Mr. Ismay: The ship receives a Board of Trade passenger certificate; otherwise she would not be allowed to carry passengers.
> Sen. Smith: Do you know whether this was done?
> Mr. Ismay: You could not sail your ship without it; you could not get clearance.
> Sen. Smith: Do you know whether this ship was equipped with its full complement of lifeboats?
> Mr. Ismay: If she had not been, she could not have sailed. She would not have received her passenger certificate; therefore she must have been fully equipped.

Sen. Smith: Do you know whether these lifeboats were the lifeboats that were planned for *Titanic*?

Mr. Ismay: I do not quite understand what you mean, sir. I do not think lifeboats are ever built for the ship. Lifeboats are built to have a certain cubic capacity.

Sen. Smith: I understand that; but I mean whether these lifeboats were completed for the ship coincident with the completion of the ship, or whether the lifeboats, or any of them, were borrowed from the other ships of the White Star Line?

Mr. Ismay: They certainly would not have been borrowed from any other ship.

First class passenger Mrs. Frederick O. Spedden stated in her account of the disaster that the numbers "3" and "5" were both attached on her boat: "Our seaman told me that it was an old one taken from some other ship, and he didn't seem sure at the time which was the correct number."

Surely it would be reasonable to believe that Lifeboat 5 must have also had the numbers "3" and "5" incorrectly attached also, but there is no evidence to support this. To have screwed the wrong numbers onto one lifeboat would have been a simple mistake, but to have done it twice defies reason. Could this have simply been an oversight while the lifeboat identification pennants and numbers were switched over from *Olympic* to *Titanic?*

Sen. Smith: Do you recollect whether the lifeboat in which you left the ship was marked with the name *Titanic* on the boats or the oars?

Mr. Ismay: I have no idea. I presume the oars would be marked. I do not know whether the boat was marked or not. She was a collapsible boat."

On a collapsible, the name was painted onto the timbers as opposed to there being a plaque as on the standard lifeboats. Was Smith trying to establish whether there was a reasonable suspicion regarding the true identity or origin of the lifeboats on board the *Titanic?*

First-class passenger Daisy Minahan stated that "Almost at once the boat began to leak and in a few moments the women in the forward part of the boat were standing in water. There was nothing to bail with and I believe the men used their hats."

Collapsible B as found by the crew of the Mackay-Bennett

The *Titanic's* lifeboats were constructed in the clinker style. This means that they were made of planks of wood, which overlapped each other. This style of construction certainly made the boats susceptible to leaking, especially when open to the weather for an extended period of time. All the *Titanic's* lifeboats had been tested for leaks prior to being fitted to the ship in February 1912. A leaking lifeboat would have been far more consistent to that of a boat over 14 months old—for example, the *Olympic.* If the ships had been switched, the original lifeboats on the *Olympic* would have remained secured below their davits, only the identification and number pennants would have been switched over.

The lack of lanterns, compasses, provisions, seaworthiness, and other essential safety equipment onboard the *Titanic's* lifeboats would be far more consistent to a ship such as the *Olympic,* which had been at sea for more than 12 months. It is certainly not uncommon for a ship's lifeboat to suffer from theft; however, this normally takes place over an extended period of time, yet all of the *Titanic's* lifeboats had been outfitted for just over 2 months prior to the disaster, and were supposed to be new—or were they?

To add mystery to the question of the age of the lifeboats and equipment, many of the ropes and tackle used to lower the lifeboats became partially jammed during their operation. Would this be consistent with equipment that was not properly or regularly maintained and serviced? If the crew of the *Olympic* believed the ship to be unsinkable, this may explain the lack of inspections and preventive maintenance that appears to have been a factor in the condition of the *Titanic's* lifeboats.

Another clue to the possible origin of the *Titanic's* lifeboats lies with the adjustable canvas sides of Engelhardt Collapsible A, which had been stored on the roof of the officers' quarters. On the night of the disaster, the collapsible lifeboat sides proved to be impossible to raise and lock into position. As a consequence of this, the lifeboat was washed overboard when the ship was sinking. Passengers who were in the collapsible boat were transferred to another lifeboat later. Collapsible A was set adrift with two, possibly three bodies remaining onboard. It would appear somewhat of a mystery why these adjustable sides could not be raised; after all, they would have been tested prior to their installation onto the ship. Could they have been the *Olympic's* lifeboats?

Another point of interest is the testimony of first-class passenger William Sloper, who described how he had seen, from Lifeboat 7, a number of passengers afloat on an inflated pneumatic life raft (not a standard or collapsible lifeboat). The fact that the *Titanic* did not carry any such life rafts therefore raises the question: Where did this life raft come from? J. Scarrott, on Lifeboat 14, described how the occupants of his boat picked up approximately 20 people from a raft constructed of air boxes, adding to the above mystery.

During the American inquiry the subject of rafts was raised by Sen. Smith when taking evidence from Ismay. The following testimony is of interest.

Sen. Smith: Can you describe those rafts?
Mr. Ismay: There were none on board the ship.
Sen. Smith: Did you see any rafts actually in service?
Mr. Ismay: No, sir.
Sen. Smith: Is it customary for the White Star Line to carry rafts?
Mr. Ismay: I believe in the old days we carried rafts.
Sen. Smith: Recently that has not been done?
Mr. Ismay: Not in the recent ships; no, sir.

Captain Rostron of the Carpathia

The *Titanic* carried 20 lifeboats: fourteen standard ones, 2 emergency cutters, and 4 collapsibles. All the standard lifeboats were recovered by the *Carpathia,* with the exception of 4, 14, and 15. The 2 emergency cutters were also recovered, but the 4 collapsibles were abandoned. This means that 7 lifeboats were left behind. All of the *Titanic's* lifeboats were therefore accounted for. However, the *Carpathia's* Capt. Rostron believed that 1 of the *Titanic's* collapsible lifeboats was not launched and remained secured to the roof of the officer's quarters when the ship went down. Rostron knew that *Titanic* carried only 20 lifeboats, and he had unloaded passengers from 18, Collapsibles A and B having been abandoned after having the passengers transferred to other boats. The total number of lifeboats recovered by the *Carpathia* and returned to New York was 13. This accounts for the 20, but if one adds the collapsible that Rostron believed went down with the ship, then that makes 21. If 1 of the collapsibles did go down with the *Titanic,* then where did the extra lifeboat come from? Could the capsized lifeboat reported to have been seen by Marian Thayer, before any of the collapsibles left the *Titanic,* have been an additional boat, which was mistakenly identified as Collapsible B? It has been testified to, and accepted, that Second Officer Charles H. Lightoller and a group of survivors balanced themselves on top of the overturned Collapsible B for most of the night before being transferred to other lifeboats. If the lifeboat on which Lightoller had balanced himself was a standard lifeboat and not a collapsible, where did it come from?

First-class passenger Marian Thayer, who was aboard Lifeboat 4, stated, "We passed an overturned lifeboat shortly after reaching the water." What could be a possible explanation for Mrs. Thayer's sighting?

Except for the reported 5 first-class women who elected to stay aboard the sinking *Titanic* with their husbands, or for other reasons, all first-class women were saved. However, 15 women (12%) were lost from second class. It would be safe to say that these women had made it to the boat deck when one considers the percentage of second-class female passengers who were scattered among the various lifeboats.

If the first lifeboats launched contained on average only 25 people, and considering that on average each lifeboat was manned by one qualified seaman in charge (normally an able seaman) and three other men provided for manning the oars, could these 15 second-class women have been lowered in a lifeboat that for some reason was capsized at the time it was launched? After all, Mrs. Thayer did see a capsized lifeboat in the water as she sat in Lifeboat 4, which was lowered at 1:55 a.m. from the port side of the ship. Could the lifeboat she saw have been the inverted Collapsible B? This is impossible, because Collapsible B was still secured to the roof of the officers' quarters at the time Lifeboat 4 was launched. If it was a lifeboat that had capsized earlier while being launched, it could have been hauled back up to the boat deck and then reloaded. Could this explain why the loading of the starboard side lifeboats was completed 25 minutes earlier than those on the port side? Could this also explain why 15 second-class female passengers were lost?

Titanic's *boats hanging from the* Carpathia *upon her arrival in New York.*

Could one dismiss the supposedly inverted lifeboat sighted by Mrs. Thayer as a mistaken witness account? No, because there is more to the story. Also in Lifeboat 14 was Jack Foley, who stated that "Scarcely any of the lifeboats were properly manned. Two, filled with women and children, capsized before our eyes."

When one carefully analyzes all of this information one realizes that there would appear to be at least one, possibly two lifeboats more than there should have been. When coupled with the 98 names listed as survivors that never appeared on the *Titanic's* passenger or crew lists, one is left with a lot of questions.

The figures given for the number of passengers and crew aboard the *Titanic* vary depending on the source. In some cases the numbers varied as the investigations moved further ahead. Some members of the crew deserted ship at Queenstown and possibly at Cherbourg. Other points of confusion surround the number saved in the lifeboats, as those numbers conflict also. Walter Lord wrote in his book *A Night To Remember* that there were 2,207 people aboard the *Titanic*. He further stated that "The British Board of Trade figure seems more convincing, less fireman J. Coffy, who deserted at Queenstown." The British Board of Trade lists the total amount of people aboard the *Titanic* as 2,201. All in all, there are many mysteries that surround the lifeboats, and the happenings of the morning of April 15th 1912. These testimonies have been added to the evidence that substantiate a switch theory, and compelling they certainly are.

Titanic's *remaining lifeboats as seen in the White Star berth in New York. At the time this picture was taken, many of the lifeboat name plates and identification markings had already been stolen.*

C H A P T E R   6

Photographic Assessment

The only way to investigate the possibility of the *Titanic* and the *Olympic* being switched prior to the *Titanic*'s maiden voyage is to analyze all the available photographic evidence on both ships. We have made every attempt to procure any available picture of the *Titanic* and the *Olympic* prior to 1913, although doubtless there are photographs that exist that may never be seen by the public, most in private hands, and some lost forever for one reason or another.

In this chapter we address theories that were brought to our attention by researchers and conspiracy theorists alike. To address some of these findings posed by others, it is important that we illustrate all the information that is controversial. As with the rest of the chapters in this book, the reader must form his or her own opinion after all the cards have been laid on the table, so to speak.

Let us now go through the various evidence, as provided by photographic history. We begin our investigation with a port side bow profile photograph of the *Titanic*, taken in May 1911, prior to her launch.

The photograph appears to reveal the name *Titanic* on the side of the ship, in bold contrast to the hull on the upper part of the bow. This photograph has been the center of discussion for years, as some historians asked "were name plates used, or weren't they?" At first glance, there certainly appears to be no evidence of a nameplate affixed to the hull of the ship. In fact, there seems to be no real evidence of plates in photos such as this over the following 3 months of the construction period. The name *Titanic*, which can be seen in this photograph, had in fact been painted or etched onto the original glass negative, most likely for identification purposes. However, close examination of this frame clearly reveals that the letters of the ship's name were incised into the ship's hull plating and are 95% obscured by the scratched-in letters.

In this view, edited for contrast and brightness, the hand printed name "Titanic" on the negative is clearly evident. Also note the rectangle that surrounds the perimeter of the letters in the shell plate.

The *Titanic*'s rigging plan clearly indicates that the ship's name letters, 18 in. high, were to be incised into the plating. Thus the letters that form the name *Titanic* may not have been painted in at this early stage. Regardless, the golden yellow paint is very hard to see in the black-and-white photographs of the era.

In this enlargement of a picture very similar to the one prior, and taken on the same day, the photographer's reference lines are seen. The letter "C" incised into the shell plate is visible to the right.

The questions surrounding the over touching of glass negatives by photographers of the time have been addressed in other publications e.g. *Titanic* – Belfast's Own, 1998 by Stephen Cameron. The use of letters painted onto rectangular steel plates also has been dismissed over the years in some reference books. However, close examination using a high DPI resolution scanner will show that there was in fact an outline from the seam of a steel plate encapsulating the letters. The same outline can be seen in close-up pictures of the *Olympic*'s bow letters. This doesn't mean that the letters weren't incised into the shell plates, as called for by the rigging plan, it means only that the letters were incised onto a separate steel plate or plates, then attached to the main shell plating. Because the two surfaces are flush, one can assume that the large shell plate was cut to accommodate the thickness of the nameplates.

There is no intent to disqualify the personal testimony of eyewitnesses over the years that a

worker slung over the side of the ship painted the name on by hand. It is very probable that the incised letters were painted after they were attached, especially because more coats of paint were to be added to the hull. A close enlargement of picture H-1712, taken while the *Titanic* was moored in the outfitting wharf in late September 1911, shows what would appear to be a rectangular metal plate making up the name *Titanic*.

Adding to the revelation that the letters are part of a separate metal plate is the fact that one can see residue dripping down the face of the fo'c'sle plating, with the metal nameplate(s) applied over the drips. It is obvious that incising letters into a smaller piece of steel is far more practical then trying to maneuver a large piece of shell plate or trying to incise the letters while the shell plate is mounted in place on the hull. It is also likely that having a precut or incised rectangle would allow easy installation of the nameplates, especially when it concerns aligning the actual word into its intended position.

However, some theorists state that the reason for the use of nameplates was due to a problem with the original lettering that may have actually been incised into the shell plate itself. If this were so, one would have to ask: Why? Was there a spacing mistake on the original routing of the letters, or was there another reason? To this date we have not received a valid explanation for this.

In order for the two sisters to be successfully switched, the most obvious starting point would have been to change the ships' bow and stern names. If one accepts as true that the bow names on both the *Titanic* and the *Olympic* had been incised into the actual hull plates, as was originally accepted, then changing the names would not have been as simple as applying black paint over the existing letters and repainting the names. The only solution would have been to either rivet new plates over the existing incised letters or to fill the letters with lead or vulcanite putty in a fashion that would render the surface totally smooth and then simply touch up the affected location with black paint. This would then leave one free to simply paint the ship's name directly onto the hull plating while decreasing the possibility of someone noticing that the depressions of the original name are still visible. Certainly, this would have been relatively simple and achievable within the time parameters we propose. However, it would be more plausible if there were some additional evidence to support this theory.

The investigation inevitably takes us to the wreck of the *Titanic* for further clues. Conspiracy theorists have stated that close examination of underwater video footage showing the *Titanic*'s port bow indicates that most of the bow letters that form the word *Titanic* have apparently disappeared. We now know that at the time of construction the bow name had been incised onto a separate steel plate; thus, it would have been impossible for any of the single letters to have literally fallen away from the hull. Even if there were three separate plates used for the name as are somewhat visible in H-1712, there would be at the very least two letters per plate, and a single letter could not fall off. Of further interest is that the video footage apparently also reveals that the letters appear to be raised as opposed to incised into the steel.

To compound the mystery further, close examination of the area where the missing letters have apparently detached from the hull reveals a mysterious area of light blue paint. It is common for areas that have been filled with lead to turn blue as a result of a reaction with salt water. Could this support the theory that lead was used to fill or cover the *Olympic*'s original letters, whether this was done on a separate plate or actually in the shell plate itself? We have tried to look at the starboard bow to verify any inconsistencies compared to the port side name letters; however, no photographs or video footage of the ship's starboard bow name were available to us. We have been led to believe by other researchers that the starboard side bow nameplate could be completely missing. If this is indeed the case, this further supports the theory of the port side letters being on attached nameplates.

While examining video of the bow section, we discovered another bit of information. We know that the *Olympic* was the first of the three ships to be built. Therefore, we can appreciate the fact that she was extensively photographed throughout her various stages of construction. However, when compared to the small number of photographs taken of the *Titanic*, historians are left rather disappointingly empty handed. Harland & Wolff's decision to take so few photographs of her seems strange; after all, she was the *Olympic* perfected. One would have thought that Harland & Wolff would have taken additional photographs to advertise this fact, as they certainly wasted no energy on photographing other less famous ships like the *Asturias, Themistocles* etc.

Olympic *during on her maiden voyage at Southampton in June 1911 still sporting 14 portholes along her fo´c'sle*

By September 1911, Titanic *would have 16 portholes along her port side fo´c'sle sheer strake*

In preparation for her launch, the *Olympic* was painted light gray to enhance her classic size and lines; this was clearly done for the eager press cameras. It was, after all, the launch of the largest vessel ever to be built at that time. After the launch, the *Olympic*'s hull would be painted the traditional hull color of black. While examining the area on the wreck of the *Titanic* where the port side bow name letters were applied, we saw what appears to be light gray paint. There is no doubt that this paint has been slowly revealing itself as the currents have worn away the top coats of black paint. There are also areas of the hull that show this light gray paint in the area of the port hawsehole. If this ship were actually the *Titanic* one should be able to see not light gray paint but a dark gray builder's primer, if not bare metal. Why has this anomaly failed to be recognized by other researchers or expeditions to the wreck?

This certainly leaves an element of doubt over the wreck's identity, and it certainly adds strength to the argument that the two ships were indeed switched. This compelling but inconclusive evidence has given us renewed enthusiasm for further investigation of the shipwreck for clues that may finally solve the conspiracy theory.

The theory of rectangular metal plates with the ship's name letters painted on certainly answers the markings seen in Picture H-1712. It also adds credence to the theory of a name switch. Whether nameplates were used, or the letters were etched into the actual shell plate, or a combination of both, any attempt to switch the name would not, with a little effort, have been impossible. In any of the above-mentioned circumstances the original lettering could be easily hidden

At the time of the *Titanic*'s launch

there were 14 portholes in the port side plating between the fo´c'sle deck and the sheer line of the hull, but by late July the same year, the ship was fitted with an additional 2 portholes, giving her a total of 16. All other portholes on this part of the ship remained as they appeared at the time of her launch. Although the ship had 14, then later 16, portholes on the port side, she had 15 on her starboard side, and this number remained consistent throughout. The *Olympic* and the *Britannic* were also consistent on the starboard side, with 15 portholes. The *Olympic*, like the *Titanic*, was fitted originally with the same 14-porthole arrangement on the port side of her fo´c'sle, but 2 additional portholes were later fitted. The reason why, and when they were fitted, will be covered later. The *Britannic*, when launched, had 16 portholes, consistent with the later port side configuration of the *Titanic* and the *Olympic*.

The porthole arrangements in the hulls of both the *Titanic* and the *Olympic* were almost identical from below the C, or shelter deck on down. To switch the ships, very little would have had to be done concerning the round portholes themselves. The only noticeable difference between the two ships' porthole arrangements was on C deck itself. This is the top row of round portholes seen in the white

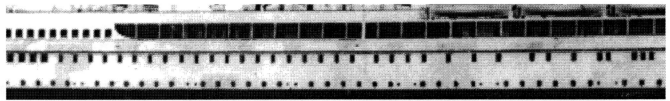

Titanic's C deck included sets of small windows along the row of large stateroom portholes
One window was for a bath, and the other for a water closet.

Olympic's C deck portholes were a bit different in the configuration of the small windows.

H-1636 - Olympic in dry dock for propeller repairs in March 1912

along the sides of the hull. The *Olympic* had a few small single sidelights positioned between the rows of larger portholes along C deck. The *Titanic* differed in that there was always a set of small portholes, side by side, positioned among the larger portholes. This was a difference that was once again never changed on the *Olympic*. Along with the C deck changes, there was also a difference in the arrangement of the portholes in the plating between the poop deck and sheer line. The grouping and spacing are noticeably different. There would have been little trouble in altering this arrangement, possibly by painting on false portholes and blocking out existing ones. It can easily be appreciated that the same deception would have been possible in regard to the arrangement on both the *Titanic*'s and *Olympic*'s C deck portholes amidships, specifically with the small portholes indicated earlier. These small portholes serviced first-class lavatories. It is also interesting to note that James Fenton stated that when he allegedly joined the ship some of her portholes had been painted on.

Olympic at New York in June 1911 – maiden voyage. Notice the lack of a large cowl and the crew galley skylight.
The breakwater railing is painted brown

The *Olympic* was seen with the newly acquired portholes in the port side plating of her fo´c´sle on her return to Belfast in March 1912. However, it is interesting to note that when we asked Harland & Wolff about the date of this upgrade to the *Olympic*, they advised that the ship did not receive these additional 2 portholes until 1914, as part of her conversion to a troop transport vessel. So why does she have the 16 portholes in March 1912? In photograph H-1636, could the 2 additional portholes have been simply painted onto the plating? This would almost certainly indicate that something was going on with these two ships. Close examination of all photographs, which show the *Titanic*'s port bow, after the *Olympic* had departed Belfast on the March 7, 1912, reveals 16 portholes. There is some doubt regarding the authenticity of portholes 3 and 5. The photographs are not good enough to make out specific window mounts, as the portholes appear totally black in some cases. The only way to satisfactorily resolve this problem is by close examination of the wreck, which would comprehensively determine whether the fo´c´sle portholes were in fact all genuine. If a close examination revealed 16, this would positively identify the wreck as the *Titanic*. If the examination revealed only 14 portholes, with the other 2 having been painted on, this would then create some uncertainty as to the true identity of the ship lying on the ocean floor, as the 2 painted portholes would probably no longer be visible. The false-porthole idea is only a theory held by some researchers looking into the switch conspiracy. There seems to be some evidence that this would be possible, but there is more information that needs to be addressed in this matter before it can be laid to rest.

Photograph H-1636 is without doubt the *Olympic*. She is clearly identified by the fact that the bridge cabs are still flush with the side of the superstructure. Because this photograph was taken on March 3, 1912—4 days before she departed Belfast for Southampton—it is quite obvious that there would have been insufficient time to switch the ships. This is based on the fact that she still has her B deck window configuration, which we know was completely different from that fitted to the *Titanic*. Therefore, there would have been insufficient time to change all the B deck applications, which would have been blatantly visible to workmen in the yard. This photograph supports the theory that the *Olympic* and *Titanic* had not been switched in either October or November 1911 or in March 1912.

Titanic's *fo´c'sle* at Southampton. Notice the crew galley skylight, the large cowl, and the white rail on the breakwater.

On the ship's fo´c'sle deck there is a breakwater, which was fitted to prevent excessive green water from running over the deck into the fore well deck. It is here that one can find another minor difference between the *Titanic* and the *Olympic*. The *Titanic*'s breakwater top railing was painted white; however, on the *Olympic* it was painted brown. Photographs of the *Titanic*'s fo´c'sle deck at Southampton offer the evidence of the white breakwater railing. Aerial views of the *Olympic* arriving in New York on her maiden voyage as well as later photographs of the *Olympic* reveal that the breakwater railing was painted brown; however, the painting of the upper part of the breakwater could have easily been altered if required. It would be interesting to view photographs of this area on the wreck today. Could there be brown paint still intact on the upper part of the *Titanic's* breakwater, exposed by the erosion of the white paint? Regrettably, available video footage shows the wreck's breakwater so corroded with rust that it is almost impossible to tell.

On the *Titanic's* fo´c'sle deck at Southampton there was a large white cowling on the port side just forward of the breakwater, yet in early photographs of the *Titanic* there is no visible cowling in this position. In early photographs of the *Olympic* the cowling also is not fitted; however, in a photograph taken of the two ships together in Belfast the *Olympic* has the cowling in place. It should be remembered that cowlings like these were easily removed, so little importance should be placed on this observation. Another difference, is the fact that the *Olympic* was not originally built with the crew galley skylight on the fo´c'sle, aft of the port side breakwater, as was the *Titanic*. This skylight does, however; suddenly appear in Frame H-1827, after the sinking of the *Titanic*. As our investigation delves deeper into the story we find that these numerous little discrepancies slowly mount into grave suspicions that the ships could have exchanged identities up to this point.

Olympic dressed out in New York on her maiden voyage. Notice the size of the swan neck ventilation head to the left of the center stokehold duct.

Next, we move aft to an area directly above the *Olympic's* bridge, forward of the #1 funnel. On the starboard side of the large rectangular stokehold duct there is a large swan neck vent. On the *Olympic* this swan neck vent was shorter in profile than that fitted to the *Titanic*; however, after the *Olympic's* return to service after the port side propeller blade had been replaced at Belfast in March 1912 the height of this swan neck vent appears to be the same height as that fitted to the *Titanic*. There is probably little significance to this, as it could easily be explained as a modification. When the *Titanic* departed Belfast on April 2 the same vent was lower than that originally fitted. What we have now is a complete reversal of the ship's swan neck vents. Why would the shipyard have taken the lower profile curl off the *Olympic* and replaced it with a higher profile one and at the same time take the higher profile vent on the *Titanic* and replace it with a smaller one? The *Titanic*'s profile was starting to look like the *Olympic*, and the *Olympic* was starting to look like the *Titanic*. If Harland & Wolff officials believed that the *Olympic* required a higher swan neck vent in this area, why remove the existing vent on *Titanic* and replace it with a smaller one?

In pictures taken of the *Olympic* during her maiden voyage there is only one cowl vent on the top of the reciprocating engine casing on the port side. In a later picture, which shows the two sisters together, one can see that there has been a cowl added to the starboard side of the roof. At some point before March 1912 this cowl was added to the *Olympic*, producing a configuration that now matched the *Titanic*'s.

H-1827 - The Olympic *at Harland & Wolff for her 1912-13 refit. Notice the additions of the large cowl, and the crew galley skylight. The fowl weather vent seen in New York on her maiden voyage is still present.*

In any of the pictures taken of the *Olympic* within her first few voyages one can see that the *Olympic*'s lifeboats are all painted completely white. When the ship returned to Belfast following her collision with the *Hawke*, the lifeboats were all painted brown around the gunwales, to be consistent with those on the *Titanic*.

Why the lifeboats on the *Olympic* were painted brown around the gunwales at this particular time remains a mystery. These lifeboats could have easily been painted at any time. It would appear that the White Star Line had been motivated for some reason to make the lifeboats on both the ships look exactly the same. When the *Olympic* sailed out of Belfast on March 7, the two additional portholes were seen on her fo'c'sle's port side plating, identical in configuration to that of the *Titanic*. The curl vents forward of the forward funnel had been reversed. The *Olympic* now had the *Titanic*'s cowl forward of the breakwater on her port side, and all her lifeboats had been painted to look similar to those of the *Titanic*. The ships were, to the casual observer, in essence completely interchangeable.

Titanic *in the fitting out wharf getting the new B deck windows added.*

Above: *By the time this picture was taken of* Titanic *in Southampton, the swan neck ventilation head was cut shorter.*

Above and Top: Titanic *in March 1912. The swan neck ventilation head is visible on the left side of the center stokehold duct.*

By the time the *Olympic* departed Belfast on March 7, the two ships were virtually identical from the exterior, the only difference being the B deck window arrangement. The *Titanic*'s forward A deck screens had not been fitted by the time the *Olympic* departed Belfast. If the ships had not been switched at this time, how could they have ever been switched at all? They were to never meet again. Could there have possibly been another window of opportunity for a switch?

As stated above, the most distinctly different exterior difference was the B deck windows. At the time the *Titanic* was launched, the windows were identical to those fitted to the *Olympic*. Work on changing these windows began in the weeks following the *Titanic*'s launch. One can see that construction had commenced on the removal of the old windows while the *Titanic* was tied up at the fitting-out wharf. As can be seen, not all the old B deck windows had to be removed, as the windows that remained were contingent to the private promenades. Bruce Ismay earlier decided that the open B deck promenade on the *Olympic* was a waste of additional revenue-producing passenger accommodations. There is merit in this observation in the fact that A deck, directly above, already had an open promenade. As a result, the cabins on the *Titanic*'s B deck were extended out to the ship's sides forming, among other rooms, luxury parlor suites, which included two private promenades, one on each side of the ship.

So if the ships were switched, the *Titanic*'s B deck windows would have to be changed to match the arrangement of those on the *Olympic*. This would have been relatively easy to do. It would be as simple as removing the existing less uniform windows and replacing them with the frames that were originally on the *Titanic* at the time of her launch. After all, they probably would have been stored away somewhere in the yard when they were removed from the ship.

An enlargement from the picture above. Olympic arriving in New York on her maiden voyage with just one cowl on the reciprocating engine casing.

The evidence that can be deducted from the actual photographs will leave one bewildered. It is in the eyes of the beholder to judge whether the pictures hold the answers to a conspiracy of a switch between the two nearly identical sisters. It is peculiar that the *Olympic* was suddenly being updated to look more like the *Titanic* prior to April 1st 1912. It is even more mysterious when one observes the imperfections in hull paint combined with the new discovery that the Olympic class liners actually did have their hull names attached to individual plates. What should be the most stable evidence to disprove a switch; the photographs in actuality add to the stability of a switch.

The two great ships in echelon, Titanic *in dry-dock and* Olympic *at outfitting wharf - March 1st 1912.*

Olympic *now in dry-dock with* Titanic *at outfitting wharf - March 2nd 1912.*

An enlargement from the top photo. The Olympic *has by this time received a second cowl over her reciprocating engine casing. The two sisters are starting to look very similar.*

Olympic's *lifeboats with white sheer planks seen on her maiden voyage*

Lifeboats with brown sheer planks on the Titanic

Olympic *in dry dock at Harland & Wolff supposedly during her repairs after the* Hawke *accident. By the time of the collision, the* Olympic's *lifeboat sheer planks or gunwales as they are sometimes called, were already painted brown.*

C H A P T E R   7

A Window of Opportunity

At the time the *Olympic*-class liners were being constructed, Harland & Wolff's workforce and outside contractors supposedly numbered in excess of 14,000 workers. To consider the possibility that the *Titanic* and *Olympic* had been switched in either October or November of 1911 or in March of 1912, one would first have to accept that the shipyard's thousands of workers were either all blind or had been paid for their silence. To accept the premise that the workers who had been working on the *Titanic* for several months had simply finished work one day and than reported back the following day, never realizing that it was a different ship, is somewhat unbelievable. It must be remembered that the same workforce that had been engaged on the *Titanic*'s construction had, without doubt, also worked on the *Olympic* during her construction.

The *Olympic* had returned to Belfast on October 6, 1911, for extensive repairs after her collision with the *Hawke*. She had departed Southampton on October 4th and, having completed the necessary repairs, returned back to service on November 29, 1911. If, for argument's sake, it was established by the yard's structural engineers and senior management that the *Olympic* was beyond economic repair, an elaborate scheme might well have been hatched to switch the ships. However, it would not have been possible to switch them at that time. Clearly, the only opportunity the shipyard had to switch the *Titanic* and the *Olympic* would have been when the two ships were together, which occurred on only a few occasions.

One possible window of opportunity would have been on the *Olympic*'s second unscheduled return to Belfast the following year, on March 1, 1912. The reason for this unscheduled visit was for the replacement of a lost port side propeller blade. However, we know that the photograph of the *Olympic* (H-1636) had been taken on Sunday, March 3, 1912, which meant shipyard workers would have had only 2 days to switch around all the B deck promenade windows on both ships. They also needed to transfer pertinent furniture from the *Olympic* over to the *Titanic*; change the names on the bow and stern; and switch any easily noticed equipment, in less than 48 hours. This would have been very difficult, if not impossible, to do. It would have involved a great number of workers to achieve this. Remember, all these major external structural alterations would have had to have been completed in front of the thousands of workmen engaged by Harland & Wolff at that time.

If this theory were to be believed, one would have to accept the story of the *Olympic* losing one of her propeller blades on February 24th as a red herring to get the *Olympic* back to Belfast to switch the ships. Even if the switch had been partially executed in the months leading up to the *Olympic*'s return to Belfast in March 1912, frame H-1636 brings the whole 48-hour switch theory to a definite halt.

If the powers that be had ever switched the two ships, one would need to look for another workable theory that addresses all of the gaping holes in the previously mentioned dates. This brings us to the only other possible switch option.

Just after noon on Wednesday April 3rd, 1912, the *Olympic*, under the command of Captain Herbert James Haddock, steamed out of Southampton for her 19th Atlantic crossing, or 10th westward passage. However, in the 5 days prior to the commencement of this voyage, a tantalising situation had presented itself.

Prior to *Olympic's* arrival from Cherbourg on March 30th, the American Line's *St Louis* had occupied pier 44. The vessel had been earlier obliged to vacate this berth prior to *Olympic's* arrival later that afternoon, being hauled to the opposite north-western corner of the dock and secured to the port side of the rafted *Philadelphia*. That morning, *Olympic* weighed anchor and departed the French port of Cherbourg just after 7:00 am inbound for Southampton. The standard duration for the Channel crossing was about five and half hours which occasionally varied depending on the weather conditions, the shipping movements around the approaches to Southampton Waters, or the tides. On this occasion, all the necessary conditions prevailed for a standard arrival at Southampton just after noon. For some unexpected reason the ship lost 30 minutes during the channel crossing. This minor delay had been addressed briefly in an obscure shipping reference found within the Southampton City Museum's archives which notes a loss of 30 minutes for the White Star Liner while crossing the English Channel.[*] Unfortunately the text within the document does not elaborate on the actual cause; the direct reference simply being a short by-line within a larger writing. As a consequence, the incident could be easily passed over at the casual glance as having no significant relevance.

Between the period 1910 -15, George Larwood, a dockside worker at Southampton later recalled to his granddaughter, C. Baverstock how he had been in the unique position during those years to witness the arrival and departure of many of the great liners of that period. On the occasion of March 30th 1912, five days before the *Titanic* berthed at Southampton (April 4th) he again witnessed the arrival of her elder sister, *Olympic*.

Upon entering the White Star Dock, *Olympic* had berthed bow first alongside pier 44. Following the disembarkation of passengers, mail and consignments, the ship was than unceremoniously moved to another berth. At the time, Larwood had reasoned that this berth change had been likely necessitated by the lingering effects and congestion brought about by the coal shortage caused by the infamous labor strike.[†]

At this point, we have identified an obscure reference to a delay between Cherbourg and Southampton, the apparently insignificant berthing arrangements upon the *Olympic's* arrival and a tantalising third hand account of the ship being re-berthed several hours after her arrival. These three incidents all appear to be somewhat unrelated when looked upon in the singular, though the considered sum, when coupled with the proceeding information, hints otherwise.

In support of Larwood's observation, a picture postcard offered for auction in 1999 presented a handsome stern starboard quarter profile of the ship at the White Star Dock. On the back of the sepia card it proclaimed, "*Olympic* departs Southampton, leaving the dock clear for the arrival of world's newest and largest ship." If the *Olympic* had been originally stern out (towards the Test) as recalled by Larwood, than the postcard reveals her position had indeed been reversed just 3 days later.

One final observation that Larwood also made was that on the following morning propeller blades had arrived dockside by rail car. This observation is mentioned because it may be very significant when considering whether something clandestine was afoot.

Mystery surrounds the *Olympic*'s reported collision in the English Channel, which resulted in her being laid up. The following statement appears in the Ulster Folk and Transport Museum's *Titanic Information Booklet*: "The *Olympic* had been laid up for repairs following a minor collision in the English Channel, so her Chief Officer H T Wilde had been transferred from the *Olympic* to the *Titanic*."

Propeller blades seen here behind London South Western Railway trucks - April 8th. Had they been dispatched to Southampton for use on Olympic?

---

[*] Presented as a web document 1998
[†] Information by correspondence (Baverstock 1987)

The term *laid up* implies that the *Olympic*'s collision damage had been sufficient to have her withdrawn from active service for possibly 3 days. Yet the damage must have been either repaired during this period or deemed insufficient to have warranted the cancellation of her Southampton–New York voyage.

The *Olympic* did, without doubt, depart Southampton as scheduled just after noon on April 3, 1912. We also know that *Olympic* had departed on schedule from New York on her prior eastbound journey having taken aboard additional coal to offset the critical shortage across the Atlantic. It has even said that coal in canvas bags had been stored in vacant third class accommodations and possibly in her reserve coal bunker. The additional tonnage of coal would have effectively provided the ship with sufficient fuel for the scheduled eastward crossing plus 36 additional hours operating within her regular service speed.

We pose to readers the following question: How badly damaged was the *Olympic* after this reported collision in the English Channel? It was obviously bad enough to have referred to her as having been "laid up." It is also interesting to try and establish whether the actual remedial work following the collision was carried out in Southampton, at the Harland & Wolff repair facility, or somewhere else. The only other likely place a ship of this size could have been repaired with all the necessary facilities would have been Harland & Wolff's yard at Belfast, in Northern Ireland. Therefore, is it possible that the *Olympic* made an unknown return trip back to Belfast for repairs and, if so, was it a trip that has never been revealed, or recorded?

CAPTAIN SMITH & OFFICERS OF THE TITANIC

Figure 1

If this were the only recorded text referring to the *Olympic* being laid up prior to her April 3rd departure from Southampton one would most likely dismiss the whole idea. However, the following statement appears in the autobiography of *Titanic's* second officer, Charles Lightoller, written many years after the disaster. He makes mention of the *Olympic* having been "laid up" prior to her departure from Southampton on April 3, 1912:

Unfortunately, whilst in Southampton we had a reshuffle amongst the Senior Officers. Owing to the *Olympic* being laid up, the ruling lights of the White Star Line thought it would be a good plan to send the Chief Officer (H. T. Wilde) of the *Olympic*, just for the one voyage as Chief Officer of the *Titanic* to help with his experience of her sister ship.

This statement gives us a vital second reference, but there are more pieces to the puzzle. Figure 1 has caused confusion in the minds of researchers for years. Most publications and TV specials label this picture as "the officers of the *Titanic*." Other historians have dismissed this picture from being the *Titanic*'s crew because of a few questions as to the identity of some of these men, and the fact is that this picture was taken aboard the *Olympic*. One point of disagreement among researchers is whether the man sitting to the right of Captain Smith is Chief Officer Wilde. There are pictures of a younger man seen in specials and publications recorded as being Henry Wilde, but they may be just that—pictures of a younger Henry Wilde. The man sitting to the right of Smith may or may not match the "younger man" pictures. Whom else could the man in this picture be? The man in this picture is wearing the sleeve stripes of a chief officer, which Wilde was on both the *Olympic* and the *Titanic*. There is very little information relating to the early officers of the *Olympic*, at least available to the public at large, and those stripes could signify nothing other than a chief officer. Again, perhaps the reason for the confusion among researchers and historians over this picture is because of the fact that it was taken on the *Olympic*.

Figure 2

If the many captions listing these men as "the officers of the *Titanic*" over the years are correct, the order of appearance, sitting, from left to right, would seem to be: Sixth Officer James Moody, Chief Officer Wilde, Captain Smith, First Officer William Murdoch and, standing, from left to right: Chief Purser Hugh McElroy, Second Officer Charles Lightoller, Third Officer Herbert Pitman, Fourth Officer Joseph Boxhall, and Fifth Officer Harold Lowe. Lowe had distinctive facial features, and the man in this photograph is *not* Fifth Officer Lowe. However, this man is wearing the cuff stripes of a junior officer. The man in this picture looks like the original intended second officer of the *Titanic*, David Blair (who was removed as second officer in Southampton).

If this is a picture of the officers of the *Titanic*, then when could these men have assembled on the deck of the *Olympic* for this picture? Charles Lightoller transferred to the *Titanic* from the *Oceanic*, arriving in Belfast on March 20, 1912. Pitman, Boxhall, Lowe, and Moody transferred from their old ship assignments, arriving in Belfast on March 27, 1912. With these dates in mind, how did these men assemble on the *Olympic* when she supposedly departed Belfast after her last recorded repairs on March 7, 1912? Could this be a third piece of evidence indicating that the *Olympic* was in Belfast at the very beginning of April, allowing enough time for a couple of photos of the new *Titanic* crew? Figure 2, possibly taken on the same day, supposedly shows, from left to right, Murdoch, Boxhall, Wilde, and Smith. Again, where did Boxhall come from when he didn't arrive in Belfast until March 27? We will address this picture of "the officers of the *Titanic*" in the final chapter.

March 27, 1912—the day that Pitman, Boxhall, Lowe and Moody signed on the *Titanic* at Belfast—was also the day the ship was registered. On the 'Agreement and Account of Voyages and Crew' papers recorded in Belfast, Captain Haddock is listed as being the original intended commander to oversee the trials of the *Titanic*. He would have then handed the ship over to Smith who, one would assume, would have still been on the *Olympic* and, hence, at Southampton. History tells us that Smith became the commander in charge for *Titanic*'s sea trials, but how did he get to Belfast if he was on the *Olympic*? What happened to Haddock? Perhaps an explanation for this is that Smith arrived at Belfast with the *Olympic* because of the damage caused in the English Channel.

Haddock sailed the disguised *Titanic* back to Southampton to meet the April 3rd departure date, and Smith went on to command the *Olympic* from Belfast now converted to appear as her younger sister. Quite literally, the two captain's handed off one ship for the other.

Upon Olympic's *berthing at New York on her maiden voyage, she struck the corner pilings of the dock and sustained a long scrape along the starboard side of her hull.*

The picture above is of the Titanic *whilst in Southampton, modified to enhance the contrast. Her paint was touched up on her port side for the benefit of the public, but her starboard side remained in the original condition from when she left Belfast. Notice the similarity between the discolored plates on* Titanic *and the area of the* Olympic's *damage above.*

Following the theory through, the *Olympic* would have had to depart Southampton on the afternoon of March 30, 1912, steam the required 570 miles to Belfast, where she would have arrived in the early hours of April 1st. Because of this extremely tight schedule, timing would have been essential. The disguised *Titanic* would have been required to depart Belfast just before, or not long after, dawn on the same day to safely return back to Southampton in time to depart for New York on April 3rd. Research reveals that the *Olympic*'s passage and navigation up the Victoria Channel and the River Lagan would have been assisted by the light of a near-full moon. The moon at this time would have set below the horizon on the morning of April 1st at 5:53 a.m.; however, sunrise at 5:56 a.m. conveniently coincided with the setting of the moon. Therefore, light should not have been a major factor in the navigation and repositioning of the two liners. On April 1, 1912, the full moon at Belfast was at 10:04 p.m.

If one is willing to accept the above, which was certainly possible, one now has to address the problem of how would the *Olympic* have safely navigated the narrow confines of first the Victoria Channel and then the River Lagan, without the use of tugs. In actuality, she could not have navigated either the Victoria Channel or the River Lagan without the assistance of tugs. So where could the necessary four or five tugs have come from? It would have been obvious to the casual observer, if these tugs had been sighted standing by at Belfast, that this would have indicated the imminent arrival of a large ship.

The *Titanic*'s sea trials had been scheduled for 10:00 a.m. April 1, 1912, and, as such, Harland & Wolff had engaged the Alexander Towing Company to supply four tugs (the *Herald, Hornby, Huskisson,* and *Herculaneum*) to assist the *Titanic* down through the River Lagan and the Victoria Channel. Although it is recorded that these tugs were alongside the *Titanic* at 9:00 that morning, it would be reasonable to assume that these tugs, which had been sent from Liverpool, would most likely have arrived at Belfast the evening before the trial itself. If this was indeed the case, could not these same four tugs have also assisted the *Olympic* into Belfast a few hours prior?

Up to this point, we have managed to get the *Olympic* out of Southampton without raising any real suspicions, and we have found the time to get the *Olympic* back to Belfast and then return the disguised *Titanic* to Southampton in sufficient time to depart for New York. We have also arranged to have the necessary tugs in place to assist her to navigate both the River Lagan and the Victoria Channel, and we have also explained how the *Olympic* was able to sail into Belfast under cover of darkness. Further – *Olympic* had taken aboard additional coal at New York, easily sufficient for a Belfast round trip.

As mentioned earlier, Larwood had stated that *Olympic* had been reberthed several hours after her arrival at Southampton. But reberthed to where? The postcard mentioned prior also supports her position at the dock had indeed been reversed from the 30th to her departure on the 3rd of April.

We know that the *Titanic* was scheduled to steam out of Belfast for her sea trials on the morning of April 1st so, with this in mind, one can reasonably expect that if the tugs were to be alongside at 9:00 a.m., the boilers would have been up to operating temperature and pressure with the fires slightly banked to avoid popping off the safety valves. Assuming that firing would have begun 8–12 hours prior, as was the norm with Scotch boilers, the first shift in the boiler rooms would have started work some time between 9:00 the previous night and 1:00 that morning. Therefore, the ship could have made the required steam to get under way in a reasonably short period of time.

It is known that there were high winds on the morning of April 1st, and therefore White Star management decided not to proceed with the *Titanic*'s sea trials, as this would have warranted an unnecessary risk to the ship's hull. Could the cancellation of these trails have had anything to do with the fact that by this time the ships had already been switched and that the 24-hour delay in the sea trials allowed further internal and external modifications to take place? Was the cancellation of these trails a scheme instigated to reduce the planned 2-day sea trials to only 1? With the trials reduced by more than 50% they, and the onboard inspections, would have been rushed. Many obvious examples of the ship being more than 12 months old, such as the boiler rooms, hull paintwork, lifeboats and their emergency equipment, and so on, could have gone totally unnoticed.

It might well be that the White Star Line could not afford to run the risk of a full 2-day intensive sea trial, believing that the structurally compromised hull of the *Olympic* may well have given indications of serious hull trouble at some point.

It should be remembered that the *Titanic* had been virtually completed by the evening of March 31, 1912, and that 99% of the workers assigned to the *Titanic*'s construction would have finished their assigned work on board the ship by the close of the shift on Saturday March 30. They would have been reassigned to a different work location or project in the yard at the start of their shift on Monday April 1st and would never set foot on the *Titanic* again. The only exception to this would have been a selected workforce who would have continued to make last-minute adjustments and provide a skeleton crew on board for the sea trials and the subsequent voyage from Belfast to Southampton.

If the *Titanic* and *Olympic* had been switched before the yard's workers had reported back for duty on the morning of Monday, April 1st, and if the *Olympic* had been altered externally to look like the *Titanic*, apart from those actually involved in the switch who among the yard's 14,000-strong workforce would have ever realized that the ship now sitting at the outfitting wharf on Monday morning was in fact the *Olympic* masquerading as the *Titanic*?

To add to the intrigue of this situation is the fact that very few people were allowed to visit the *Titanic* in Southampton. She was never opened to public view. Her paint and funnels were touched up and she was repainted on her port side only while at Southampton. The port side was of course facing the dock. Why was this done to a new ship? Was someone trying to hide something before the hoards of passengers arrived on Wednesday April 10th?

This theory manages to address how the White Star Line and Harland & Wolff may well have achieved the greatest switch of all time. Although we have attempted to present a possible alternate theory, it should still be remembered that there would have still been hundreds, if not thousands, of people actively involved in this switch, giving a true meaning to the phrase 'April Fool's Day'.

C H A P T E R   8

The Conspiracy Put to rest

It is most important that we step back from the mindset of the last quarter of the 20th century so as to judge the events of 1912 in the perspective of the time. Since the latter half of the past century many people, especially Americans, have grown to judge their world on the basis of feelings and how things affect them personally. This attitude is marred by an inability to see the forest for the trees as the truth and the reality of human nature are completely shrouded in the emotions of the modern age.

At the turn of the century the civilized nations were undergoing a growth of dramatic proportions. The Industrial Revolution was pushing inventions ahead at an alarming pace. With this new era came, as one can imagine, carelessness and mistakes. Quite frankly, mankind was unprepared for what it was getting into and had a lot of lessons to learn. Even to this day, mankind finds itself caught up in technology, tempting fate and one's own ability far too much. Just as after the sinking of the *Titanic*, man has time and time again had to step back to call on his common sense and keep himself in step but, as usual, it never lasts very long.

The Edwardian age was an era of very rich men and very poor immigrants. The antitrust laws were not in effect yet, so the dash to create monopolies was prevalent. The "Atlantic Ferry" was a very profitable business with the huge inrush of emigrants flocking to America. These emigrants, most of whom were poor, were segregated from the first and second classes, and this was accepted as common practice. This is the way it was in 1912, and people expected it. The emigrants were treated well aboard the *Titanic*—many of these people had never even seen an actual operational toilet before. Those who were wealthy were not supposed to mingle with the emigrants, and there were valid reasons why. Though some 1st class passengers traveled into the 3rd class for a peak of the simpler life, the ship companies did not condone the practice. The upper classes were informed that intermingling with 3rd class could cause delays at New York with the health inspectors. Though the emigrants were checked by medical officers before embarking, there was still a chance of some of them having any number of common diseases and ailments of the time such as: diphtheria, tuberculosis, typhoid, measles etc.

The name of the game in the passenger trade was money and competition. To make money, a company had to appeal to the emigrant and the millionaire alike. To achieve this they needed speedy travel time and a luxurious ship. Even though the *Olympic*-class liners had no chance of breaking the records set by Cunard, they still had to cross the Atlantic in a reasonable amount of time, or else customers would find passage with a competitor.

Captain Smith had been at sea for many years. He was a Salty Dog, well respected by his repeat passengers. He had been at sea long before there was wireless telegraphy aboard ships. When he was in command of the *Titanic* across the Atlantic on her maiden voyage, he was doing what he always did, and what the captains of other passenger liners always did: sail at a pace to keep to schedule. Keeping on schedule was another factor that pressured captains to arrive on or ahead of schedule regardless of the conditions encountered. Charles Lightoller even made mention in his book, written years later, that he considered the passenger liner captains to be reckless with sailing their ships—not because they wanted to be, but because they had to be.

When one reads the testimonies of the many captains who attended the British Inquiries one notices that they spoke of what the captains of the time did when they were sailing the North Atlantic passenger route. These captains sailed as fast as possible, assigned men to the lookout, and carried on until someone sighted something. At that point, if ice were found, they would take the appropriate action. Unfortunately, on the night of April 14, 1912, the ice was spotted too late. Everything just happened to go wrong on that fateful night. It is well to remember that Rostron sailed at full speed, too, while en route to the *Titanic*'s radioed position. What precaution against collision did he take? He put lookouts at the "eyes of the ship" and put his trust in them to sight any obstructions ahead. Smith had no reason to believe that his lookouts would fail him; after all, this is the way it had been done for many years. The chances of a liner of that size hitting a huge iceberg and sinking were slim to none. In fact, the people of the age literally thought these huge ships to be unsinkable. Along with this attitude of invincibility, sinkings caused by impacts with icebergs were very rare.

It is amazing how the story of the lack of binoculars is thrown around in the modern times as a symbol of incompetence. Have we forgotten how binoculars work, or what they are used for? Binoculars are not magic eyes, pulling objects out of the air like X-ray lenses. One cannot use binoculars for their designed purpose unless one has spotted an object first! Binoculars are useful in positively identifying that which one has already sighted with one's unaided eyes. Unless of course one wanted to put them up to the eyes and just wait for something to appear in the lenses. They are completely useless on moonless nights when there is nothing on which to train them. One will not be able to see anything with binoculars on a pitch-black night that one cannot see first with one's naked eye. The absence of the binoculars is completely irrelevant. Perhaps if Frederick Fleet had had high-technology night vision equipment, the collision wouldn't have happened.

Smith was known to be a bit overconfident in his own abilities, and a bit reckless to some people. Even though it is true that most of the problems he had with the maneuvering of his past ships were actually the fault of the harbor pilots, Smith had his own bit of miscalculations. However, he was not the only captain who was in a hurry to get across the Atlantic in good time; after all, that was the name of the game. It is only those who do not know of the methods of the early passenger liner captains who can't understand this. We have found that people who have little knowledge of steamships create a lot of misinformation.

The *Olympic–Hawke* Collision

The collision between the HMS *Hawke* and the *Olympic* on September 20, 1911, is certainly an area that provokes scrutiny. It must be stated, and reiterated throughout, that these *Olympic*-class ships were a new frontier. The size of the *Olympic* was far greater than anyone had seen before or had been used to dealing with. There were a couple of accidents that occurred to the *Olympic* in her first few voyages that were based on the inexperience of those working with her.

While the *Olympic* was being positioned into her berth at Pier 59 in New York, on her maiden voyage, an accident happened in which one of the harbor tugs was severely damaged. While the harbor pilot attempted to assist the tugs with maneuvering the *Olympic* into the slip, the order was given for "ahead, dead slow," followed by an immediate "stop!" This was an attempt to give the *Olympic* a nudge into the slip. However, the 103-ft tug *O.L. Halenbeck* was to close to the hull of the *Olympic* and was pulled under the stern counter. The tug's ensign mast was snapped off as she was driven into an underwater cable. The motion of the *Olympic*'s propellers drove the *Halenbeck* down into the water, causing her decks to become awash. Luckily, the tug was able to right herself and managed to limp to a pier in the area. The tug's stern frame was smashed, and her rudder and wheel shaft were disabled. This incident was the first of a number of accidents resulting from the unfamiliarity in handling ships of the *Olympic*'s immense size.

The *Hawke* collision was just one more example of this type of inexperience on the part of the *Olympic's* harbor Pilot and the *Hawke's* captain. It is evident that the collision was the captain of the *Hawkes* fault, as he should not have attempted to pass the *Olympic*. However, because he did not know about the effects of suction regarding the forward movement of the White Star liner, and considering the lack of space he had, it is understandable that he just didn't know any better.

There are plenty of pictures that show the damage inflicted on the *Olympic*'s starboard stern quarter. While looking at the photographs, one can obviously see where the bow of the *Hawke* entered the side of the *Olympic*. We know this to be the case even above the visual evidence, in that the collision tore off the cement-reinforced ram from the *Hawke's* bow. Because the *Olympic* was still in forward motion when the *Hawke* caught the side of the *Olympic*, she was spun around, snapping off the ram. The *Hawke's* ram, and perhaps her hull, were responsible for damaging the propeller blades and the shaft boss plating. It is worth noting that the damaged section of the propeller shaft was located directly beneath the damaged shaft boss plating. This section of the shaft was most probably bent along with the plating as a direct result of the collision rather than as the result of the propeller making contact with any portion of the *Hawke*.

There are pictures that show the *Olympic* in Southampton after the collision, and the stern is noticeably down in the water. The bow is up and shows no sign of damage and certainly no breach in the plating. The layup of 2 weeks is completely understandable, as the stores and passengers had to be offloaded. The patchwork done to the hole was only temporary and could not be expected to be fully watertight. One can even see in the Harland & Wolff photos of the damaged area where wood had been pounded into the open rivet holes to seal them off.

As discussed in chapter 3, the *Olympic* would more than likely sail to Belfast with only the port engine in operation. We believe the simple answer as to why the center turbine was not engaged was based on the fact that the ship could produce sufficient speed without it, and that although it was feasible to operate the turbine on the exhaust of just one engine, it was deemed unnecessary for a run of such short a distance. To provide the answer to the never ending question of "why didn't the *Olympic* use the center turbine also, when returning to Belfast?" we turned to Scott Andrews, a trustee of the *Titanic* Research and Modeling Association, who stated:

> It's possible that the port engine may have been able to supply sufficient steam to run the turbine at low power, but in order to do this, it would have been necessary to block steam from backing up in the starboard engine's exhaust manifold and condensing into water. The only valve we know of that could have accomplished this would have been the changeover valve, but both the port and starboard valves were worked in tandem. When one was in the "operate" (open) position so was the other, which would have caused a feedback loop, allowing steam from the turbine case free access to the idle starboard engine's manifold. With the change valves in the "maneuvering"(closed) position and the sluice valves between the turbine exhaust ports and the main condensers closed, each reciprocating engine would work independently through it's own condenser which would also allow for operation of either reciprocating engine while keeping the other (and the turbine) free and dry of condensation.

> I also don't think the strainers located at the bottom of the main inlets to the turbine would have been able to deal with the kind of run-off that this return of condensation from the idle starboard engine's manifold would have caused. The strainers were there to break up small water droplets, which tend to form in the low-pressure steam coming from the reciprocating engine exhaust. Even these tiny droplets are capable of causing severe damage to the blading inside a rotating turbine. These strainers weren't designed to deal with what would have been a small stream of water pouring back out of that pipe.

> As far as channeling steam from an idle starboard engine, this wouldn't have been possible. Steam was delivered to the throttles at over 200 psig. The steam from each reciprocating engine had been expanded down to 9 psia and was delivered to the turbine in tremendous volume. The only other means of supplying low-pressure steam to this turbine would have been the lines which provided steam for "warming up" purposes. (The rotor was turned over by the turning motor while a small quantity of steam was bled into the case to evenly heat up the internal components prior to getting under way.) These lines would have been incapable of providing steam in the sort of quantities needed to provide any meaningful additional power to the turbine.

> In all likelihood, the turbine could have been configured to run at much reduced power from the steam of one reciprocating engine. Indeed, this might have been desirable had it been necessary to return the ship to Belfast over a long distance, say from New York. However, this would have required disengagement of part of the changeover valve linkage and manually jacking the affected valve into the proper closed position. The work involved in the derangement of this and other machinery just to gain a knot or two in speed would have been impractical given the short distance to be traveled from Southampton back to Belfast. Contemporary accounts state that the Olympic proceeded back to Belfast at a cautious eight to ten knots. Either reciprocating engine was capable of generating that much power by

itself without the help of the turbine. By all indications, the Olympic probably went back to Belfast on only one engine.

The drawings acquired from Harland & Wolff for this book do show damage forward of the bridge on the starboard side. However, we have to believe this drawing is accurate. This is a leap of faith based on the hope that Harland & Wolff's Technical Services representative knew what he was doing. With this in mind, it was never said when this forward damage occurred. Just because Harland & Wolff repaired damaged shell plates forward at the same time they were repairing the *Hawke* damage doesn't mean that these were a result of the same incident. There is no doubt that when the *Olympic* was brought in for the extensive repairs to her stern Harland & Wolff would have made maximum use of the time to repair any other damage caused from earlier incidents. These same types of small repairs were generally addressed at the end of each season when a ship was brought in for annual maintenance. It is not economically feasible to bring in a ship for repairs after every minor dent and ding received.

All ships are prone to bent and dented plating, especially these huge liners. The waterways of the late 19th and early 20th centuries were inadequate in most places to safely maneuver these ships. Though shipbuilding was advancing in great strides, the port authorities were generally slow in making the required improvements to waterways and dock facilities necessary to safely maneuver these giant liners. Compounding the situation, the captains of other vessels operating within these same waters were unfamiliar with what constituted a safe distance to maintain from these liners, and as a result there where quite a few groundings and collisions in those days.

More than one accident occurred to the *Olympic* while she was entering the dock at Pier 59 on her maiden voyage. Besides the collision with the tugboat during her maiden arrival, which was addressed previously, the *Olympic* caught the corner of the pier pilings and scraped her hull for a good distance along the starboard side.

It can clearly be seen that, while in the process of docking at the White Star pier, the *Olympic* struck the leading end of the pilings. Examination of the photograph shows a long scratch approximately 15 feet above the water and extending as far aft as her third funnel. Even by the time the photograph had been taken, *Olympic's* stern is still only just clear of the pier. One can also clearly see the discolored plates just above the waterline. These light patches are the result of paint which had peeled off during the voyage.

There is absolutely no evidence that the forward plating as seen in the Harland & Wolff drawing had resulted from the collision with the *Hawke*. A well-known fact concerning the Hudson River and the corresponding docks in New York is that the fast current and tidal changes constantly created havoc for captains who were attempting to maneuver ships into their berths. In some cases, captains would purposely position the forward portion of the hull against the corner pilings of the pier and let the current swing the stern around straight. This made it easier for the tugs, but it certainly created problems with the shell plates sooner or later. It is important to note that the current of the Hudson River changes with the tide, as the Hudson has two tidal intervals. You can bet that this wasn't the last time that the *Olympic* would get a scrape from the pier.

When looking at the damage to the *Olympic's* stern quarter after the *Hawke* collision, it can be clearly seen that there was no damage anywhere near the keel. The theory of torsional shock from the propeller striking a solid object, or of the vibration of the bent shaft having caused material damage to the engine mountings or keel, doesn't stand up to close scrutiny. The mass of the ship's structure alone was more than sufficient to absorb such a blow before any meaningful amount of shock could be transmitted directly to the keel.

It is easy to understand how this could be when one understands the design of the ship and her machinery. First, the wing propellers, which were driven by the reciprocating engines, were composed of manganese bronze blades bolted to a steel hub. This hub was keyed and locked onto the tail shaft, the last segment of the propeller shaft. The tail shaft was bolted to a series of hollow tubular segments of shafting supported on plummer blocks, or bearings. Propeller shafts are made in segments for ease of manufacture and to facilitate installation and removal aboard ship. Each segment is held to the other by a series of bolts passed through flanges. In turn, the line of shafting is coupled to a thrust shaft and thrust block assembly. The thrust block assembly transmits the thrust created by the propellers to the hull and insulates the engines from shock created by any fore and aft movement of the shafting. Torsional loading, which is created by the torque of the engines working against the resistance of the propeller cutting through the water, is dissipated largely through the normal twisting of the propeller shaft as it is put under load. In extreme cases, such as that created by a propeller striking a solid object, the blades of the propeller, being of a softer material, would yield first, bending or breaking off of the hub. Should even this have failed to dissipate all of the shock, the bolts coupling the shafting would have been broken somewhere along its length. As a matter of course, these bolts are designed to sheer off before causing damage to the shaft. All of this is designed to happen long before any detrimental effects are felt by either the machinery or the ship's structure.

None of the engines were mounted right to the bottom of the hull at the level of the keel. The engines were mounted to the engine beds on the tank top plating, which in this area was some 6 ft above the keel plate. The weight of the machinery was supported by the tank "floors," or frames, which were attached to the center keelson and extended out to the tank margin. Intercostals running parallel to the keel joined the floors to one another. It is to these "floors" that the internal tank top plating and exterior bottom plating were attached, creating an incredibly strong, yet resilient structure. The engine bedplates did not connect directly to the keel, neither did the boss arm castings.

Harland & Wolff was a shipbuilder's shipbuilder. They were pioneers in lengthening ships, cutting them in half, and fitting in new sections. A case in point demonstrating the abilities of Harland & Wolff is the White Star liner *Suevic*, which grounded on the rocks off the coast of Lizard Point in 1907. Harland & Wolff built a whole new bow section to fit on this vessel after wreckers had to blast the ship in two to release the aft section, which contained the boilers and machinery, from the rocks.

Another demonstration of the ability of Harland & Wolff took place in 1924–1925, when shipyard workers removed the *Olympic*'s cracked stern frame and replaced it with a new one. All of these tasks required work on and around the keel. It is an undeniable fact that Harland & Wolff had the expertise to repair a keel if it were necessary. The old idea of a ship being permanently weakened because she "had a broken back" came from the days of wooden vessels, and was not relevant to steel ships whose keels were assembled from separate plates.

The wreck of the Suevic

66

The new bow of the Suevic *leaving the Lagan under tow for Southampton. Is this evidence of a shipbuilder who couldn't repair keel damage?*

The aft section of the Suevic *entering the Trafalgar dock in Southampton on April 4th 1907*

Further demonstrations of Harland & Wolff's abilities to repair serious damage are the repairs completed on the ships *China* and *City of Paris*. Both these ships went aground, the former on Perim and the latter on "The Manacles." In both cases, the bottoms of these vessels suffered major structural damage to both the exterior plating and the structural portions of their double bottoms. The *China* was so badly damaged that the boiler room floors were visibly distorted and the boilers were unseated. Harland & Wolff rebuilt both of these vessels and returned them to service.

The famous *Baltic*, one of White Star's "Big Four" was launched by Harland and Wolff on November 12, 1903, and was also branded with the term "practically unsinkable". She was the largest ship in the world at the time. The reason she earned this designation was partly due to an early modification. Her construction had already begun when White Star gave the orders to enlarge her. Harland & Wolff proceeded to cut the already-completed keel in half amidships, moved the after portion 28 feet, and then inserted a new connecting piece. For it's day, it was an amazing piece of surgery.

The *Titanic* did not break into two pieces while sinking, as was theorized for some years. She was broken into three sections. The middle section was found a distance from the two larger segments of the wreck, and had been overlooked for a long time. When the middle section was found, it was lying upside down. The keel was exposed and found to be twisted at the breaking point. This indicates that the keel was one of the last things to break apart as the ship was foundering; in fact it was probably the last thing connecting the pieces together as the ship was falling to the bottom. The *Titanic* certainly did not break in two because of any inherent weakness in her keel.

Nowhere is it recorded that during repairs following the *Hawke* incident that Harland & Wolff used one of the *Titanic*'s propeller blades as a replacement on the *Olympic*, because there were no spares. The publications available only mention the requisition of a few segments of the *Titanic*'s propeller shafting to replace those on the *Olympic*, which had been damaged in the collision. This was understandable, as using some of the *Titanic*'s shafting was the most expedient way to return the *Olympic* to service. As the *Titanic* was still months away from completion, there would be more than adequate time to fabricate a replacement for the donated shaft. There is no reason to believe that spare propeller blades weren't put aside for the *Olympic*. We know that there were spare blades made for the *Titanic,* because after the *Titanic's* loss Harland & Wolff donated several to be melted down;

the bronze was used to make some of the many memorials to those who were lost. Spare blades were made in sets for each ship, because they needed to be balanced to one another, and they all had to have the same overall installed diameter and pitch. That's why the blades were numbered in the first place. Unlike with a mass-produced automobile, most parts are not usually interchangeable from one ship to another even when they are made from the same drawings. Everything is individually fitted together as a unit.

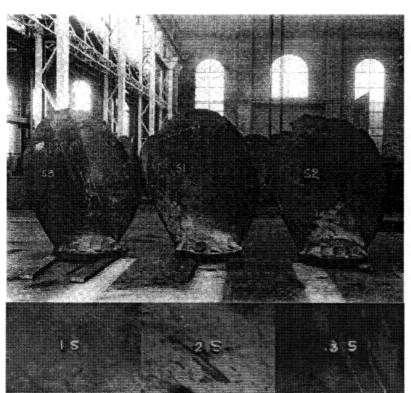

Olympic's *starboard propeller blades damaged in the* Hawke *collision. The large identification numbers of "S1, S2, and S3" have been written on with chalk for the benefit of the photograph. These identification markings were cast into the base of each blade, and were used to identify where on the propeller hub the blade was to be bolted.*

Another area of question has been the size of the *Olympic's* propellers compared to the *Titanic's*. Statements have circulated that the diameter of the two ships' propellers were different. This has been found to not be entirely accurate. The fact of the matter is that the *Olympic's* propeller diamters were changed, but only after the *Titanic* disaster. The replacements occurred during the 1912–1913 refit. The two wing propellers were reduced in size from 23 ft, 6 in. to 22 ft, 9in., and the center propeller was changed to a three-bladed design at a diameter of 17 ft, 0 in. from its original configuration of four blades at 16 ft, 6 in. The three-blade propeller arrangement of the *Olympic* as of 1913 may have been a temporary feature, as the four-bladed prop is seen again in photographs by 1924.

Icebergs and fog weren't the only dangers faced by ships traveling the North Atlantic. The *Olympic* supposedly hit a submerged wreck on February 24, 1912, while out in deep water. This was possible, even common in this era. However, one must not assume, when the newspapers said, "hit a wreck", that they were talking about sailing in shallow water. What most people don't realize is that the officers of the *Olympic* believed they hit a derelict wreck, not a submerged wreck lying on the sea bed. *Derelicts* are wrecked and abandoned ships that stubbornly remain afloat. In some instances, wooden sailing vessels do not founder immediately. Instead, the remaining buoyancy in their wooden construction allows the wrecked vessel to lay just at the surface or slightly below, awash from the surrounding sea and all but invisible to other ships. Often, cargo such as a hold full of lumber or empty wine casks could keep one of these vessels in this floating state of limbo for months. Yes, the *Olympic* could have hit a derelict wreck.

The paint shade differences observed on the *Titanic* while at Southampton are nothing out of the ordinary. The varying shades of black could have been brought on by a different batch of paint or could indicate an area that required a move of the painter's platform or lighter, depending on if this area was painted in the dry dock or in the fitting-out wharf.

The paint used in the early part of the 20th century and even years later did not come out of gallon pails bought at the local marina. Though commercial paints were available, Harland & Wolff hand mixed their paint using lead powders and linseed oil. They actually had a paint shed in the yard specifically for this purpose.

The similarity of the damage sustained to the *Olympic's* starboard hull, and that of Titanic's paint shading at Southampton is curious, but not evidence of foul play. There is no reason to believe that *Titanic* and *Olympic* didn't hit a few pilings or the caissons of the Thompson Graving Dock at Harland & Wolff. Incidents like these were not uncommon and would not be generally known outside of the shipyard.

The mere presence of propeller blades on the dock seen in the *Titanic* picture from chapter 7 does not mean they were intended for an *Olympic* class liner. With the Harland & Wolf facility being practically right next-door, these things may have been brought to Southampton for the repair yard. After all, *Olympic* was required to travel to Belfast for her thrown propeller blade replacement in March because that was the only place with a dry-dock large enough to hold her and do the work.

The Coal Bunker Fire

The *Titanic's* famous coal bunker fire is a staple for many conspiracy theorists. Coal bunker fires were far more common than coal dust explosions. The theory that a coal dust explosion was responsible for blowing a hole in the starboard side of the *Titanic's* hull is based on misinformation. It has been speculated by some people that the hole seen on the starboard side of the wreck today, at about the area of the forward well deck, was the result of such a coal dust explosion. Some even speculate that it is the result of an intended detonation!

There is plenty of testimony addressing the coal bunker fire, to the point that no one can deny that it didn't happen. However, the presence of a coal bunker fire should not be confused with a raging wood fire onboard a ship, with the staterooms going up in smoke. Fire is a major concern to mariners, this is true, but a coal fire can be easily contained within the steel bulkheads of the bunker. It is quite possible the surveyor, either at Belfast or Southampton, knew of the fire, but that he let it go, considering that these types of incidents were not uncommon aboard coal burning ships.

When decomposing organic matter is stacked, creating weight at the bottom of the pile, spontaneous combustion can result. Even piles of grass clippings can spontaneously combust, and have. Have you ever seen a pile of freshly cut grass clippings appear to smoke? This can happen with coal also; it is, in essence, a chemical reaction. This is the same reason why freshly cut and baled hay is left out in the field for a time rather than immediately stacked in the barn.

The process used to extinguish a coal bunker fire is quite straightforward: A number of men are required to remove the coal from the bunker as the top layers are sprayed with water to contain the hot embers at the bottom. This was the case with the *Titanic*.

It is quite possible that the stokehold crew believed they had the fire out before arriving at Southampton but, after reprovisioning the new coal, they found it was still active. At this point, extra men were assigned to the task of extinguishing the fire once again. As has been testified to, it was out by the following Saturday. It is probable that the heat damaged the bulkhead, but research tells us that the damaged bulkhead had little or no bearing on the fate of the *Titanic*.

If the crew had failed to extinguish the fire by the time the *Titanic* arrived in New York, it is possible that the New York City fireboats would have been called out to extinguish the smoldering coal. This would have been achieved by closing the internal bunker access doors in the affected bunker, opening the coal chute from the outside, and simply dumping water down the chute into the bunker.

The theory of a coal dust explosion is not supported by the facts. In order for a coal dust explosion to occur, two requirements must be met. First, there must be a certain ratio of airborne coal dust present in respect to the surrounding air. Second, there must be a source of ignition present. The presence of a fire smoldering within a bunker would seem to satisfy the second requirement. However, while fighting a coal bunker fire, water is continually sprayed over the top of the coal pile being worked as the burned material is raked out. This continual wetting of the surrounding coal would have precluded any dust being created within the immediate vicinity of the fire. Even had the proper conditions existed to create a coal dust explosion, the odds of this occurring at the very moment the *Titanic* just happened to be passing an iceberg would have to be astronomical! An occurrence of this type would be just too coincidental, unless one were to believe that an explosive was put in the forward part of the ship intentionally. Even entertaining this bit of fantasy, one would have to ask how an explosion of this magnitude could have taken place without someone's notice. The coal dust theory should be put to rest once and for all.

The explosions heard by the survivors while the *Titanic* foundered would have been the steel tearing and the rupture of the main steam pipes that were still in use at the end. The amount of force caused by the sudden release of steam is immense. The second explosion aboard the *Lusitania* also falls into this category. When it is referred to that the boiler exploded, the people of the time are not speaking of an instance where the boilers were literally blown to pieces; they are speaking of a breach in a pressurized device. In an instance where a pressurized boiler actually blew apart, one will find the cause to be old equipment and/or improper upkeep or operation of the boiler.

The Lifeboat Mystery

Why Captain Rostron didn't save lifeboats 4, 14 and 15 is anyone's guess. There was a problem with some of the boats having water in them, and perhaps it just wasn't worth the effort to try and retrieve them. In fact, the added weight of the water inside of a boat may have made retrieval very difficult. Apparently lifeboats were considered expendable at the time, or else Rostron would have made more of an effort to bring the three boats aboard. If it were necessary, no doubt he would have found room to stow them on the deck of the *Carpathia*.

It is evident that the White Star Line wanted to downplay their liability in the sinking as much as possible. When they removed the boats from their guarded post at the White Star dock in New York the remaining lifeboat markings were removed, and then the boats were stored in a warehouse away from the souvenir hunters. However, probably the biggest reason they were stored is so they could be kept away from the eyes of the public and press.

The whereabouts of the *Titanic*'s lifeboats will go on as a mystery throughout time. They were most likely either taken back to Belfast, sold to a yard in New York as part of the requirements of the Limitation of Liability law, or destroyed.

The White Star Line and Harland & Wolff truly didn't believe that anything could ever sink their new liners (nor did anybody else for that matter). It is probably because of this idea that they didn't bother to make sure that the boat lamps were in good working order. The reason why many of the lifeboats were not provided with lamps, was because White Star was not required by law to keep them in the boats. At the time the lamp trimmer came around with the lamps in his hands, many of the lifeboats had already been launched.

Mrs. Frederick O. Spedden's reference to the wrong number being on her lifeboat in chapter 4, may or may not be accurate. However, if it were accurate, it is possible for someone to make a mistake, especially with the outboard numbers. With the fact that the *Titanic* was hurried through the process of her final fitting out, it is possible that the numbers were mismatched on the outboard sides of the lifeboats.

If there were any instances of the falls being jammed while the lifeboats were being lowered, it would be more because of crew inexperience than because the ropes were old. Actually, new rope falls tend to be very stiff and try to coil back on themselves, which is a far bigger cause of jamming in blocks than old rope, which has weathered and relaxed. It was well known among mariners that these old types of tackle were prone to tangling. This would be an issue that brought about many new patents of non-tangling lifeboat falls after the *Titanic*'s demise.

Adding to the evidence that the attending crewmen were inexperienced is the incident with collapsible A. No one was able to get the canvas sides locked into position. Perhaps the hardware was faulty, but more than likely, there was no time to try and figure out how to manipulate the gear, as this boat was practically brought down with the ship. The people aboard this half-sunk collapsible appeared not to know how to pull up the frame, or perhaps were just too cold to try and figure it out.

Captain Rostron thought one of the collapsibles went down with the ship. Second Officer Lightoller is said to have stated that he did not think collapsible A made it off the ship. It is possible that he never saw it leave the roof of the officers' quarters. In fact, Lightoller may have been the one who passed this on to Rostron while onboard the *Carpathia*, which would explain why Rostron thought one of the collapsibles went down with the ship. Another consideration to be taken into account is that Rostron testified that this information was relayed to him on the *Carpathia*. In fact collapsible A was not launched from the *Titanic* in the correct definition of the term, but floated off. With all due respect to Rostron, he seems to not have known what kind of supplemental lifeboats the *Titanic* was carrying. Rostron thought the *Titanic* was fitted with Berthon collapsibles. This is absolutely not true. Rostron apparently was not familiar with the Engelhardt collapsibles, just as those on board the *Titanic* weren't. Engelhardts were new to all of these people, and their testimony confirms this. Berthons were well known among mariners with Naval experience, because they were commonly seen on Admiralty ships. A Berthon was a true collapsible boat, as it literally folded longitudinally along its whole length. An Engelhardt collapsible was really a raft constructed with airtight divisions within its hull, with collapsible canvas bulwarks. Many of the crewmen of the *Titanic* rightfully called them "rafts", because that is what they technically were. This is what Scarrott and Sloper were referring to when they testified to seeing people on a raft. As for the overturned boat Mrs. Thayer stated she saw in a writing done years after the sinking; who knows if she has her facts correct. There are cases of testimony from other survivors that was taken after a period of time following the tragedy illustrating contorted information.

Did Rostron testify to seeing an overturned standard lifeboat, revealing a mysterious 21st boat from another ship? No. If one is going to use testimony from the Board of Trade transcripts as a reference to a theory, one should make sure they read the whole testimony, and not just that part which can be used to create a situation that didn't exist. Rostron's testimony at the British Board of Trade hearings is as follows starting from line 25476.

The Attorney General: Altogether how many boats did you pick up?
Rostron: We got 13 lifeboats alongside, two emergency boats, two Berthon boats. There was one lifeboat which we saw was abandoned, and one of the Berthon boats, of course, was not launched from the ship, I understand. That made twenty altogether.
The Attorney General: My impression is there is one collapsible still unaccounted for in that?
Rostron: Oh, yes; I beg your pardon, one bottom up; one that was capsized. That was in the wreckage. That was the twenty.
The Attorney General: You picked up and actually took on board the *Carpathia* 13 of the *Titanic*'s lifeboats?
Rostron: Precisely.
The Attorney General: One of them you saw; the occupants of the boat were rescued and taken on your boat, but the boat was left in the water?
Rostron: Yes, she was damaged.
The Attorney General: You did not bother any more about her?
Rostron: No.
The Attorney General: That made the 14 lifeboats. Then there were the two emergency boats; were they taken on board the *Carpathia*, or abandoned?
Rostron: I cannot say which were the boats we took up. I took them as they came along, and after the whole thing was over we got as many boats as we could. I did not notice which they were.
The Attorney General: There were two emergency boats, and besides that there were -?
Rostron: The two Berthon boats.
The Attorney General: The two collapsibles?
Rostron: Yes; and there is one Berthon boat which we saw amongst the wreckage bottom up. It was reported to me that there was another Berthon boat still on board the ship.
The Attorney General: That makes 19 out of the 20?
Rostron: No, excuse me. It makes the 20 if you reckon the one still left, but I am not reckoning that. It comes to the same thing. If you reckon that one in, of course it accounts for the lot.
The Commissioner: The one collapsible boat was not launched in the proper sense of the word; it got into the water, very likely?

Starting at Line 25568 Rostron is questioned by Sir Robert Finlay in an attempt to clarify his lifeboat testimony.

>Finlay: I wish you would tell us again what you know about the collapsible boats. There were four collapsible boats on board the "*Titanic*"?
>Rostron: Yes.
>Finlay: How many came alongside your ship, or did you get alongside of?
>Rostron: Two.
>Finlay: Did you see any collapsible boat adrift?
>Rostron: We saw one adrift bottom up amongst the wreckage of the *Titanic*.
>Finlay: Then you only know of three boats?
>Rostron: We only know of three collapsible boats.
>Finlay: As to what became of the other boat you know nothing?
>Rostron: Nothing whatever, my Lord.

Nowhere in Rostron's testimony does he state he saw a capsized regular lifeboat. In fact, Rostron is describing 19 boats, and cannot account for the fourth collapsible. This was probably boat A which was abandoned during the morning some time before the *Carpathia* arrived.

It is important to also address statements regarding flooded lifeboats. There is no evidence to believe that the reason some of the lifeboats flooded was because they were the older boats of the *Olympic*. There are a couple of facts that need to be addressed that seem to have been left out by certain conspiracy theorists. One is that the boats lowered from the starboard side of the ship were getting caught on the rivets because of the list of the ship. This would have created havoc on the clinker planking. The other fact is that some of the drain cocks were not installed immediately because they couldn't be found in the crowded lifeboats. One must not dismiss the fact that these lifeboats had plugs!

Some people testified to not having bailers, and other provisions. In most cases, it was merely a case of not being able to find these items in crowded lifeboats. The compasses were only required to be provided, not necessarily installed in the boats. The same holds true for the biscuits. These requirements changed after April 15th 1912 of course.

Mystery or History?

The story printed in an Australian newspaper about the recollection of James Finch is really intriguing. It spurs the imagination, but it holds no relevance to an actual switch.

The response to Finch's story is discussed at length in chapter 4. The only points that need to be expounded on are the birth of the switch theory itself and the "painted-on portholes." The theory of a cover-up or a switch has been around for a long time. Although not published aggressively, one can be sure that someone thought about it long before 1972.

The idea that there were painted-on portholes is a farce. There was no need to paint portholes on a ship. The process of cutting out a porthole is relatively simple: A pneumatic cutting device is positioned against the side of the hull, and the porthole is simply carved out. Afterward, bolt holes for mounting the sidelight are drilled around the periphery of the opening, and the sidelight is bolted in place. This process is not that complicated, can be performed from either outside or inside the hull, and can be undertaken at any place where one of these cutting devices is located. Cutting out portholes did not require a stop in dry dock. With the proof in the photographs of the *Olympic* having the added two portholes by March 1912, this idea of the painted holes should be laid to rest. It is important to mention that according to the "The Drawing Office Notebook", a book kept by Harland & Wolff outlining the changes done to the *Olympic* through 1913, the sidelights on the port side of the fo´c'sle were added by January 23, 1912.

The second half of chapter 4 addresses the testimony from some passengers regarding a severe vibration on the starboard side of the ship in the area above and around the reciprocating engine room. We must remember again, as stated earlier, that the engines would not have been affected by the *Hawke* collision. The only parts that were affected, besides the obvious shell plates and propeller blades, were some sections of propeller shafting. No one will ever know the truth behind the claims of the vibration, if these claims are even accurate. However, it was the *Titanic*'s maiden voyage, and these were the types of problems that were on notice. Vibrations aboard steamships were quite common in those days. The *Olympic*-class liners, although built in a fashion to prohibit unnecessary vibration, were still vulnerable to these kinds of occurrences. There is not enough evidence to state that damaged engine components caused these vibrations. A ship is highly complex machine, and there are many things that can cause vibration. It would appear that things of this nature were largely perceptual—the vast majority of comments regarding vibration on the *Titanic* were in reference to how remarkably free she was from this particular problem!

The theories of whether Ismay was on the bridge before the *Titanic* struck the iceberg can never be substantiated. Ismay was not known to be the type of person who would go aboard the bridges of his ships. If he did go to the bridge at some point, that is irrelevant to a switch. If it is true that Smith was seen in the lounge at a time that is not concurrent with testimony, and if the times indicated by passengers don't match up, what does this mean? Nothing. One has to wonder if the passengers adjusted their watches to the time changes in which the *Titanic* was traveling through. In any case, there is still not enough information to substantiate these statements.

Photographic Assessment and the Wreck

When we were researching information for this book, we called on several well-known maritime historians who posses information not accessible to the general public. We hit wall after wall when it came to obtaining copies of information, or even just being allowed to view the documents, books, and video.

As fate would have it, we did get to view rare footage that shows the name on the port side of the wreck of the *Titanic*. After reviewing the tape a number of times, we found that the name is still intact on the port side of the hull. In fact, the letters are correct and evenly spaced. The only reason why someone may think the letters are spaced incorrectly is because they didn't take into account the lens used to protect the camera from the pressure of the deep sea. The lens is of course round, or fish-eyed, which thus causes an exaggerated sense of dimension and space.

The letters are incised into the plating. However, they are hard to see, because in most cases the letters are darker than the steel that surrounds them. In the case of a few of the letters there is what appears to be light-colored paint that was exposed after the black hull paint peeled away. The reason for the loss of paint may have much to do with the fact that an expedition team scrubbed the port side name for the purposes of removing rusticles from the name letters. The black paint peeled in the areas where it wasn't strong enough to withstand the scrubbing.

If one were to look at the exposed undercoat of the bow area, one would think the paint color is white or light gray. This strikes an *Olympic* chord, but there are some answers to this light-colored paint.

The primer used on these vessels, and on many other vessels, was not a dark, dark gray or black like it appears in the old black-and-white photographs. The film of the day did not show true shading. The primer used on the *Olympic*-class ships was a medium gray. The *Olympic* was painted in an even lighter color than this medium gray when launched. In fact, the *Olympic's* paint was so light that some people considered it to be white. With the addition of the fact that the paint was mixed by hand with lead powders and linseed oil, it is not hard to understand how this medium gray could have washed out after being submerged under the salt water of the ocean for more than 90 years. The lighting used by the submarines is of high intensity; this also adds a false sense of a lighter color.

On April 14, 2000, Ralph White was personally interviewed by one of the authors as to the name on the starboard side of the *Titanic*'s hull and was asked some other questions revolving around this matter. White, who was with Dr. Robert Ballard when he found the wreck, was the American submarine commander in the IMAX movie *Titanica* and has been down to the wreck some 28 times.

White advised us that the letters of the name on the bow of the *Titanic* are in fact incised. He went on to state that the reason why the starboard side name is never seen in any video footage is because of the severe current running over the bow on that side of the wreck. He stated that it is very difficult to navigate the camera in place to video the starboard name letters. He also stated that he was not able to find the stern name and port of registry letters.* It is very dangerous to maneuver the submarine under the counter of the wreck, so it is entirely possible that he just didn't get close enough. White substantiated all of the information he gave by sharing his personal slides of the wreck and the evidence of the name on the bow. So we have not only video but also the personal collection of Ralph White available to help us with our research.

The wreck of the *Titanic* will show the astute observer that many of the fittings that made the *Titanic* different than the *Olympic* are still visible, even after many years under the cold Atlantic water. The angled steel breakwater forward of the No. 1 hatch coaming is still intact; the teak sill of the wheelhouse is still present, showing the different configuration from what the *Olympic* originally had; and even the round skid lights that were specific to the *Titanic* are still visible.

When referring to the propeller videotaped on the ocean floor, it has been said that the blades and hub had been originally buried in the silt, then suddenly uncovered to expose the number 401 on one of the blades. The truth of the matter is that Ballard just plain missed the propellers when he searched for them back in 1986. He was in the wrong place when he searched the side of the hull. It must be remembered that the *Titanic* was huge, and the visibility was not good at that point. These problems are compounded by the difficulty of trying to maneuver the submarine in the unstable current.

Is the number 401 incised on the thrust side of the propeller as is seen in wreck photos? Yes. Yard numbers were generally indicated on propeller blades. Each blade also had an incised port and starboard designation, and position indicated at the base where the blade attached to the hub. In fact the *Titanic's* exposed starboard propeller also shows a position number for placement on the hub on the face of the blade. The foundries producing parts for ships would stencil the ship numbers on the products with paint. This was purposely done while the material was still hot. The result of this procedure literally baked the paint on, and it became part of the material it was applied to. However, propellers were cast in sand and were thicker than needed when they came fresh from the molds. The bronze of the propeller was shaved and dressed to the intended thickness and shape. The number 401 seen on the thrust side of the propeller blade of the *Titanic* is the remnants of a founder's handiwork, and would not have easily come off as the result of the blade pushing through the water. These numbers were cast or etched into the blades for identification purposes.

The process of retrofitting the *Titanic* and the *Olympic* is not out of the ordinary. The *Olympic* underwent constant changes from 1911 to 1913. These changes were all the result of trial and error. It is not surprising that the *Olympic* would turn out looking like the *Titanic* at some point, as the *Titanic* was fitted with upgraded parts as she was being built, just as the *Olympic*. The starboard side swan neck duct seen ahead of the forward funnel is an example. The *Olympic* did have a much smaller swan neck duct and fan housing during her first voyages, but this was changed to a different diameter fan and a larger duct by January 1912. However, her duct in this area never matched the *Titanic's*; they were close, but never the same size. This was a constant throughout both ship's careers.

The lifeboats on the *Olympic* were in fact painted white where the sheer planks were concerned. Why White Star painted them white is not known, but brown sheer planks were the usual color for White Star lifeboats, and those of other shipping lines for that matter. It is not odd that the *Olympic* had her lifeboat sheer planks painted brown at some point. What is odd is that they were painted white to start with. It is possible—and this is only a guess—that the White Star Line wanted to keep the presence of the ship's immensity by painting the *Olympic's* lifeboat sheer planks white. The brown would break the appearance and the smooth lines of the ship. Later the sheer planks would be painted brown to match the teak railings and the other lifeboats of the line.

---

* Since this book was written, the stern lettering indicating the name *Titanic*, and the port of registry had been located during James Cameron's 2001 IMAX dive. However, photographic evidence has yet to be presented.

The Belfast Switch

The possibilities of a switch happening in October 1911 during the *Hawke* repairs, or in March 1912 during the propeller repairs has been addressed. The writings that speak of the *Olympic* being "laid up" prior to the April 3rd voyage from Southampton leave one in suspense. Certainly the Ulster Folk and Transport Museum, and Lightoller, had to get this information from somewhere. The story of the *Olympic* hitting an object in the English Channel may very well be true; however, it is never mentioned what these two sources meant by the term *laid up*. This does not mean that the *Olympic* had to return to Belfast to have her hull checked for damage. In fact, if the *Olympic* was required to depart Southampton on April 3rd under the command of Captain Haddock, she would in no way have had time to return to Belfast for repairs. One must remember that the *Olympic* was returning from a past voyage and had to have the onboard passengers disembarked, be reprovisioned, laundry washed, rooms cleaned, and so on. Remember that the passengers had to arrive early in the morning so that the luggage could be loaded and the proper presailing activities carried out. One must also understand that these ships were not returned back to dry dock after every bump. Harland & Wolff would have, without a doubt, sent down a diver to inspect the hull and the propelling equipment while at Southampton.

Captain Smith traveled aboard a transport from Southampton to Belfast to take over his new command. It is true that Haddock signed on as the original commander to take the *Titanic* on her sea trials and on to Southampton. For whatever reason, Smith was written in at the end papers of the registration document, taking over the command from Haddock. This explains nothing more than a change of mind on the part of White Star.

The picture mentioned in chapter 7 (figure 1) has indeed been mislabeled as "the officers of the *Titanic*" in many publications. The theory that all of these men identified in this picture were officers of the *Titanic* is only partially correct. The truth of the matter is that only three of the men pictured were on the *Titanic*. The man identified as Lightoller is not him, although he does bear a close resemblance to good ol' "Lights." Neither is the man with the mustache, thought to be Chief Officer Wilde, actually him. The uniforms worn by these men show a variation from the uniforms worn on the *Titanic*, the difference being the color of the hats. In the mystery picture, the hats are white. The reason for the white hats probably has more to do with the month of the year more than anything. The white hats would have been part of the transition to the summer white uniforms. The hats worn on the *Titanic* were navy blue, as the uniforms being worn were still for the winter–spring season. The mystery picture is of the *Olympic*'s maiden voyage crew. The picture was taken on May 28, 1911, while the *Olympic* was at Harland & Wolff. The officers in the picture are, standing left to right: Purser Hugh McElroy (later of *Titanic*), Third Officer Henry Cater, Second Officer R. Hume, Fourth Officer David Alexander, and Sixth Officer Harold Holehouse and, seated from left to right: Fifth Officer A. Tullock, Chief Officer Joseph Evans, Captain Edward Smith (later of *Titanic*) and First Officer William Murdoch (later of *Titanic*). Figure 2, photographed on the same day as figure 1 is from left to right: Murdoch, Evans, Alexander and Captain Smith

This information came from the collection of George Behe, who owns a copy of the original newspaper in which the mystery picture was printed. It is amazing how we find that once again there has been published misinformation throughout the years.

Looking back on the Belfast switch: It sounds feasible, but it is a far stretch at best. Even if the White Star Line was able to get the *Olympic* back to Belfast and send a disguised *Titanic* back in time for the April 3rd voyage to New York, there would not been time to do the identity switches completely enough to convince everyone.

In the memoirs of Violet Jessop, a stewardess who served aboard the *Olympic* and survived the sinking of the *Titanic* and the *Britannic*, she mentions that there were changes in accommodations made to the *Titanic*. She wrote of the admiration for "Tommy" Andrews and how he paid attention to the needs of the victualling department. Jessop described how Andrews would walk around in the working areas of the ship and listen to the suggestions of the crew. She described how she was very pleased to see that she had a private wardrobe in her room, which she shared with another stewardess. This was a problem on the *Olympic*, according to her, as she had to share her accommodations and wardrobe with her roommate. A direct quote from Jessop's memoirs tells it best:

> Eagerly we joined the new ship—hundreds of curious eyes, each looking for what interested them most. Yes, there was my bunk placed the way I had suggested for privacy and there was the separate, though small, wardrobe for my companion and myself, one of the immeasurable blessings when two people of absolutely different tastes have to live together in a confined space. No longer would there be anxiety as to whether a companion's clothes bore testimony of her devotion to whiskey and smoke.

Miss Jessop went on to write about a social call she made while onboard the *Titanic*, to a friend who was a second-class bartender both on the *Olympic* and the *Titanic*:

> It was not strange, therefore, that I should seek him out to exchange opinions about our new venture. He alone knew I did not like big ships, that I was secretly afraid; however we drank a toast to his happiness and *Titanic*. Then he proudly showed me all his new improvements to make his bar work easier and chaffingley added that we women were not the only ones with something to show off about.

It is apparent in Jessop's writings that, if there was a switch, they also fooled her. After all, she would know, as she had just been transferred from the *Olympic* after serving aboard her since the maiden voyage.

The Ship That Never Sank?

It is no secret that this volume was written in response to other books written about a switch conspiracy. We have no intent to do a review of these books, however, we will answer some of the opinions found to be less than accurate. On the other hand, some information in the "pro-switch" books has become outdated since they were published, thus being negated. We have addressed many of the opinions of these books in the latter chapters, but we will revisit some of the stronger arguments here again:

After the *Olympic–Hawke* collision in 1911, and the subsequent departure from Southampton to Belfast, the *Olympic* would have used only the port engine. This is completely feasible, because the engineering work required to configure the center turbine to utilize the exhaust steam from only one engine was not practical for such a short trip. The keel is not connected to the engine beds, neither are the boss arms. There is no way the keel could have been damaged by the collision. It is not surprising that the patch did not hold as well as might be expected. They did not have underwater welders at that time. Many of the open holes were patched with wood or steel; the repair workers did the best they could with the resources they had.

The extra two portholes seen on the port side of *Olympic*'s fo´c'sle were added by the beginning of 1912. The added B deck accommodations of the *Titanic* were not removed to disguise her as the *Olympic*. The B deck staterooms that extended out to the sides of the *Titanic* are still on the wreck to this day. The *Olympic* did not have her forward B deck staterooms extended out to the edge of the ship until 1928.

The torn plates and bent ribs from the *Hawke* collision would have been straightened or replaced. This is what Harland & Wolff should have done, and did. One does not "patch" a center turbine propeller shaft. This is not necessary. Even if the center propeller shaft were damaged, Harland & Wolff would have needed to replace only some of the detachable shaft sections.

If it is true that the B deck windows of the *Olympic* were refitted to give the ship the appearance of the *Titanic*, and the space behind the windows was merely an open promenade deck, as was particular to the *Olympic*, then White Star had a problem. One would have to wonder if the passengers who booked rooms in the B deck accommodations along the outsides of the hull wanted their money back! One would assume that the passengers who booked these rooms would have noticed the open promenade when opening their stateroom windows. This theory, as written in one certain publication, is more than a little lacking. If Steward Alfred Crawford saw lifeboats being lowered past the B deck windows, there is no reason to doubt him. After all, the windows would not be obstructed from the hallway if the doors were open, regardless of whether a room was present. Then again, many of the *Titanic*'s crew didn't even know the proper deck letters, as their testimony at the British hearings attest to.

It is true that a propeller repair is an easy task that could have taken 1 day; however, one must consider the change of tides and the weather conditions that hampered the *Olympic*'s removal from the dock, not to mention the fact that she grounded out on submerged rocks on the first attempt to leave Belfast, causing her to be returned to the dry dock. This would more than certainly explain the lapse of a week for such a minor repair.

Even if the lifeboats aboard the *Titanic* were actually the older lifeboats of the *Olympic*, they would not leak from dry rot, because even the *Olympic*'s lifeboats were not that old. The simple fact of the matter is that the drain cocks were not installed properly, and this was the reason for the flooding—unless of course your lifeboat was the one that was stuck under the condenser exhaust while it was being lowered.

It's All About the Rockets!

The reason why Captain Lord did not respond to the distress rockets of the *Titanic* is still open to debate. The theory that he was waiting in his location to rescue the soon-to-be-scuttled *Olympic* does not qualify for comment, as it is proven in this book that the ship that sank in the morning of April 15, 1912, was truly the *Titanic*.

We do not dispute that there was most certainly one other ship, if not more than one, in the area of the sinking *Titanic*. The identity of this ship is not known; perhaps it was the *Mount Temple*. The reason why this mystery ship ignored the *Titanic*'s call for help may be none other than human error, or greed. Perhaps the individuals on the mystery ship just wanted to see the competition suffer a loss. Or better yet, perhaps the people aboard the other vessel thought the *Titanic* couldn't sink!

The fact of the matter for Captain Stanley Lord of the *Californian*, is that he was negligent in his duties as a captain. Lord's errors are human, and his supporters should be commended for their support of him, however, the rules are the rules. A captain is ultimately responsible for the actions of his crew. If a crewman makes a mistake, the captain must answer for it even though he may not be directly responsible.

It makes no difference if the *Californian* was 5 miles or 18 miles away from the *Titanic*'s actual position. It does not matter which ship it was that 2nd officer Stone and apprentice Gibson were seeing from the *Californian's* bridge. It makes no difference what color the rockets were, or how high they were fired. The fact that a report was not heard is irrelevant since distress rockets were not required to provide a sound signal. The Rules of the Road for ships in 1912 stated that one option for issuing distress signals was rockets of any color throwing stars. The "stars" were visual signals that consisted of a cluster of lights such as a modern day firework. Though rockets that emitted stars produced a report from the detonation which dispersed the chemicals, this was not the purpose of the signal. The illumination of stars was what fulfilled the distress requirement, not their height above the water, or the sound they made.

Another option specified by the regulations was the use of detonating rockets used in lieu of guns. These devices should not be confused with rockets emitting stars. The rockets used in lieu of guns were an option if the steam ship companies did not want to install detonation guns (that looked like a small cannon) on their ships. These rockets were sound signals, which when used for distress, were to be fired at "about one minute intervals". They emitted a very loud detonation, but did not emit pyrotechnic stars. Detonation rockets had other signaling purposes, and were not specific for distress. The distress rockets that emitted a cluster of stars, were specified for use only in cases of distress, and did not have any other signaling purpose. This specification alleviated confusion with other pyrotechnic or detonation signals.

Flares and Roman Candles were supplied to the *Titanic*, and were generally used as company signals, and for calling a pilot at night. They were not used for distress purposes, and were not of the same design as rockets, which emitted a cluster of stars. Flares were stationary signals, and Roman Candles emitted a ball of light, one at a time.

When the *Californian's* officer on watch saw the distress signals, he should have taken appropriate action in making sure the captain reported immediately to the bridge. When the 2nd officer and the apprentice were watching distress signals, they were in fact watching a ship in trouble. They literally stood there and watched the *Titanic* sink, though they may have never actually seen her lights. Would the *Californian* have made it to the scene in time to save those who perished that morning? Perhaps not – but what about the people who succumbed to exposure in the lifeboats?

People such as Leslie Harrison have defended Captain Lord to the end, and the *Californian's* case was even re-investigated by the Department of Transport Marine Accident Investigation Branch. The Lord incident was reviewed by two different investigators, and though differed in their opinions of the distance between the *Californian* and *Titanic*, both came to the same conclusion- Lord ignored the distress signals and did not take the appropriate action.

Lord turned into a scapegoat, which is why many people who support him are upset. Lord may not have deserved the lashing he received by Lord Mersey or the newspapers, but the fact remains that he was the one who was caught. If someone could have proven the identity of the other mystery ships present while the *Titanic* was sinking, then Lord may have been let off the hook.

Many books have been written about the *Californian* incident, and people have literally become enemies over the disagreements on how Lord was treated. After all is said, and the mitigating circumstances are brought on the table, the truth of the matter still remains - it's all about the rockets.

It has been alleged that the *Titanic* hit a waiting rescue ship that was darkened out. This is one theory that would make a good movie. If this mystery ship was responsible for puncturing and bending the plates under the *Titanic's* waterline, she must have been a good size. The next question is: What part of the other ship could have extended out far enough to reach below the curves of the *Titanic's* hull and penetrate the plates that far down in the water without affecting the plating above the waterline? The mystery ship would have collided farther up along the side of the *Titanic's* hull before coming into contact with the area below the waterline, which planed inward at that point. Was it the propellers of the mystery ship that would have extended out the side in order to be wide enough to damage the *Titanic*, without the ship first hitting the *Titanic's* upper structures?

The damage that caused flooding in the fireman's passage would have to be the result of an opening that falls within the 12 square feet puncture area calculation first introduced by Edward Wilding at the Board of Trade hearings, subsequently upheld by the Marine Forensic Panel's research in the 1990's. The fireman's tunnel was in fact about 3½ feet within the hull at its furthest forward point, and was located at the centerline of the ship above the double bottom. Anything that could penetrate that far in to cause flooding would no doubt be felt by many people. In fact, when the *Olympic* struck an attacking U-boat in WWI, the shock was enough to nearly throw the *Olympic's* captain off his feet. The only damage sustained by the *Olympic* was a bent stem. Imagine the force that would have to be delivered to penetrate the *Titanic* some 3-5 feet into her hull? Some researchers believe the flooding was caused by the *Titanic* grounding on an ice shelf, the bottom plating having been breached and the floors of the inner bottom becoming loose enough to allow water through their watertight caulking. Though this theory is certainly more believable than a rescue ship's propeller tearing a hole in the side of the *Titanic's* hull, it does not coincide with the testimony of fireman Charles Hendrickson.

Starting at line 4890 of the transcripts from the British Board of Trade inquiry, Hendrickson is questioned by Mr. S. A. T. Rowlatt. In Hendrickson's testimony it was stated that the water was "falling" in. This would indicate it was coming from on top of the fireman's tunnel-starboard side.

Rowlatt: But what I want to get from you is this. You said you saw the water coming from the ship's side; do you mean that. You saw it coming through the ship's side?
Hendrickson: No, coming from the ship's side.

Rowlatt: That was merely the direction from which you saw it traveling?
Hendrickson: Yes.
Rowlatt: That is, into the space into which the spiral staircase is descending?
Hendrickson: Yes.
Rowlatt: You could not tell whether the water was coming through the fore and aft bulkhead at the bottom of the staircase, could you?
Hendrickson: No, I could only see the direction it came from.
Rowlatt: Was it coming hard?
Hendrickson: Yes, it was more than rushing in; it was falling in.

The more reasonable explanation comes from general knowledge of *Titanic's* structure. There was a forward fresh water tank, known by some as a "saddle tank" which was 6ft. wide and extended clear across the beam of the ship, but only extending to the Orlop deck level. The fireman's tunnel was built through this tank. With the tank having reinforced framing and swash plates, it is quite conceivable that a side impact could have pushed the internal framing of this tank against the watertight plates of the fireman's tunnel, breaching its integrity. The flooding inside the watertight fireman's passage was most likely internal, being fresh water from the 7th water tank.

It has also been written that the ice on the fore well deck and the forecastle (after the collision) came from the *Titanic* herself. It is stated that the ice fell off of the shrouds, stays, and Marconi aerials. One has to ask: Where did the accumulated ice come from? Where is it stated that the *Titanic* passed through an ice storm? Ice does not just accumulate on rigging out of nowhere, especially not an estimated 1–2 tons' worth. Did this ice come from condensation on the rigging? If so, how did the rigging become heated to cause the condensation? What's even more amazing is the thought that the vibration of the *Titanic's* engines being put into full reverse loosened the ice. Anyone with knowledge of these old steam engines will know that the engines cannot be reversed in that little amount of time, certainly not in less than 30 seconds. If the engine telegraphs were put into the full-reverse position in the time given at the hearings, one can rest assured that the *Titanic* never had time to start in a reverse motion before striking the iceberg.

The fact of the matter remains that the ship that sank was the *Titanic*. There were too many differences in the two ships, too many passengers and crew who had traveled aboard both sisters and would have known the difference. Whatever it is that certain passengers saw, heard, or felt must be taken with a grain of salt. These passengers were not seamen, and they certainly were inexperienced in regard to the operations of ocean liners.

Whatever the theories are that came out of the years and years of testimony and quotes, one must remember that stories change when witnesses exchange notes. It is a well-known rule for police investigators to separate the witnesses after an event occurs that requires interviews. If not, the investigator will notice peculiar similarities in a story. The worst thing that ever happened to the testimony of the survivors was the days spent onboard the *Carpathia*, and the members of the press who twisted the information to meet their needs.

Another piece of information to substantiate the identity of these two ships are the remaining pieces of woodwork and furniture. A large amount of the wood fittings and pieces of paneling from the *Olympic* have survived to this day. Looking at the back sides of these objects, one can see that nearly every piece of wood has the number 400 stamped or painted on the surface, as well as the location of where the piece was fastened aboard the ship.

In the end, the pictures hold the evidence that there was no switch. There were many differences between the sisters that were different at time of launch and never changed. Pictures of the *Olympic* taken before and after the sinking will prove this. Many of these differences never changed throughout the *Olympic's* career. Some of the dissimilarities were minor and are not noticed by the casual observer. Switch theories and tales of insurance scams are entertaining to read. One must remember, however, that these theories are based heavily on misinformation and do not stand up to scrutiny. Why?

Because the *Titanic* IS the ship that sank.

Penciling on the back side of a wall cabinet from Titanic found floating at the wreck site in 1912. It indicates "1ˢᵗ Class Baths – Bridge Dk. 401". The front of the piece is shown below.

A panel from one of the Olympic's *sitting rooms in the Louis XIV design from C deck.*

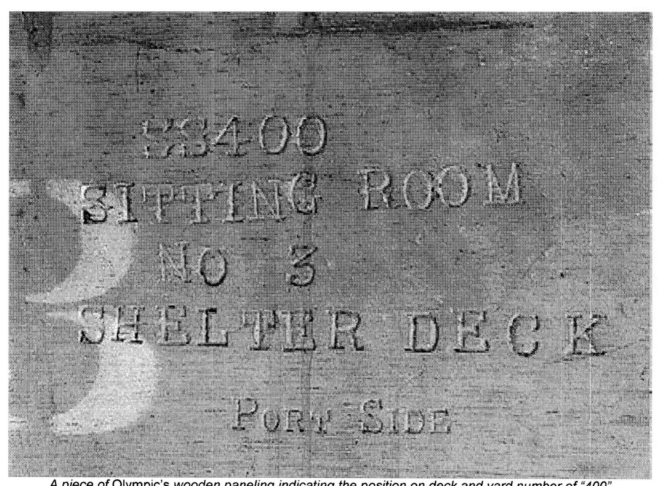

A piece of Olympic's *wooden paneling indicating the position on deck and yard number of* "400"

A P P E N D I X   I

Almost Identical Sisters

For more than 90 years photographs of the *Olympic* have been misidentified as being of the *Titanic*, and vice versa. In some cases this is understandable, as to the general public the two sisters appeared nearly identical externally. The White Star Line substituted pictures of the *Olympic* for the *Titanic* in early postcards and promotional brochures, even when it came to photos of the *Titanic's* internal room arrangements. With the *Olympic* being the first liner built of the class, there were many more pictures taken during her construction than during the *Titanic's*. White Star deliberately initiated the picture switch, because it was certainly more frugal to spend the money on only one liner, when both were so much alike. This would have been even more true if the *Olympic* had been fitted with A deck promenade windows, which likely would have happened had not the sinking of the *Titanic* intervened.

Of the 100-odd photos of the *Titanic* that exist today, only a handful were taken by Harland & Wolff's main photographer, Robert Welsh. An even smaller number were taken of the actual interiors. Identifying one sister from the other can get tricky depending on what area of the ship one is looking at. In any case, one would have to research these ships in detail to really understand how different they actually were.

One must remember that the main structural components of the first two *Olympic*-class liners were built from the same set of plans. Some of the original builders' drawings for yard Nos. 400 and 401 still survive in the archives of Harland & Wolff. When viewing the plans, the common notations of 400–01 are always present at the top of the drawing. In the instances where upgrades were made to the *Titanic* based on experience with the *Olympic*, there are notations drawn in pencil, usually indicating a date also. A case in point would be the *Titanic's* forward A deck promenade bulkhead. This bulkhead, which the *Olympic* never had, is dated in pencil as being drawn on a supplemental plan on February 14, 1912. A change would not necessarily be penciled in on a main drawing but instead would have been drawn up on a supplementary sheet. Other additions may have been carried out as an afterthought and may never have even made it to paper. Because few of these supplemental plans for the *Titanic* exist, we will probably never know just how abundant they were.

The *Olympic* was a continuous experiment while on her first voyages, at least up until 1913 when most of the alterations would finally be completed. What was learned from the *Olympic* was applied to the *Titanic*, and the *Olympic* would see upgrades brought on by her own experiences as she went along.

A close examination, including the very minute details, will uncover many differences. In fact, there are quite a few details even in the *Olympic's* hull that were different than those of her younger sister and were never changed throughout the *Olympic*'s glorious career.

When comparing the *Olympic* and *Titanic*, it is only practical to demonstrate that which can be seen in the photographs. Although there were differences below decks that are known from testimony or from technical journals and plans of the period, it is only through the photographs that these details can be proven without debate.

Olympic *1911*

Titanic *1912*

Two postcards of Olympic *labeled as* Titanic. *This was not a mistake, but done intentionally as most people would not notice the difference in the two ships.*

Because the *Olympic* and *Titanic* were so similar in appearance, at least from a distance, conspiracy theorists have had a field day with dreams about switches and insurance scams. Although the switch theory is interesting, it falls short when debated against the actual differences in the two ships, differences that almost always go unnoticed by the average person.

The fittings that were the most visible as being different on the two ships were the many air ventilation devices servicing the accommodations. The ducting seen on top of the boat deck and deckhouses of the *Olympic*-class liners were referred to as *Sirocco* fans. Sirocco was a brand name of the company—Davidson and Co., Ltd., Belfast— that built the devices. The fan motors were of the Allen type, designed in accordance with Harland & Wolff's specifications.

To fully appreciate the Sirocco fans one must be familiar with their different configurations and uses. Although the air input or output attachments were different, the internal fans and housings were basically the same.

The commonly recognized Sirocco attachment was the *cowl vent*. These cowls were attachments that were secured to the tops of the Sirocco fan housings and looked like the bell of a Sousaphone. Cowl vents were attached to air *exhaust* fan housings and serviced 10-, 20-, 30- and 35-in. diameter fans located within the base unit. Foul air was drawn from the rooms below by the fan while the direction of the cowl opening, usually facing aft, assisted the motor by creating a natural suction effect while the ship was underway. The cowls could be rotated to adjust the amount of natural suction they produced, or rotated away from strong following or quartering winds to prevent

A Sirocco ventilator attached to the corner of a casing

Straight Duct

Stokehold ventilation duct on Olympic – forward of 1st funnel

Swan Neck Ventilator head

Thermotank and corresponding Sirocco fan

reversed flow. When needed, some of the cowls could be rotated to the forward position to take air in while at sea.

There are examples of the cowl vents being attached to air *supply* fan housings on the *Olympic* later in her career. Cowls mounted to air supply fan housings served a different purpose, acting as wind "scoops" to create a positive pressure at the fan's intake opening, and were only seen in use on the *Olympic* after the 1913 refit. This configuration was an exception to the original design and was presumably done to increase the volume of air intake.

Located above the officers' deckhouse were a couple of examples of what some call a *curl duct, or swan neck* ventilator. This type of attachment was rectangular in shape. It connected to one side of the Sirocco fan housing, extended upward, and then "curled" back down. The opening would usually face outward or downward. These attachments were fitted with a protective screen to keep debris out of the fan below. In a few cases the duct attachment would just project upward, having a simple screened rectangular opening, eliminating the "curl." For purposes of this discussion, they will be termed a *straight duct*.

Galley flue pipe Olympic-1911

Cowl ventilation head

The stokehold Sirocco fans were located on F deck and consisted of huge 40-, 50-, and 55-in. diameter fans. The topside ductwork that serviced these huge ventilation fans were referred to as *stokehold ducts* and were located fore and aft of the first three funnels. These were wide, quarter-circle ducts, sometimes referred to as *whale back ventilating ducts*, with the rectangular openings again covered with a protective screen. It was against the stokehold duct forward of the first funnel that Second Officer Lightoller found himself pinned up as the water poured down to the bottom of the ship through the protective screen. Lightoller also testified that he was freed from the stokehold duct by a blast of hot water coming up from below. However, Lightoller found himself again trapped on a foot grate by the inrush of water pouring into the Fidley, servicing boiler room No. 6, located just aft of this forward stokehold duct. A Fidley is a term used to describe an air space and service shaft that was fore and aft of the first three funnels. The shaft containing a ladder, topped off with a foot grating. This shaft served as the exhaust for the air being drawn into the boiler rooms through the stokehold ducts.

Located in the corners of the funnel casings were steam-heated tube bundles. This is the reason why one sees Siroccos of one form or another located in the vicinity of the four corners of a casing. The Siroccos in these areas served as warm-air intakes. The air would be drawn in from the side of the quarter-circled Sirocco fan housing, through a round hole on the opposite side of the motor, or a duct. One can see these Siroccos tucked in their corners with the intake holes hidden or fenced off to limit access by passengers. In a few cases, where it was not practical to position the intake hole out of reach of the passengers, one sees a swan neck attachment or straight duct installed on the fan opening.

Another version of these warm-air Siroccos was the *thermotank*, a self-contained heating device consisting of a drum or tank, containing steam-heated coils, with a Sirocco mounted on one side to supply the air. The fan, usually of 30 in. diameter, would draw in air, force it through the thermotank, and then distribute it through an insulated duct system to service the associated rooms.

There were many other smaller ducts and ventilating devices seen on the deckhouse roofs and in the well decks. Many of these were the same on the two ships. However, the more visible were the large Sirocco ventilators.

It is necessary to identify yet another device seen on the ships that were not specifically vents but chimney flues. There was one located directly to the port side of the fore mast, used to service the ovens and stoves of the crew galley located under the forecastle. The second chimney flue was located above the fireplace in the first-class smoking room. The flue pipe rose out of the raised roof aft of the fan room on the boat deck, bent at a 90° degree angle forward, and then entered the base of the fourth funnel horizontally.

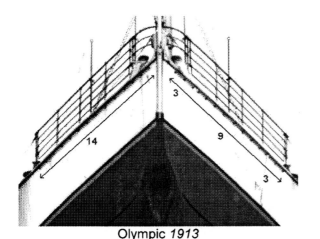

Olympic *1913*   Titanic *1912*

The Forecastle

Located on the outboard plating at the forepeak of the ships were jackstays. These were merely steel bars mounted horizontally against the plating by numerous brackets. They were used when it was necessary to fasten a canvas splash shield on the forepeak railing. When viewing the *Olympic's* port side jackstays one will notice that the brackets are broken up into groups because of the removable door for the center anchor. In this instance, the division of the brackets on the port side show, from fore to aft: three, nine, three. When one looks at the *Titanic* for purposes of comparison, one notices that the grouping consists of four, eight, and three. Looking at the starboard side of the ships, one will notice that *Titanic* had 15 mounting brackets for the continuous jackstay, and the *Olympic* had 14. This is a minor detail, but still a difference, a difference that never changed on the *Olympic* throughout her years of service.

Olympic's *hatch cover in 1911*

Olympic's *hatch cover in late 1912*

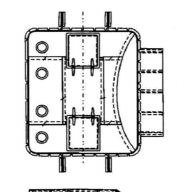

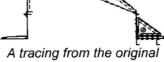

A tracing from the original plan of the Titanic's *No.1 hatch cover*

Titanic's *No.1 hatch coaming as it appears today.*

When the *Olympic* left on her maiden voyage she sported a No. 1 hatch cover with squared fore and aft sides. It is highly probable that the configuration of the square forward side of this cover changed because of an incident that happened on January 14, 1912. It is reported that Captain Smith encountered tremendous seas in gale force winds and blinding snow. The waves were so fierce that green water tore off the *Olympic's* No. 1 hatch cover, throwing it onto the forward well deck. The wave also tore a steam winch and anchor windlass from their mountings while washing away the forward port side railing. Although there are no pictures that definitely show the configuration of the *Titanic's* No. 1 hatch cover, there is a set of plans that show the "alterations made to the forward watertight hatch cover over the No. 1 hold." The *Titanic's* cover differed in that it had a forward face that was angled at nearly a 45° angle. This would create less resistance when hit with an exterior force like that encountered when being overtaken by green water. To add to this, the *Titanic* had an added steel plate breakwater, also angled at 45º, mounted on the deck against the No. 1 hatch coaming. The *Olympic* would be seen with a cover much like the *Titanic's* when she was photographed in 1913 during the post disaster refit, the difference being in the round skylights located on the forward angled face. The *Titanic* did not have these same windows, according to the plans. The *Olympic* would also show, in the pictures from 1913, that the angled steel breakwater was still not added to the forward hatch coaming. However, the breakwater does appear later, in aerial photographs taken in the early 1920s.

The *Olympic's* main breakwater running the width of the forecastle had an upper lip that was originally painted brown. The *Titanic's* breakwater was painted completely white, as is seen in photographs. The *Olympic* would show the brown upper lip even after the disaster.

The Olympic's *fo´c'sle taken on her maiden voyage in New York. Notice should be made of fittings present or absent as compared to* Titanic.

1. *the breakwater top rail is painted brown*
2. *A foul weather ventilation head and no crew galley skylight*
3. *The crewman's galley chimney pipe is straight the whole length and has a distinctive head.*
All of these features, though small, will play a part in identifying the two sisters from each other. Harland & Wolff utilized the time the Olympic spent in dock for repairs or to make updates, and it is these supplemental fittings that Titanic *was built with from the beginning which made these ships look even more alike. However, there are some things* Olympic *had, that* Titanic *would never see.*

In a photo of the *Olympic's* forecastle, taken while the ship was in New York on her first voyage, one can see that there is no crew galley skylight located aft of the port side breakwater. Curiously, there is a foul weather vent located in this area instead. There also is no large cowl vent forward of the port side breakwater. The large cowl vent would appear on the *Olympic* in pictures taken in March of 1912, when she entered the graving dock for propeller blade repairs. Also appearing for the first time in the pictures of the *Olympic* taken in March of 1912 is a small cowl vent located at the far port side of the forecastle aft of the breakwater, by the waterway. It appears, after looking at the photo of

Titanic's *fo´c'sle as photographed in Southampton. Some fittings were different than those on the* Olympic.

1.   *The breakwater top rail is painted white.*
2.   *A crewman's galley skylight*
3.   *A large cowl*
4.   *The base of the crewman's galley stove chimney is curved at deck level.*
Olympic's rectangular foul weather duct is not present here. Titanic's chimney flue pipe has a distinctive curve at the base, and though it can't be seen here, the top of the pipe had a different design of ventilation head-one that Olympic was not fitted with, and never would be.

the *Olympic's* forecastle in 1913, that the crew galley skylight had been added like that seen on the *Titanic*. Surprisingly, the small cowl and foul weather vent were never removed. The *Titanic* never had these two additional features.

B Deck

As is well known, the *Olympic* had an open promenade extending the length of B deck. It would not be until the 1912–1913 refit that the Café Parisien and á la carte restaurant would be extended out to the sides of the ship, cutting off the free passage along the full length of this promenade. The noticeable difference between the *Olympic* and the *Titanic* in this area, while looking aft from the forecastle to B deck, is that the *Olympic* had bulkheads fitted on either side, each with a door and a window, seen aft of the crew stairs. These were the entrances to the open B deck promenades. The *Titanic*, which had staterooms in this area, was fitted with a single window on a solid bulkhead on either side. These windows are visible in photographs.

The very forward bulkhead of B deck differed on the two liners in that the *Titanic* had two doors with round windows among the row of rectangular stateroom windows, providing access to the corridors inside. The *Olympic* did not have doors in this area, only a row of rectangular glass windows servicing the rooms. The *Olympic* would never have doors fitted in this area.

The sides of the hull along B deck were different on the *Titanic*, but not at first. Looking at launch photos, one will notice that the windows along the length of B deck are uniform, just as seen on the *Olympic*. With the later addition of the staterooms on the *Titanic*, the windows would be reconfigured in a manner to accommodate the alterations. The windows on the *Titanic*, commonly known as "Utley sliding glass windows," were much thinner on the forward section, and spaced differently, as is evidenced in photographs taken as early as September 1911.

In this classic photo of Titanic *taken at Southampton, details can be seen that were unique to her alone.*

1. *The bulkhead of the B deck promenade sporting a window for an added stateroom. This was an upgrade that* Olympic *would not see until her 1928 refit.*
2. *The weather screen for the A deck promenade containing a door and window.* Olympic *would never have this fitted.*
3. *Round windows in doors that were exclusive to* Titanic. Olympic *had no doors in this location but a continuation of the rectangular windows. This feature would never change on her.*
4. *The wing cabs have been moved over the side of the ship by about 18 inches.* Olympic *would not see this until her post sinking refit.*

Olympic *during her post sinking refit on December 1*st *1912. H-1826*

1. A small cowl was added – an Olympic *specific fitting*
2. The rectangular foul weather duct was retained as originally fitted
3. A crewman's galley skylight has been added as Titanic.
4. A large cowl has been added like Titanic.
5. The breakwater top rail retained the brown paint.
6. The forward end of the hatch cover is slanted, but the forward fitted windows were not on Titanic.
7. Notice the bell is mounted to the fore side of the mast. Titanic's bell was mounted on the aft side.
8. A duplicate of the weather screens Titanic had on A deck. Here it is used for Olympic's B deck promenade. Further-if one looks real close at the same location on the right side of the photo; daylight can be seen streaming in through the promenade windows.
9. No A deck promenade weather screens. The Olympic never had the type fitted to Titanic. But would later sport canvas in this area to act as a wind and spray barrier.
10. A rectangular window is in place where doors with round windows were on Titanic. This never changed on Olympic.
11. Harland & Wolff workers have removed the bridge cab roofs in preparation to extend these structures outboard, as was Titanic's.

A Deck

The *Olympic* was never fitted with the A deck promenade weather windows along the sides of the superstructure as was the *Titanic*. This was in response to the loss of the unobstructed view to the open sea on the Boat deck after the installation of the added Welin davits and lifeboats, as well as the problems associated with loading passengers into lifeboats through the window openings, as experienced on the *Titanic*. It was quite evidently a compromise to tolerate the sea spray in order to accommodate the view of the open water for first-class passengers. It seems that the spray problem was partially reduced in any case, as the *Olympic* would be fitted with a canvas splash shield extending from the forward corner of the crew staircase enclosure and attaching aft to an outboard stanchion. On the *Titanic*, with her added windows, there would also be a doorway bulkhead with a window at the forward end of the A deck promenade, seen on both sides of the ship. This was the exact type of bulkhead that the *Olympic* had on her B deck promenade.

The internal windows and doorways along the A deck promenade were much the same on the two sisters, except for a few room configuration changes that are evident only on deck plans, not in photographs. Of course, the rooms that were used by Thomas Andrews and Fr. Browne aboard the *Titanic* were originally part of the aft first-class entrance foyer. This arrangement was not on the *Olympic* at first, but was added either by January 1912, or after the disaster.

Officers' Deckhouse On the Boat Deck

A small detail, which commonly goes unnoticed but is key to identifying the *Olympic* from the *Titanic*, are the bridge wing cabs on both sides of the forward superstructure. The *Olympic* was built with wing cabs that were flush with the sides. The *Titanic's* bridge cabs extended over the sides about 2 ft. The *Olympic* would see this upgrade during the 1912–1913 refit. In picture H-1826 one can see that the roofs of the cabs have been removed. This was no doubt done in preparation to extend these structures.

The wheelhouse on the *Olympic* underwent three different design changes throughout her career. When one looks at the earliest plans one will find that the wheelhouse contained recessed doors on both sides, with a flat forward bulkhead. This structure extended to the sides, even with the bridge roofline above. However, before the wheelhouse was built on the *Olympic*, the forward bulkhead was changed to a rounded configuration. This is the way it is seen in photos taken during the ship's construction and later during her maiden voyage. It appears that this configuration was not practical, as the *Titanic's* wheelhouse would have a flat forward bulkhead, a reversion to the original design plans of the *Olympic*. However, the port and starboard bulkheads were recessed inboard under the roofline with flush mounted doors, the width of the *Titanic's* wheelhouse being only as wide as the funnel casing located aft.

The *Olympic's* wheelhouse was greatly transformed during the post-disaster refit, so that it eventually matched that on the *Titanic* to some degree. Unknown to many *Titanic* researchers is the fact that the *Olympic's* officers' deckhouse was approximately 9 ft shorter than the *Titanic's*. With the addition of first-class staterooms on each side located at the aft end of the deckhouse, the whole of the *Titanic's* officer's quarters was pushed forward past the edge of the forward funnel casing. This is probably the main reason for the flat forward wheelhouse bulkhead, as there was less space for a curve. It would have been necessary for an officer to be able to see across the ship from one bridge cab to the other, for maneuvering and docking purposes.

When comparing pictures of the *Olympic's* officers' deckhouse windows with those of the *Titanic*, one can see a different window spacing, which is the result of the added rooms. The skid lights that were mounted at the deck level of the officers' deckhouse were used to allow light into the inside bank of first-class staterooms below on A deck. The *Olympic* was fitted with oval skid lights, much like those on the *Oceanic*, whereas those on the *Titanic* were round. Again, because of the different room and length configuration, the *Titanic's* skid lights would have a different spacing than that of her older sister. To add to the window placement differences of the officers' deckhouse, the *Olympic* had a window on the forward port bulkhead, abreast of the wheelhouse; the *Titanic* did not.

During the 1912–1913 refit the *Olympic* had her officers' deckhouse extended forward, like the *Titanic's*. This would bring about the third change in the design of the *Olympic's* wheelhouse. As with the *Titanic*, the curved bulkhead was removed for the placement of a flat bulkhead, again because of the necessity to see through the navigating bridge from wing cab to wing cab.

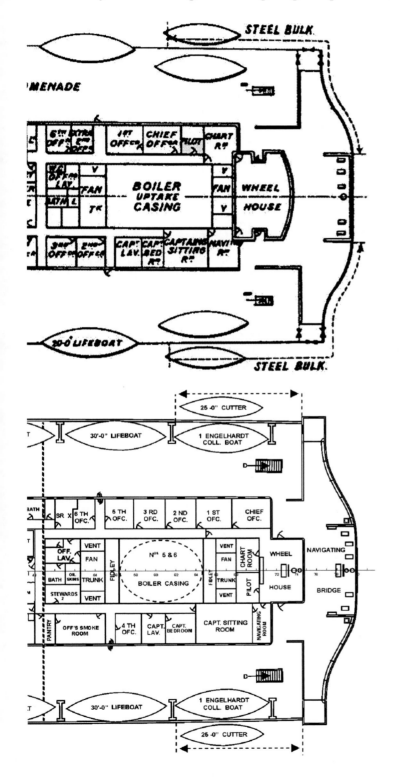

Partial plan of Olympic's *officers' deckhouse*
As Built

1. The wheelhouse extends to the sides, even with the navigating bridge, and the doors are recessed.
2. The forward bulkhead of the wheelhouse is curved.
3. The officers' deckhouse proper terminates right forward of the fan trunk casing.
4. The bridge wing cabs are flush with the sides of the ship.

After the 1912-13 refit, nearly the whole of the internal deckhouse arrangement would change. With the forward extension of the deckhouse, there would be room to add first-class staterooms aft of the officers' accommodations.

Partial plan of Titanic's *officers' deckhouse*

The differences are quite apparent between the two ships in these plans. Titanic *was an improvement over* Olympic *to say the least. But the* Olympic *would not be left out, as she would see the majority of these upgrades after her 1912-13 refit.*

93

The Olympic *while under construction showing the wooden footing for the wheelhouse complete with recessed doors and curved bulkhead. Another difference in the two sisters was Olympic's port side deckhouse window that faced forward from the chart room.* Titanic *lacked this window altogether.*

The senior officers preparing for Olympic's maiden voyage in 1911. L to R: Murdoch; Evans; Alexander and Captain Smith. Note the curved wheelhouse bulkhead to the left of Murdoch.

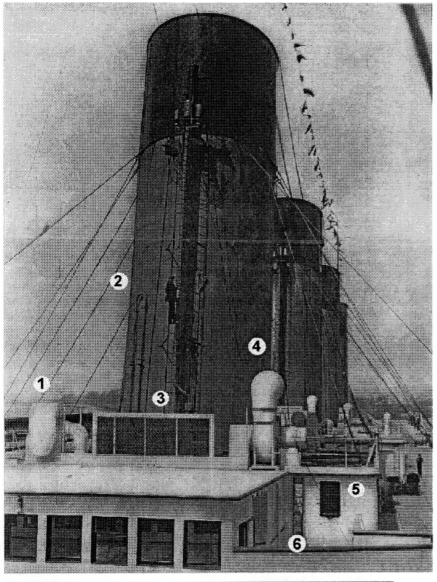

The Olympic at New York
Maiden Voyage-June 1911

1. A swan neck ventilation duct that was an original Olympic fitting, but later replaced before April of 1912.
2. Notice the height of this water main. The top is about centered between the two ladder support brackets.
3. The Olympic's No. 6 stokehold ventilation duct. The screen is divided by reinforcing mullions creating a visual appearance of (from starboard to port) one narrow and three evenly spaced rectangles.
4. A Sirocco ventilation fan with a cowl head. The housing is positioned longitudinally, and the motor is athwartship.
5. Window facing forward from the chart room, a fitting Titanic did not have.
6. The outboard bulkhead of the wheel house is seen here being about flush with the roofline, and the door is recessed in an alcove.

Captain Smith on the bridge of the Titanic. The flat bulkhead of the wheelhouse is visible to the right.

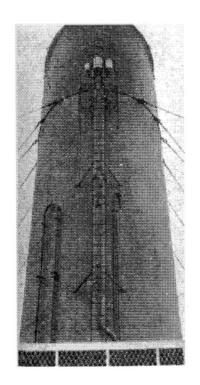

Titanic's *bridge roof at Southampton*

Note that the roof of the navigating bridge is overhanging, by a considerable margin, the outboard bulkhead of the wheelhouse. In fact the wheelhouse bulkhead cannot even be seen here. The chart room window is also missing, a definite difference between the Olympic *and* Titanic. Titanic's *chart room was not located in this part of the deckhouse. The large starboard side swan neck ventilation head is seen here, along with the large port side cowl. In this instance, the motor is facing longitudinally and the fan housing is athwartship. The large Sirocco ventilator aft of the cowl was another fitting* Olympic *would never have, at least not in this form.* Olympic *would see a ventilation fan in this position but with a large swan neck duct attached. On* Titanic, *this fan had an open intake hole facing forward, the top half being obstructed by a hood.*

Right- Titanic's *No.1 funnel looking up from the roof of the wheelhouse. Note the height of the water main being closer to the top ladder support, and the screen divisions of the No. 6 stokehold ventilation duct. In this instance the screen division consist of (from starboard to port) three wide and one thin rectangle. Directly the opposite of* Olympic

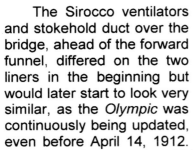

The Sirocco ventilators and stokehold duct over the bridge, ahead of the forward funnel, differed on the two liners in the beginning but would later start to look very similar, as the *Olympic* was continuously being updated, even before April 14, 1912. The *Olympic* sported a 30-in. cowled Sirocco on the port side of the stokehold duct above the wheelhouse. This lone Sirocco was mounted to the side of the stokehold duct, parallel to the centerline (longitudinal). The *Titanic* had the same 30-in. Sirocco cowl in this area, but the fan housing was mounted athwartship. This is a distinct difference clearly seen in photographs prior to, and after, April 14, 1912.

The protective mesh on the face of the stokehold duct in the center of the casing, ahead of the forward funnel, consisted of three mullions that divided the screen into four rectangular columns. In the case of the *Olympic*, these columns appeared, from starboard to port: thin, wide, wide, wide. The *Titanic's* screen divisions were completely opposite: wide, wide, wide, and thin.

On the port side, ahead of the forward funnel, the *Titanic* was fitted with a large 35-in. Sirocco with a swan neck duct. The *Olympic* was originally fitted with a smaller 30-in. Sirocco with a duct that was unique in shape. It is apparent that this duct did not provide enough air flow, as it was replaced with the same type of 35-in. Sirocco as on the *Titanic*, again before March 1912. However, it should be noted that the *Titanic's* swan neck duct in this location was shorter than the one later fitted to *Olympic*. The *Titanic's* shorter swan neck duct did not match the original Sirocco fitted to the *Olympic*. They did not look alike and were of a slightly different design.

Aft of the forward funnel, the *Olympic* originally had a small 30-in. Sirocco feeding out of the center stokehold duct on the starboard side. This again was upgraded to a 35-in. fan with a larger swan neck duct, just like the *Titanic*. The port side roof over the officers' deckhouse, aft of the forward funnel, was the home of a thermotank and its subsequent Sirocco fan housing. The two ships had the same size thermotank and fan; however, the *Titanic's* was installed so that the fan housing was perpendicular to the centerline of the ship, and the *Olympic's* was installed so that the fan housing was parallel with the centerline of the ship. This configuration never changed on the *Olympic* and remained as such until the end of her career.

Just forward of the port side thermotank was another sort of air intake Sirocco. The one on the *Titanic* consisted of a 35-in. fan housing and a large swan neck duct, exactly as was seen on the starboard side. The *Olympic* had a smaller Sirocco fan housing, probably a 30-in. unit, minus the ventilation head. The pictures show a simple intake opening on the opposite side of the motor. This was updated prior to the sinking to include a swan neck duct.

Located on the starboard side, aft of the second funnel and over the first-class gymnasium, was another air intake fan. As with the other air intakes originally seen on the *Olympic*, Harland & Wolff upgraded this Sirocco with a larger fan and swan neck duct. This was done before March 1912.

It is more than apparent that the *Olympic's* ventilating system was inadequate at first. With the process of trial, error, and evolution, the *Olympic* was upgraded as she went along. As previously stated, what was learned from experience with the *Olympic* was applied to the *Titanic*, and it certainly is plainly evident in the photographs of the period.

Olympic *during her sea trials in 1911*

1. *The grand staircase dome cover has sidelights and rectangular louvers fitted.* Titanic *did not.*
2. *The awning rafter extends from the top of the No. 5 stokehold duct, over the Gibbs ventilation head, and connects to the edge of the dome cover.* Titanic's *awning rafter ended on the Gibbs ventilation head and did not pass over it.*
3. *This water tank did not last long on the* Olympic, *and would never be fitted to* Titanic.

A major structure that helps any White Star enthusiast identify the *Titanic* from the *Olympic* is the grand staircase dome cover, forward of the second funnel. The *Olympic* had a series of portholes, or sidelights, installed on all four sides of the structure. Along with the sidelights were devices to enclose the windows to protect them from the weather and to close out the glare of the light from inside at night. These appear as square boxes when looking at the sides of the dome cover. The *Titanic* never had these sidelights and retractable devices on her dome cover. Instead, the *Titanic's* dome cover was plain, with only two sidelights located on the aft side, protected only by the apparatuses surrounding them.

Just forward of the dome covers on these two ships was a Gibbs extractor vent situated over the elevator motor room. Seen in many pictures of the two ships is a pipe that has always been believed to be part of this Gibbs vent. On the *Titanic*, this pipe leads from the top of the ventilator and extends forward horizontally, ending on top of the stokehold duct aft of the forward funnel. This pipe was not part of the ventilating apparatus. In fact it was merely a hollow pipe that rested on top of the Gibbs vent, used only to support a canvas awning. The *Olympic's* pipe differed in that it actually mounted on the forward edge of the dome cover, passed over the Gibbs vent, and then connected to the center of the stokehold duct aft of the forward funnel. This is the way the configuration remained on the *Olympic* throughout her career, the difference with the *Titanic* again being that the pipe mounted on top of the Gibbs and then extended forward. A close examination of the railings that lined the officers' deckhouse in this area will reveal a series of eye loops. These were used for securing the awning at the outboard edges.

Olympic photographed in Southampton shortly after the Titanic *sank. It should be noted that though there are some vent size increases, the fittings that were present in her pre-sinking era are still there.*

1. *The cover over the grand staircase dome still has the sidelights and the rectangular louvers.*
2. *The motor for the cowl ventilator is still facing athwartship, and the fan housing is still longitudinal.*
3. *The outboard bulkhead of the wheelhouse is still extended out to the roofline.*
4. *The screen divisions in the stokehold duct are still the same as in 1911.*
5. *This upgraded swan neck ventilating head is new, but taller than* Titanic's *was.*
6. *For information purposes: these two lifeboat falls are a dead giveaway to identify pictures of the* Olympic *post sinking, and pre refit. In the dash to get lifeboats for all, and to make the existing equipment safer, these two portable falls were secured to the funnel shrouds to accommodate the Engelhardt collapsible boats on the roof of the officers' deckhouse.*

Raised Roof Over the First-Class Lounge and Reading and Writing Room

This area of the ship was photographed on the *Olympic*, both before and after April 14, 1912. As with many of the Sirocco fan dimensions, there were upgrades and enlargements. The raised roof on the *Olympic* encompassed the outline of the rooms below. Because of this, there was an alcove on both sides of the raised roof that corresponded with the bay windows of the first-class lounge on A deck. When Harland & Wolff planked the steel decks on the *Olympic* they framed the wood around the alcoves, leaving the space open. On the *Titanic*, this was done differently: The alcoves were planked over. The alcoves were still there, but they were now enclosed at the top. This little bit of open space between the decking of the raised roof and the decking of the boat deck did not go unused, as there were ducts occupying this space that fed into 20-in. Siroccos with cowls, positioned on both sides of the *Titanic's* raised roof. The *Olympic,* on the other hand, with her exposed alcoves, had only one cowl in position on the port side. This configuration remained throughout the *Olympic's* career, because a starboard side 20-in. Sirocco was never added.

Located just forward of the *Titanic's* raised roof on the port side was a 20-in. Sirocco and cowl. The *Olympic* never had a ventilator in this position.

Titanic in Belfast April 1ˢᵗ, 1912

Among other differences, the Titanic *had no sidelights in the dome cover of the grand staircase.*

Titanic *above, and 1911* Olympic *below*

It is rather obvious that there were more differences in these two sisters than just the A deck promenade screen windows. The majority of upgrades made to Olympic *which resembled the* Titanic *would not be done until the 1912-13 refit.*

Olympic *maiden voyage* left, *and post sinking* right.

Observe the window just forward of the door. This was the Captain's lavatory window on the Olympic. *Lavatory windows in this deckhouse were unique in that they did not have the round locking mechanism at the bottom of the frame. It can be seen in the same position in both pictures. Not only is this evidence that the deckhouse remained the same through these periods of* Olympic's *history, but also illustrates a different window configuration than* Titanic. *The reason for this was because of different room arrangements between the two sisters. The* Olympic's *officers' deckhouse, though modified, would never truly match* Titanic. *Special attention should be given to the elliptical "skid lights" at the base of the bulkhead.*

Captain Smith and Chief Purser Hugh McElroy on Titanic

The window just forward of the door to the extreme left had a round locking mechanism and was the 4th officer's cabin. The window just forward of the 4th officer's cabin was Captain Smith's lavatory. The round "skid lights" can be seen clearly in this photo.

Captain Smith on the Titanic.
A round "skid light" is behind him.

Olympic *later in her career looking aft from the starboard side on the boat deck.*
The originally fitted officers' deckhouse windows would never change as this photo indicates.

Olympic's *port side raised roof. H-1543*
May 1911

1. Titanic *would have a 20 in. Sirocco fan and cowl in this position.*
2. *This swan neck ventilation head would be replaced on* Olympic *in the months to come to match* Titanic's.
3. *20 in. fan with cowl attachment. This had a mate in the exact same position on the other side on* Titanic, *but* Olympic *would only have a port side cowl here, and this configuration never changed throughout her career.*
4. *The divisions of the screen of the stokehold duct were different on* Titanic.

Titanic's *raised roof-port side.*

1. The ventilation head that can be seen just behind the cowl was an upgrade.
2. The divisions of the stokehold duct screen were different on Olympic
3. A 20 inch fan and cowl is added just forward of the roof over the reading and writing room. Olympic *was never fitted with this ventilator.*

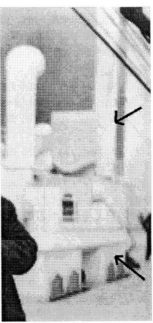

Left -Olympic *1911*
Right -Titanic *1912*

Observe the alcove on the boat deck formed by the bay windows extending up from A deck.

On Olympic, *the decking of the raised roof was cut around the perimeter of the alcove. On* Titanic, *the same space was decked over.*

The Olympic *did not have a cowl on the starboard side of the raised roof, but* Titanic *did.*

Note the large swan neck ventilation duct on the roof of the tank room. This was another Titanic *only feature.*

Titanic's *raised roof ventilators-starboard side. A 20 inch cowl Sirocco ventilator can be seen on the roof, matching a counterpart on the port side. This was a* Titanic *only feature.*

The Third Funnel Deckhouse

The third funnel deckhouse on both ships contained the officers' mess, stairwells, a pantry, a deck chair storeroom, and a machinery room for the motor that operated an electric lift. There were no significant differences in this deckhouse except for the configuration of the Siroccos that fed the heating elements at the corners of the funnel casing. As mentioned before, these Siroccos differed in size and configuration in regard to their swan neck ducts and air intake apparatus. As with the many Siroccos on the roof of the officers' deckhouse, Harland & Wolff felt it necessary to enlarge or upgrade them to increase airflow, creating slightly different fan housings and attachments.

At the very aft side of the third funnel deckhouse, along the face of the stokehold duct, which was built into the casing in this instance, was an opening for a crew stairwell. Pictures show that the *Olympic* did not have this stairwell after construction; however, the *Titanic* did have it. The original builder's plans show the addition of the stairwell on the *Titanic* dated September 26, 1911. The stairwell is not seen on the *Olympic* in pictures until the 1920s, but it was added at least by the 1912–1913 refit. It is not known if the *Olympic* had the stairwell added before the post-disaster refit, as it does not appear in the Drawing Office specification notebook.

Reciprocating Engine Casing, Tank Room, and Engineers Smoke Room

This structure holds one of the many openly visible differences in the two ships. It would be proper to address the roofs of the tank room first and foremost. To explain the orientation of the tank room it is best to describe it as actually consisting of two different rooms, connected by a narrow catwalk. These rooms flanked the reciprocating engine casing on the port and starboard side and contained the water supply tanks for the passenger and crew accommodations, specifically, the fresh water, washing water, and saltwater used for baths. The tanks were located on the highest deck of the ship as a simple gravity process supplied water to the many outlets. Located on the aft side of the third funnel was a series of main feed water pipes that supplied these tanks. The *Olympic* had a very simple arrangement of these pipes in that she had only one set of loops per side, mounted on the funnel, the port and starboard sides being divided by the steam escape pipe mounted to the aft and center of the funnel. These pipes appear in photographs as an upside down *U*. Located directly to starboard of the steam escape pipe was an even smaller series of pipes that appear as a *P*. This P-shaped pipe was an overflow. Any place on the funnels where these P-shaped pipes are seen indicates an overflow, whereas the "U," or "loops," represent main water feed for a water tank.

The sets of main water feed pipe loops on Harland & Wolff ships were mounted so that the topmost bend was above the level of the water tanks. The pipes were kept in place by hangers on the aft side of a funnel. In the case of the *Olympic*-class liners this was the third funnel. From here they led aft, over the deck space between the third funnel deckhouse and the tank rooms. The *Olympic*, having only one set of pipes per side, connected to the roofs of the tank rooms right at the forward edge of the deckhouse. The starboard tank room of the *Olympic* was completely utilized by water tanks. However, the *Titanic* differed in that there was an engineer's smoke room added to her starboard side, occupying more than half of the space forward. Because of this upgrade, the *Titanic's* water pipes are seen extending farther aft along the roof, over the top of the area encompassing this added room. The port side tank room on the *Titanic* also differed in that the pipes extended farther aft along the roof to accommodate a different arrangement of the tanks. The *Olympic* would not see the addition of the engineer's smoke room until she was refitted in 1912–1913. The locations where the water pipes entered the roofs of the tank rooms would always remain different.

Even though the *Olympic's* water main loops would later look much like those of the late *Titanic's*, they were never exactly the same. One example is the P-shaped overflow on the starboard side of the two ships' funnels, as the *Olympic's* and *Titanic's* were opposite of each other. Another example of how the *Titanic's* water pipes differed was that she had an extra set of loops on the port side of the funnel, giving her two sets, whereas the *Olympic* had only one set prior to the sinking.

The addition of the engineer's smoke room on the starboard side of the *Titanic's* reciprocating engine casing also meant that there was a difference in the windows along the bulkhead, as well as an extra door. When looking at pictures of the starboard side, one can see the longer water pipes and two doors, one for the aft section tank room and one for the engineer's smoke room. Another difference in the windows occurred with the forward bulkhead of the deckhouse, in that the *Olympic* had only one window per side and the *Titanic* had two windows on the starboard side and one window on the port side. Although the *Olympic* was later fitted with the engineer's smoke room, the window configuration on this forward bulkhead never changed throughout her career. However, the *Olympic* would have the starboard window and door arrangement of the *Titanic*, but only after the refit.

From the beginning, the *Titanic* had a set of cowls located on the aft section of the roof that encompassed the reciprocating engine casing and tank rooms, one cowl per side. The associated Sirocco fans were located internally. The *Olympic* would start out with just the port side cowl, the starboard side being added by March 1912, as is evident in photographs.

The aft bulkhead of the tank room and reciprocating engine casing sported a combination of a ladder and a window on both sides, port and starboard, flanking the aft first-class stairwell dome cover. The starboard bulkhead of the *Olympic*, from inboard to outboard, had a ladder and a window. The *Titanic* had the exact opposite arrangement in this same area, a window and then a ladder. The *Olympic's* configuration remained consistent throughout her career.

Included as part of the reciprocating engine casing for the purposes of this book is the aft first-class staircase dome cover. Just as the *Olympic* had sidelights completely around her forward dome cover, such was the case with the aft dome cover. The *Titanic* did not have any sidelights on the port and starboard sides of her aft dome cover. It is not known whether the *Titanic* had two sidelights on the aft side of the cover, because there are no pictures that show this area. The *Olympic's* portholes in this structure would also remain unaltered until the end.

Olympic *1911*

1.   *Notice the placement of the ladder and the window.*
2.   *This water pipe arrangement was particular to the* Olympic *in this stage of her career.*

Titanic 1912

1.   *Notice the arrangement of the window and the ladder. Although slight, it was different than the* Olympic.
2.   *The water pipes on* Titanic *were much different and expanded more then the* Olympic's. *The* Olympic *would see a similar arrangement after her post-sinking refit, but the pipes would never look like this.*

You will notice a few differences in ventilators between these two pictures also.

Titanic *1912*

1. Notice the position of the light and the window.
2. This large swan neck ventilation head was particular to Titanic.

Olympic *1911*

This photo is commonly mislabeled as the Titanic. *However, it is far from it. Besides the white painted lifeboat sheer planks we can see:*

1. No large swan neck ventilation head.
2. A slight variance in the deck light position in relation to the window as compared to the same on Titanic.

Olympic's *return to service 1913*
How many things changed, and how many stayed the same?

1. *The water pipes are expanded, but do not match* Titanic's
2. *The "P" of the hot water overflow is still facing starboard.*
3. *The 20-inch cowl has not been added to the starboard side of the raised roof, nor have the alcoves been decked over.*

The Fourth Funnel Deckhouse and Raised Roof Over the Smoke Room

The fourth funnel deckhouse is commonly known as the *fan room*, because the deckhouse almost entirely contained Sirocco fans for the ventilation of the galleys and the turbine engine room, among other areas. Because the fourth funnel was nothing more than a large ventilating shaft, the fan room could contain a vast assortment of Siroccos that fed into it.

When examining the roof of the fan room on the original configuration of the *Olympic*, one will see two rectangular box ducts with louvers, which were located one on either side of the roof forward of the funnel. On the very far port side of the roof, outboard of the box duct, was a single rectangular duct, which exited out of the roof at the forward edge. This duct served the large Siroccos inside the deckhouse and then ran horizontally aft, connecting to the base of the funnel itself.

The starboard bulkhead of the *Olympic's* fan room contained two doors, a series of rectangular teak-framed windows, and a thermotank. The port side bulkhead of the fan room consisted of a thermotank, a series of teak-framed windows, and two doors, the forward door leading to a spiral staircase for the use of the crew.

The *Titanic* was very much different in that her fan room roof consisted of two 20-in. Sirocco fan housings with corresponding cowl vents located just forward of the funnel. In the center of the forward section of the roof was a huge 35-in. Sirocco fan and a swan neck duct with an opening that faced to starboard. Instead of a single long horizontal rectangular duct on the starboard side like that on the *Olympic*, the *Titanic* had one on each side. Both of these ducts fed out of the Siroccos in the fan room and ran along the roof horizontally and connected to the base of the funnel.

The *Titanic's* starboard bulkhead had the addition of a 20-in. Sirocco and cowl located forward of the thermotank. Along with the added vent there was an extra door on the aft portion of the bulkhead, giving the *Titanic* three doors.

The port side bulkhead differed from the *Olympic* in that there was one fewer window mounted on the bulkhead. This was in the area between the thermotank and the door to the spiral staircase. As an added note, the series of windows on the bulkheads of the *Titanic's* fan room were not teak framed but recessed.

The *Olympic* was fitted with a different configuration on her fan room roof by March 1912. Pictures of her entering the dry dock for the thrown propeller repair show that the rectangular duct with the louvers on the starboard side was replaced by a 20-in. Sirocco and cowl. A large 35-in. Sirocco and cowl were installed in the center of the roof on the forward section. This configuration would remain with the *Olympic* throughout her career and would always be different than the configuration of the *Titanic*. Because of this slightly different design on the *Olympic*, there was room to mount a railing around the forward roof of the fan room. The *Titanic* did not have a railing in the same location.

After the 1912–1913 refit the ventilating apparatus for the *Olympic's* fan room would see a Sirocco added forward of the thermotank on the starboard side, in the same place where the *Titanic* was fitted with the 20-in. Sirocco and cowl. In the case of the *Olympic*, a wider fan housing would be fitted with a large swan neck duct that faced forward.

A point of confusion for structural researchers of the *Olympic* and *Titanic* is the presence of what was thought to be a Gibbs extractor located aft of the fourth funnel deckhouse rising out of the raised roof over the smoking room. It was commonly thought that a pipe exited the top of this Gibbs vent, bending forward and then leading into the aft side of the fourth funnel. As with the theories of the forward Gibbs vent at the forward grand staircase dome cover, this is not true. In actuality there was no Gibbs extractor vent in this location at all. The object in this position was a chimney flue from the fireplace located at the very aft of the smoking room. The pipe exited the deck vertically, bent forward, and then entered the aft side of the fourth funnel. The base of the flue pipe had a protective sleeve fastened around it that extended the height of the bend where the pipe headed forward. This sleeve was probably made of asbestos and protected passengers from heat.

The difference between the two ships in this regard is that the *Olympic* did not have a flue pipe running into the funnel at first. She had a simple stand pipe that exited the deck vertically to a height above the second-class entrance deckhouse located aft of the raised roof. The stand pipe had a damper attached to the top that would open when hot smoke came out and close when not in use. The *Olympic* was upgraded to the *Titanic's* configuration only after the 1912–1913 refit.

When Dr. Robert Ballard photographed the stern section of the *Titanic's* wreck, little did he know that included in the pictures would be another difference in the two sisters, one that is certainly missed by many people. A photograph showing the remains of the aft second-class entrance on the boat deck shows the vertical plating that was once the aft side of the raised roof of the Smoking Room. In the photo there can be seen three skid lights that were mounted in the steel. These skid lights, like the ones along the base of the officers' deckhouse, were right at about the level of the deck. In the wreck photo, the steel aft end of the raised roof has been bent back, exposing the skid lights from the inside. Pictures of the *Olympic* from both before and after the sinking show that she never had these three round windows.

Olympic *Maiden Voyage*

1. The smoke room fireplace chimney flue standpipe with veined damper. This was the only operational fireplace within a passenger compartment on the ship.
2. A single door, and general arrangement of the aft and of the deckhouse was different than Titanic.
3. A large louvered ventilation duct that was soon to be removed, but never fitted to Titanic.
4. These windows appear to be framed out in teak.

Left: *both* Titanic

1. A mystery box that was never on Olympic
2. The fireplace flue exhausted to the base of the No. 4 funnel. This feature would be added to Olympic *later*.
3. The aft end of the deckhouse is a bit different than Olympic and had an extra door.
4. The windows were not trimmed in teak. They are merely set into the steel. The ventilation ducting above was different on Olympic, as can be seen in the picture just to left. Titanic's large swan neck ventilator is plainly visible.

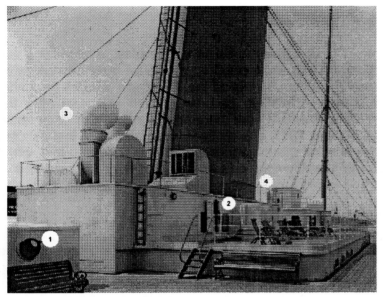

Olympic *pre April 15th 1912*

This is a transition picture, probably taken during the propeller blade repair in March of 1912.

1. One of the sidelights in the aft dome cover. Titanic *did not have these fittings.*
2. *Teak trimmed windows*
3. *A large cowl has been added by the time of this photo, and the louvered duct on the starboard side has been replaced with a 20-inch cowl and fan.*
4. *The chimney flue standpipe is present.*

Olympic *arriving in New York on her maiden voyage.*

In this photo one can clearly see the starboard louvered duct on the top of the No. 4 funnel deckhouse. As stated above, this was removed in place of a cowl prior to the Titanic's *demise.*

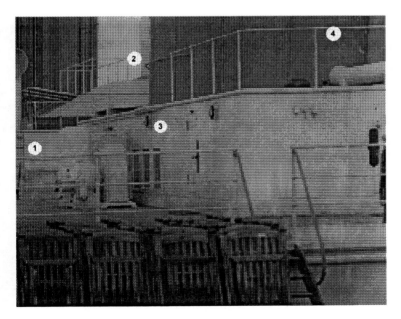

Titanic

1. *After dome cover with no sidelights.*
2. *The outward curve of the fan housing for a 20 inch Sirocco and cowl.*
3. *Windows minus the teak framing.*
4. *The chimney flue leading into the base of the funnel.*

The Aft Well Deck

The aft well decks of the *Olympic* and the *Titanic* appear to be nearly identical, except for a few things. First, the locations of the propeller spanners that were mounted on the aft bulkhead are seen out toward the sides of the ship. Although there are no pictures of the *Olympic's* aft well deck that show a starboard spanner before the *Titanic* sank, there are pictures of both spanners after the disaster. It is believed that the starboard spanner was added after the propeller repair was undertaken in March 1912, or after the *Hawke* collision in October 1911. The main point of this find is that pictures *do* exist showing the positions of the *Titanic's* propeller spanners mounted on the bulkhead and, when one compares the positions with later photos of the *Olympic*, one notices that they are mounted at different heights and angles.

The Poop Deck

It is a common occurrence for authors and archive personnel to misidentify the *Titanic* and the *Olympic* when they are looking at pictures of only the poop deck, the aftermost deck of the ships. However, there are a few very visible differences. It only takes a careful eye to notice them.

The docking bridges on the sisters hold what is probably the most noticeable difference at the stern of the ships, this being the width of the docking bridge itself. The *Olympic's* docking bridge did not extend over the sides of the hull but ended right at the supports on each side. The *Titanic's* docking bridge was upgraded in that it extended over the sides of the hull by a number of feet. This was a permanent fixture for the *Titanic* added in September 1911. However, with the *Olympic's* flush docking bridge ends, she was fitted with removable boards that could be lowered to provide an extension over the sides of the hull.

An additional difference is the placement of the life rings mounted on the docking bridges of the two sisters. Readers will notice that they are positioned in slightly different areas on the railing.

Below the overhangs of the docking bridge, just inboard of the supports, were gooseneck ventilation pipes seen one on each side of the ship. These pipes resembled candy canes. The *Olympic's* faced forward, whereas the *Titanic's* faced aft.

The cylindrical base platforms of the cranes located on the poop deck had a difference in the location of the watertight doors used to service the internal motors. The *Olympic's* crane platform doors faced forward, whereas the *Titanic's* faced outboard.

The docking bridge length, crane platforms, cowl vents, and the candy cane overflow pipes were different on the *Olympic* from those seen on the *Titanic*, as stated above, and they remained different throughout.

The Hull

Photographs of the *Titanic's* hull that have the clarity necessary to fully count each of the strakes and rivets are not available; however, there are enough photos that show the bow and stern well enough to discern subtle differences. Before we scrutinize the shell plates and doublers it is necessary to point out one of the more visible differences in the hulls of the two ships. This is the porthole arrangement in the plating just below the poop deck. The *Olympic's* portholes were positioned in a different order than the *Titanic's* and remained different throughout her career.

Along the sides of the hull at C deck in the area of the lowest level of portholes to be surrounded by white paint can be seen large portholes with flattened fore and aft sides. Intermixed with these large portholes are a number of small portholes. These small portholes were for the lavatories. On the *Olympic* one will be able to find only single small portholes situated in the line of large portholes. On the *Titanic* one will notice that wherever there is one small porthole there will be a second, creating a set at every interval where they appear. This configuration never changed on the *Olympic*. The "Big Piece," which was raised from the depths of the *Titanic's* resting place, is a part of the hull that included a set of these small portholes.

The gangway entrance doors to the first-class entrances on D deck present another difference: The *Olympic's* doors had round portholes, whereas the *Titanic* had rectangular windows. The doors visible on the wreck today still retain these rectangular windows, as does the door that was retrieved from the wreck several years ago. The *Olympic's* remained round.

When one looks at the original builder's shell plating plans for the *Olympic* and *Titanic* one finds a notation at the doubler forward at the "Halls" patent anchors. The plans indicate an overlap of the plates, or strakes, for the *Olympic*. A notation for "401" shows a change in that the strake butted up against the doubler and did not overlap it. One can see this overlap in pictures of the *Olympic* prior to the disaster and after. Pictures of the *Titanic's* bow shows that in fact the strake butts up to the doubler evenly and is completely smooth.

Located aft, right above the stern frame casting that surrounded the center propeller, at about the 23–24 foot draft mark, was a small plate. The significance this plate holds on the identification of the hulls of these two ships lies simply with the amount of bolts. The *Olympic* shows eight bolts in this plate both before and after the sinking, whereas the *Titanic* shows five bolts in pictures of her at the time of her launch. Unfortunately, if one wanted to look for this plate on the wreck today one would have to dig some 6 ft into the sediment.

There were internal differences that escaped the lens of the camera. One exception to this may be the *Titanic's* gymnasium. An examination of pictures of the *Titanic*'s reveals that there was a rowing machine, whereas the *Olympic* had different exercise apparatus. Less obvious, but important just the same, is the glass lighted map seen on the inboard bulkhead of each gymnasium. If one compares the shade of grays in the black-and-white pictures, which represent the colors in which the countries of the continents were painted, one will notice that the *Titanic's* continents had light colors painted within, and those on the *Olympic* had darker colors. The lighted illustrative sign to the right of the map was different on both ships also. Adding to the differences in the two gymnasiums was the furniture: The *Olympic* had wicker furniture and no wooden bench, whereas the *Titanic* had a bench and leather fitments.

The *Olympic* and *Titanic* were much the same in the big picture, certainly to the novice, but when one researches the ships in detail one sees that they were very much different.

Olympic *in New York on her maiden voyage*

1.   *This bulkhead is where a propeller spanner was fitted on* Titanic. *It is absent here on* Olympic. *There is, however, a spanner on the corresponding port bulkhead.* Titanic *would have a spanner on the port side also, but mounted at a different position.*
2.   *Special attention should be given to the location of the doors on the crane platforms, as this is a certain way to identify one sister from the other. Many* Titanic *historians have labeled* Olympic *as* Titanic *based on cropped photos of this area which show the doors facing forward.* Titanic's *doors faced outboard.*
3.   *This is a passive ventilation head made by "Gibbs". It was particular to the original configuration of the* Olympic, *but would be replaced by a 10-inch fan and a tall cowl.* Titanic *followed suit with the 10 inch fan from time of construction, never having the "Gibbs".*

Titanic *at Queenstown*

1. The propeller spanner on the starboard side. The object just to the left is a water fountain for 3rd class, another fitting Olympic would do without.
2. The doors of the crane platforms faced outboard. There was another door on each platform witch is not seen in this picture. All crane platforms had two doors.
3. The docking bridge is extended over the side of the hull permanently by about 2 ft-a Titanic only feature. Also, the location of the life rings on the rail are different than Olympic.

Titanic's *port side well deck with spanner and water fountain circled. The spanner is hung at an angle.*

Two different views showing the Olympic's docking bridge. It was unique in that the sides were flush with the hull of the ship. A teak platform was extended over the side for taking soundings and so fourth. This feature was upgraded on Titanic to a permanent extension of the bridge. This is another identification point commonly missed by Titanic researchers. The configuration on Olympic never changed throughout her career.

Right-Olympic *after the Hawke collision*

Below-Olympic *maiden voyage.*

The Olympic *in the 1930's. The position of the crane platform doors have remained the same since 1911 and the propeller spanners are placed on the bulkhead in positions unique to this ship.*

Olympic *during her sea trials in 1911. Note the position of the portholes along the sheer strake of the poop deck.*

Titanic at Belfast. Note the position of the portholes in the sheer strake of the poop deck, and how they differed from the Olympic.

Olympic *in the 1920's. Note that the position of the portholes along the poop deck sheer strake have not changed since 1911.*

D deck gangway doors
Olympic *1911*

D deck Gangway doors
Titanic *1912*

D deck gangway doors from Olympic *at the beginning of
W.W.I.*

The round windows never changed.

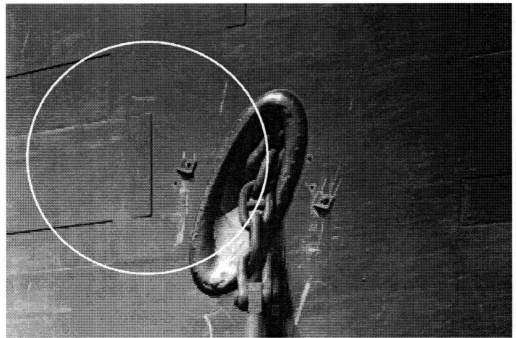

Olympic *in dry-dock 1911*

An overlapping doubler just forward of the anchors was a specific feature to this ship.

Titanic *prior to launch 1911.*

The overlap in the same area was smooth on Titanic because the plates were butted flush with each other. This change was specified in the original Shell Plating Plan of these two ships.

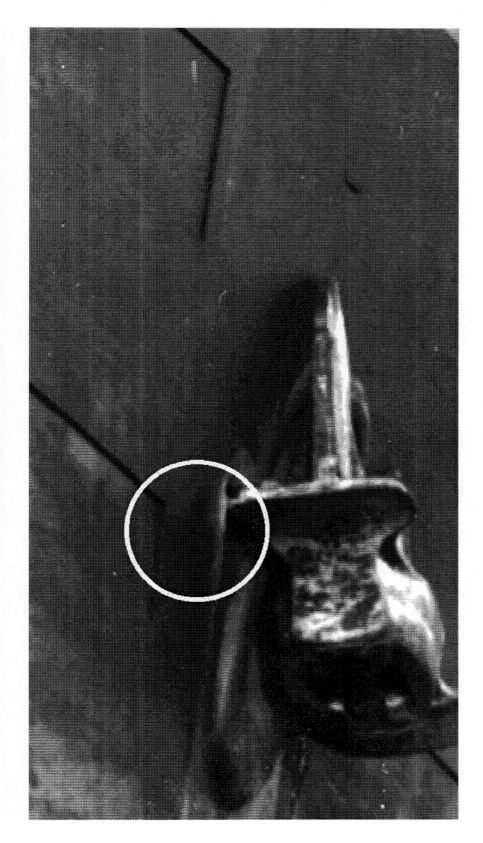

Olympic *December 1912*

Though the overlapped doubler is hidden behind the stowed anchor, the shadow of the butt lap is still discernible.

Top-Olympic *1911,* middle-Titanic, *and* Olympic *1924 bottom.*

This zinc plate on Olympic *had 8 bolts, and the matching plate on* Titanic *had 5. Even up until 1924, the count and alignment of the bolts did not change on the* Olympic.

The illuminated signs in Titanic's *gymnasium. Notice the color shading of the map and the illustrations to the left showing a cut-away of the ship.*

Olympic's *illuminated signs in 1911*

Olympic's *illuminated signs circa 1920's. Notice the absence of* Titanic's *name on the illustration, and the map of White Star Line routes.* Titanic's *signs were unique to her design.*

A P P E N D I X   I I

Olympic: The Last Grand Lady

The White Star Line started a new era in Atlantic travel with the building of the *Olympic*-class liners. Little did they know at the time of the launch of the first ship in a series of three that the *Olympic* would be the last grand lady built for the White Star Line. There would be other ships, some obtained through war reparations, but none as grand for White Star as the *Olympic*. The two younger sisters of "No. 400" and, subsequently, the dreams of J. Bruce Ismay and Lord Pirrie, would sink before they matured to their full potential as Atlantic passenger liners, their lives cut short as victims of circumstance. Such is not the case for "Old Reliable."

The beginning of the *Olympic*'s career has been well covered in almost all of the *Titanic* books that have been published since 1912. It has been widely discussed within circles of ocean liner historians whether the *Olympic* would have ever gained the fame she did if not for the sinking of the *Titanic*. Would the *Olympic* have been just another name on the list of White Star ships? Would she ever have gained the level of intense study she did since the *Titanic* sank? Probably not. However, the *Olympic* does have a history after the *Titanic* and *Britannic*. Not only was she the first of an era, but she also was the first at a number of other events in history as well. The *Olympic* is at the forefront of nearly every ocean liner collector's priority list. Her postcards, emergency escape maps, furniture, china, menus, and other surviving memorabilia command top dollar. Probably the best thing that ever happened to perpetuate the memory of this ship was the sinking of the *Titanic*. Therefore, we begin our discussion of the *Olympic*'s history just before April 15, 1912.

At 3:00 p.m. on April 13, 1912, the *Olympic* left New York heading east on the Atlantic, toward England. There was talk on the *Titanic* that the *Olympic* might pass within view on April 15, while the *Titanic* was on her maiden voyage westbound to New York. On the evening of April 14, 1912, the passengers on both ships turned in for the night as another day of ocean travel wound to an end, but those on the *Olympic* would wake on the morning of April 15 to be stunned with the news that the *Titanic* had sunk. During the time that the *Titanic* was frantically calling for assistance, Captain Herbert James Haddock of the *Olympic* found that he could do very little, because his ship was more than 500 miles from the *Titanic*'s position. Haddock radioed the *Titanic,* advising that he was en route with all boilers fired, in an attempt to rescue passengers of the stricken ship. However, before Haddock arrived at the wreck site, he was informed of the bad news from Ismay via Marconi transmissions from the *Carpathia*. At this point, the only manner in which the *Olympic* could give assistance was to relay the list of survivors to Cape Race. Out of respect for the *Titanic*, all festivities on board the *Olympic* were canceled. Crew and passengers alike were struck hard with the news, as many of the crew had friends and family on the *Titanic*. Unable to assist with the survivors, the *Olympic* carried through on her voyage to Southampton, arriving early on Sunday, April 21. The *Olympic* arrived at a city in a total state of mourning as all of Southampton appeared to be affected by the disaster.

The *Olympic* had to be readied to depart Southampton on April 24 but, because of the circumstances, some fast modifications to her lifesaving apparatus had to be made. Under the direction of Captain Maurice Clarke, the marine surveyor who had cleared the *Titanic* less then 2 weeks earlier, 40 extra Berthon collapsible lifeboats were fastened to the *Olympic*'s boat deck. Originally, the White Star office had stated that only 24 extra boats had to be fitted, but because more boats were brought in then was necessary, rumors started to circulate that some of these collapsibles were rejected by Clarke as not being fit for use. The extra boats were not new—they had been borrowed from naval vessels located in the area. By the morning of Wednesday, April 24, the boats had all been fitted, and extra hands were signed on. Extra wire falls were installed to ensure that the boats could be handled in case of an emergency. These extra wire falls would include a set attached to the middle shrouds of the No. 1 funnel to accommodate the Engelhardt collapsibles on the roof of the officers' deckhouse. (The *Titanic* had fittings to accommodate wire falls for the same reason, but

these were never used.) Even with all the extra effort put forth by the White Star Line to accommodate the extra collapsible boats, trouble was still in the air. At 7:00 a.m., when Clarke came aboard the *Olympic* to inspect the boats. In this instance, he put the boats and davits through a trial of higher intensity. As the passengers were beginning to arrive, Clarke had the appropriate crew muster on deck to have them uncover and lower a number of different boats to make sure that everything operated smoothly. Clarke estimated that it took an average of 12-½ minutes to lower each boat. At 11:50 a.m., Clarke was just about going to hand Captain Haddock his certificate of clearance when a message came to the bridge that the stokehold crew had deserted the ship. A meeting was arranged between the fireman and officials from the White Star Line. Even after Clarke insisted that everything was in order and that the boats were safe, the men refused to board the ship unless regular open lifeboats were installed. Because of the desertion of the stokehold crew, the *Olympic*'s journey had to be postponed for a day. It was decided to move the ship out of the berth to be anchored out of the way off of Spithead. This also ensured that there would be no more desertions, because the ship was now in the open water. Second Engineer Charles McKean remained on shore to muster a replacement stokehold crew. By the early morning of the 25th, the situation on the *Olympic* had not changed much. Clarke had remained on board to ensure that the ship could be cleared immediately after the new crew was in place. Wasting no time, Clarke again had some of the crew mustered on the boat deck to once again practice lowering the boats. This time the drill did not run as smoothly as the initial try. It took the

Above and Below- *A Berthon collapsibles put aboard the* Olympic

Firemen leave the Olympic *under protest of the lifeboat accommodation on April 24th 1912.*

crew almost 2 hours to prepare and lower the boats. By 8:00 a.m., some of the passengers were starting to roam the decks, and Clarke had the drill stopped so as not to alarm anyone. Later that morning a delegation from the union came on board to negotiate a settlement. During the discussions, six of the collapsibles were lowered to the water and kept afloat for 2 hours. On examination, it was found that five boats were completely dry, although the sixth had some water seepage. With the little amount of water that came in through the tiny hole in the boat during the 2 hours, it was agreed that less then 3 minutes of bailing could remedy the flooding. After a quick conference in the captain's cabin, the union delegates agreed to advise their members that the lifeboats were safe as long as this one faulty boat was replaced.

At 10:00 p.m. the tender finally arrived with a replacement stokehold crew of 168, including extra manpower to allow the *Olympic* to achieve a faster speed in order to make up the 36 lost hours. All of this effort would prove to no avail, because at midnight another message came to the bridge. This time 53 men were deserting the ship. Among the men were 35 able seamen, 5 quartermasters, 5

Testing a Berthon collapsible from the Olympic

lookouts, 2 lamp trimmers, 4 greasers and 2 other engine room personnel. These men were boarding the same tender that brought the replacement crew from shore. The problem this time was not with the lifeboats but with the replacement crew. These deserters refused to sail with men whom they considered the "dregs of Portsmouth." Many were inexperienced in sailing ships of this size, and some didn't even have sign-on books. It seems the second engineer had picked literally any man he could find to replace the first round of

deserters, and this second batch of deserters would not tolerate it. The recent deserters refused two attempts by Captain Haddock to order them back to their posts. The men expressed their due respect for the captain, but they just would not work with men who were unfit to operate the *Olympic*. A spokesman for the deserters stated that they wholly agreed that what the firemen did when they deserted at the dock was "a dirty low down trick," but they felt that going to sea with such men would be very dangerous. Haddock was at his wits' end with these men, so he signaled for the assistance of the commander of the HMS *Cochrane*, which was lying a half mile away, off Spithead. Within half an hour, Captain W. E. Goodenough boarded the *Olympic* in an attempt to mediate the dispute and try to convince the men to return to their stations. Goodenough found, while talking to the men, that even though some of them were concerned about the boats, many of the men were more concerned with the abilities of this new replacement crew to carry out their assignments. They were concerned that many of them were not even union members, which probably was more the true underlying issue. With this statement, Capt. Goodenough found the reason for the desertion to be based more on the worries that the men would get in trouble from their union than on the other problems. The men showed all due respect for the two officers, but even the threat of a charge of mutiny did not affect the outcome, neither did the officers consider force, as there was no call for it when no one else was hurt or threatened.

With the situation now facing White Star, officials had no other choice but to recruit yet another bunch of men. By 11:00 a.m. the next day, a tender arrived boarding more than 30 new men, although Captain Clarke failed to pass a few as fit for duty. About an hour later, Clarke received orders from his office to clear the *Olympic* as soon as he felt the ship was sufficiently manned. However, now that the ship was already 2 days behind schedule, it seemed less than likely that the *Olympic* would be able to make the journey. At 3:00 p.m. the news arrived from the White Star office that the voyage was canceled, so the *Olympic* returned to the berth at Southampton to disembark the passengers. It was here that she would remain, being fitted with union-approved crewmen and boats, until her next scheduled voyage, on May 15.

The mutiny incident was over, but in order for the White Star Line to save face after the loss of the *Titanic*, they had to take action. In this case, the 53 crewmen who deserted while the *Olympic* was anchored off Spithead were brought up on charges in the Portsmouth Police Court. The case began on Tuesday, April 30. The accused men were present and required to answer to the charge that "they were guilty of willful disobedience to the lawful commands of Captain Haddock, the Master of the steamship *Olympic*, contrary to section 225 of the Merchant Shipping act, 1894."

Olympic berthed at Southampton after the disaster. In the foreground are lifeboats possibly standing by to be loaded onboard a ship.

The defense attorneys argued, on the basis of Article 458 of the same act, that the owners of the White Star Line were required to ensure the seaworthiness of their ships. Allowing the *Olympic* to go to sea with an incompetent crew would be nearly as bad as the *Olympic* having sustained a hole in her hull. The attorney for the White Star Line, Norman Raebarn, called Captain Benjamin Steele, the White Star marine superintendent at Southampton, to testify as to the adequacy of the lifeboats and that there were enough crewmen to handle them. The second engineer testified that it was true that some of the men he picked were nothing more than Yorkshire miners. He did not consider the job of fireman to require that much skill, but in a statement that amused the court, he did acknowledge that it was hard work. The verdict came down on May 5th in favor of the White Star Line but, instead of fining or imprisoning the mutineers, the judge decided to strike any form of punishment because he believed that the men had probably been stricken with a case of nerves because of the recent loss of the *Titanic*. The mutiny case ended up fading into the background, because the testimony for the British Board of Trade inquiry was commencing. The lawyers for the White Star Line would need to work their hardest in order to save the reputation of the company in this heavily publicized arena. On May 14th a question was tabled in Parliament by George Terrell to Prime Minister H. H. Asquith as to what action would be taken against the officials of the British Seafarers Union who had prevented the *Olympic* from departing with His Majesty's Mails. Terrell's question was referred to the Board of Trade, who decided that, on the basis of the outcome of the court decision at Portsmouth, no prosecution would be undertaken.

On May 6, Lord Mersey traveled to the *Olympic* from the *Titanic* hearings in order to witness a lifeboat drill and to view the lifesaving apparatus on the ship. After the lowering of starboard boat No. 9, Lord Mersey returned to London after he had lunch on board the ship with Harold Sanderson, leaving Captain Haddock to prepare for the next departure. Sailing day came and went on May 15th as the mooring lines were slipped off of the *Olympic*. She arrived in New York 7 days later without incident.

Lord Mersey and his assessors testing one of the Olympic's *lifeboats.*

It was not unexpected to see all the added attention the *Olympic* received as she arrived at New York for the first time since the loss of the *Titanic*. However, it was a complete surprise to Captain Haddock when on Saturday, May 25, Sen. Alden Smith, chairman of the Senate Congressional Committee that was in charge of investigating the loss of the *Titanic*, appeared on the ship without notice only hours before the *Olympic* was to set sail. Captain Haddock was advised to give Sen. Smith every assistance as Philip Franklin rushed out of the International Mercantile Marine offices at 9 Broadway to get to Pier 59. Sen. Smith requested a lifeboat to be lowered with a full load of 65 men inside. Smith timed this operation at exactly 18 minutes. The esteemed guest, escorted by Chief Engineer Robert Fleming, was then taken down to the working areas of the ship to witness the safety features. Fireman Frederick Barrett was also on hand for questioning as he was previously on the *Titanic* in boiler room No. 6 the night of the collision. Barrett demonstrated what he had testified to in the inquiry, after which a watertight door was lowered for a demonstration. Sen. Smith left that afternoon satisfied with what he had seen, to prepare his speech, to which he would deliver to Congress 3 days later. The *Olympic* returned to England 1 week later with the temporary arrangements working properly but, to build confidence back up in the *Olympic*— and soon, the *Britannic*—some permanent modifications would be necessary. The *Olympic* remained in service for only six more journeys before the next step in her permanent upgrading was undertaken.

By the end of the summer season it was decided to bring the *Olympic* back to Belfast on October 9th for what would be the first of four major refits that the ship would see throughout her career. This overhaul would take the better part of 6 months, costing approximately £156,500. The refit would incorporate all of the lessons learned from the *Titanic* along with heavy reconstruction to the inside of the hull. An extra transverse bulkhead dividing the dynamo room in two was added, and many of the remaining transverse bulkheads were raised to an appropriate height above the waterline, some as far up as B deck.

Olympic *after the* Titanic *disaster but prior to the refit.*

The biggest feature of this refit would be the addition of an inner skin that extended amidships from the forward end of the No. 6 boiler room, aft throughout the full length of the boiler and engine rooms. The inner skin was riveted to inner frames placed inside the hull and extended to above the waterline. This inner skin was unlike the longitudinal bulkheads fitted to Cunard's *Lusitania* and *Mauretania*. The longitudinal bulkheads on the Cunard ships also formed the inner walls of the coal bunkers, which required the fitting of numerous watertight doors in these bulkheads to provide access for the trimmers and coal-passers to work the bunkers. The inner skin fitted to the *Olympic* was intended purely as a safety feature. Requiring no working access openings, it was sealed off from the inside. This was thought to offer even more safety, making the *Olympic* one of the safest vessels afloat. The subsequent loss of internal space caused by the inner skin required the removal of the center boiler in boiler room No. 5, to be replaced with a boiler of a smaller diameter, allowing the outer boilers on either side to be moved inward. Boiler room No. 5 was located at the point in the hull where the sides began to narrow toward the bow. There would be a significant revision to some of her ventilating fans as many of the swan necked ventilation ducts were enlarged or reconfigured. Extra cowls were added, and Sirocco fan housings were enlarged to accommodate the needed ventilation found to be insufficient in the past. The officers' deckhouse was extended forward by approximately 10ft allowing for a few more first-class staterooms to be incorporated at the aft end of the structure, similar to those on the *Titanic*. The rounded forward bulkhead of the wheelhouse was removed, and a flat bulkhead was fitted in its place, in the same manner as *Titanic*'s. The *Olympic*'s bridge cabs were extended over the sides of the superstructure about another 2 ft, also just like those on the *Titanic*. The large á la carte restaurant provided on the *Titanic* was said to be a popular feature with the first-class passengers, so the *Olympic's* á la carte restaurant was enlarged. It now extended all the way out to the port side, and passengers were afforded an open view of the ocean, just as were those on the *Titanic*. Along with this was a reception room, which was added to the starboard side at the expense of a wine cellar and 2 three-berth rooms. To further mirror the *Titanic*, the Café Parisien was added by enclosing the starboard side promenade opposite the á la carte restaurant. This feature eased the turnaround time for setting the tables in the restaurant, because coffee could be served out on the wicker tables. The exterior A deck promenade weather screens, so prevalent as the significant difference between the two sisters, were never added to the *Olympic*. Additional staterooms were added in places, and some were removed from others. Externally, the *Olympic* appeared practically unchanged except for the additional windows along the B deck superstructure encompassing the Café Parisien on the starboard side, the extended restaurant on the port side, and the obvious removal of the bulwarks on both sides of the boat deck where extra lifeboats were added. However, because of the high demand for lifeboats at the time, only 16 of the 32 planned boats were available. To have the *Olympic* ready for her next voyage, Harland & Wolff had to install 10 Berthon and 6 Henderson collapsible lifeboats as a temporary measure until the proper boats were ready for delivery. The *Olympic* would be fitted with a lifeboat capacity of 3,538 in 1913, and with the increased passenger accommodations the gross tonnage would jump from the original 45,324 to 46,359.

Olympic *at Harland & Wolff in December of 1912 during the refit.*

Throughout the refit, the White Star Line maintained its service from Southampton to New York with the *Oceanic, Majestic,* and *Adriatic.* In March 1913 the work on the *Olympic* was completed, so on the 22nd she left Belfast for Southampton, where she would resume her service scheduled for April 2nd. White Star advertised the newly refitted liner in many publications of the time. Much attention was given to the new inner skin and added safety features. However, she soon lost her status as the world's largest ship, because 1 month after the sinking of the *Titanic* the Germans launched the 52,000-ton *Imperator.* Even though she lost the "largest" status, 1913 turned out to be a good year for the *Olympic,* as she started to regain some of the popularity that she had enjoyed in the beginning of her career, all while still being under the command of Captain Haddock. (However she didn't match her 1911 popularity until 1920-21)

The prospects for the White Star Line appeared to be improving in 1914 despite rumored financial problems with the IMM. On February 26th, the *Britannic* was launched in Belfast and, if all went well, she would be in service within the year. Plans for a new *Germanic* were well underway to replace the *Titanic*. White Star appeared to be moving on, and the *Titanic* tragedy was becoming a thing of the past. This rediscovered confidence was distracted, however, by what would happen next.

On August 4, 1914, Great Britain and France entered into a conflict against Germany and Austria–Hungary that would come to be known as World War I. The British economy soon was centered on supplying the war effort as the merchant fleets prepared for a long struggle ahead. The *Olympic* was en route to New York when war broke out, and even though they were close to reaching the coast, Captain Haddock ordered blackout conditions aboard the ship. After the *Olympic* reached New York, the crew spent the 4 days in port blacking out the windows and painting the funnels and white superstructure gray. On August 9th, Captain Haddock sailed the *Olympic* back to what would be her new homeport for the duration: Liverpool. Carrying no passengers and taking the safest route off the north coast of Ireland, she arrived safely in Liverpool on August 15th. The mercantile fleets were hard pressed to keep up with their war duties while still supplying service from England to America. In fact, the shipping lines were packed with Americans fleeing from Europe to go back home while, on the other hand, transporting British nationals back to England. All available berths on the ships were occupied. First-class passengers even occupied third-class berths if necessary. There was no complaining, because the unrest in Europe was escalating. The *Olympic* would make only a handful of runs out of Liverpool until October 3rd, when she had to return to a new, temporary port at Greenock because there was no longer any room for a liner of her size in Liverpool. On October 9th, the *Olympic* made her last voyage, following a zigzag course for safety, arriving in New York 7 days later. She departed New York on October 21st, setting a course for Belfast, where she would be laid up. Less than a day from safety, the *Olympic* was forced to pass through unsecured waters. In her path was the 2nd Battle Squadron, on maneuvers. The danger would increase for the *Olympic,* as the battleship HMS *Audacious,* which had struck a mine off Tory Island, was lying directly ahead. Because of the possibility of U-boat attacks, the Admiralty had ordered the fleet to leave the area while the light cruiser HMS *Liverpool* and a number of smaller vessels remained to assist the damaged warship. At 10:30 a.m. the *Olympic* was sighted by the *Liverpool* and ordered to help evacuate the crew of the *Audacious.* After approximately 250 of the *Audacious*'s crew were taken off the wounded ship, the destroyer HMS *Fury* succeeded in attaching a cable between the *Audacious* and the *Olympic* in an attempt to tow the *Audacious* back to port. They headed westward toward Lough Swilly, and everything seemed to be running smoothly until the steering gear on the *Audacious* failed. At this time the sea was starting to get rough and, as the wind made the *Audacious* unmanageable, the tow cable snapped. A second attempt was made to tow the warship, but within 15 minutes the cable became entangled in the cruiser's propellers and sheared off. A third attempt was made to secure the vessel, this time to the collier *Thornhill,* but again this line gave way to the now-foundering battleship. Captain Haddock was advised to stand by, as another attempt would be tried. By 5:00 p.m. the quarterdeck of the *Audacious* was under water, and it was decided to evacuate the remaining crew. By 6:30 p.m. the rest of the crew was taken aboard either the *Olympic* or the *Liverpool.*

This was a stroke of luck: At 8:55 p.m. there was a massive explosion aboard the *Audacious* in her magazine, and the ship sank stern first.

The *Olympic* anchored in Lough Swilly that evening to disembark the portion of *Audacious*'s crew, which she was carrying. Captain Haddock was ordered to stay out of sight of the Grand Fleet that was also anchored in the area, because there was a fear that some of the German-American passengers aboard *Olympic* may be sympathizers and would inform the Fatherland of the military activity they witnessed. As American citizens, they could not be arrested, but they could be held for questioning if necessary. It was already too late to keep them from seeing what had happened to the *Audacious,* and needless to say they could not be relied on to keep their silence.

While at Lough Swilly, Captain Haddock had to keep his passengers occupied as they basically were marooned on their own ship. Also, White Star officials were not in any hurry to get the *Olympic* back to port, because she was planned to be laid up anyway. No communications were permitted to be dispatched, and passengers were not allowed to leave the ship at the lough. The only people exiting the ship would be the crew of the *Audacious* and Chief Surgeon John Beaumont, because he was being transferred to the *Celtic.* On November 2nd, the *Olympic* was finally allowed to leave Lough Swilly to go to Belfast, where the passengers were disembarked. Captain Haddock stayed on at

Belfast, where the Admiralty appointed him to lead a squadron of merchant ships that were disguised as warships in an attempt to mislead the enemy.

It was at this time that the *Olympic* joined her incomplete younger sister, *Britannic*, as both were laid up and could be seen berthed side by side. The *Olympic* waited silently with only a maintenance crew from Harland & Wolff aboard.

The *Olympic* remained dormant for another 10 months as the Admiralty decided what to do with the large merchant liners that were unsuitable for military service. The *Oceanic* was declared a total loss after grounding on a reef off the island of Foula in September 1914. In another incident, the *Aquitania* collided with the Leyland Line's *Canadian*, illustrating just how unsuitable these huge liners were for patrol duty. In fact, the *Aquitania* remained as an armed merchant cruiser for only 2 weeks. Because of the size of these great liners and the high cost of operating them, by the spring of 1915 the *Olympic*, *Britannic*, *Aquitania*, *Mauretania*, and *Lusitania* were either laid up or kept in standard company service.

As a repercussion of the sinking of the *Lusitania* on May 7, 1915, Cunard announced that the *Mauretania* would be continuing with the next scheduled sailing to New York, but before this came to fruition the Admiralty officials announced they had other plans for Cunard.

In May 1915, Cunard agreed to assign the *Mauretania* to the Admiralty as a troopship. The Admiralty offered a specified rate per gross ton, and Cunard weighed the costs and signed on. The *Mauretania* was officially requisitioned as a troopship on May 11th for the Mediterranean. The only problem with ships of this size carrying such a large complement of men is that they were subject to submarine attacks, and if one should fall victim there would be a substantial loss of life. There appeared to be no other feasible alternative, as the use of many smaller ships would be needed to achieve what could be accomplished with liners of the *Olympic*'s size. The advantages of using the large liners would be the speed at which they traveled and their carrying capacity. They could transport more men, faster, and could be fitted out more cheaply than many smaller vessels. Considering this, the Transport Department finally conceded that the use of the liners was a necessity, and on June 18th the *Aquitania* was also requisitioned as a troopship.

While the *Aquitania* was being prepared for war service, messages were starting to come into the White Star office regarding the *Olympic*. Harold Sanderson conferred with Harland & Wolff and advised the Admiralty that the *Olympic* could be refitted without a problem. Her onboard cabin arrangements could be converted into table and hammock accommodations for up to 7,000 troops. The ship's bunker capacity would allow her to maintain a speed of 21 knots from Southampton to Mudros and as far back again as Gibraltar. The only problem was that the *Olympic* had spent many months idle at the yard and would need to be dry-docked for removal of the accumulated growth on her bottom. The tide would not allow the use of the Thompson dry-dock until the end of the month, and the Gladstone dock in Liverpool was occupied by the *Aquitania*. Unfortunately, on June 22nd, the Admiralty informed the White Star Line that the *Olympic* would not be needed.

The tide of the war was changing dramatically. The troop movement to the Mediterranean was heavy, and by autumn the increasing number of casualties was beginning to overwhelm the Transport Division. Earlier in the war, the Admiralty had used some 20 merchant vessels, called "Black Hospital Ships," to transport stores and troops to the battle areas and return with sick and wounded soldiers. The problem with this procedure was that the ships were unmarked even while carrying casualties, which opened them to attack from the enemy and allies alike. To solve this problem, the Admiralty requisitioned vessels to be used exclusively as hospital ships. This new classification of liners would be painted in Red Cross colors and therefore protected under the terms of the Geneva Convention. With the high speeds of the *Mauretania* and *Aquitania*, they would be ideal for this use. In September 1915 both were converted to hospital ships, leaving an opening for other ships to serve as troop transports.

On September 1, 1915, Harold Sanderson was instructed to get the *Olympic* ready for war service. While Harland & Wolff progressed with preparing the *Olympic*, Sanderson negotiated the terms of the ship's charter. It was agreed that the Admiralty would pay only about £23,000 per month, out of which the White Star Line would have to pay the crew. The Admiralty did agree however, to pay any costs the insurance company would not cover in the instance of the ship being lost.

Harland & Wolff was working steadily on getting the *Olympic* ready for her new assignment. Many of the peacetime fittings were removed and stored, and the portable third-class accommodations were cleared for thousands of men while the public rooms were fitted with mess arrangements and hammocks. However, the completion could not be carried out at Belfast. There still was the problem of the fouled hull, and the Thompson graving dock was not available. In any case, the *Olympic* would need to return to Liverpool for provisioning and coal. The *Olympic* left Belfast on September 12th and, on arrival at Liverpool, was placed in the Gladstone dock, recently vacated by the HMS *Barham*. Harold Sanderson originally intended Captain Haddock to resume command of the *Olympic*, but the Admiralty turned him down, because Haddock was needed to command the "ghost fleet." Sanderson thus decided on his second choice, Captain Bertram Fox Hayes, formally of the *Adriatic*.

Olympic *as a troop transport vessel in gray paint.*

When Captain Hayes boarded his new command in Liverpool, he found the situation to be one of "utter confusion." He had a run-in with the principal naval transport officer over the fact that he was not in uniform. It was common for captains of the merchant fleet to wear civilian clothes while not on the ship; therefore, it was in this state that Hayes reported to the naval officer. Needless to say, the naval officer was not happy. Hayes also had to talk up for his officers who were not in the naval reserve. Hayes insisted that if his assistant commander was not given a rank higher then sub lieutenant, then Hayes would have him wear his company uniform while on duty to command a higher rank. The principal naval officer shook his finger at Hayes and said: "Take care, sir. Remember you are talking about the King's Commission, and if you are not careful your commission may be taken away from you." Hayes retorted that the reserve had done nothing for him in way of money—in fact, it had been an expense to him—and although the naval officer could take away Hayes's commission, he could not take away Hayes's employment, which provided his livelihood.

When the *Olympic* departed the Gladstone dock ready for her voyage to the Mediterranean, she was provisioned with a 12-lb gun on the forecastle and a 4.7-in. gun aft. At 10:00 a.m. the *Olympic* departed Liverpool for service designated as transport T2810. On board were 6,000 troops, mostly from the Southern Counties Yeomanry, and a couple of troops from the Welsh Horse Division with their glee-singers, who provided entertainment on the ship.

On October 1st, while steaming off Cape Matapan, crew members on the *Olympic* sighted lifeboats from the French steamer *Provincia*, which had been sunk by an Austrian submarine at 9:00 that morning. Hayes ordered the *Olympic* stopped while the 34 survivors were picked up, climbing aboard by means of the pilot ladder. The gun crew on board immediately sank the boats after the men were aboard, and the *Olympic* continued the journey to Mudros. Although this was a gallant move by Hayes, in doing so he had left his ship wide open for a U-boat attack. In fact, while proceeding back to Mudros on this day, a U-boat was sighted. Hayes altered his course and outran the U-boat later in the evening after firing the guns at it. The torpedo the U-boat fired missed the *Olympic*, passing some distance off the stern. The French Admiral recommended that Hayes should be given the Medaille de Sauvetage by a grateful French government. The Commander-in-Chief in the Eastern Mediterranean however, was not pleased that Hayes left his ship open for attack with more than 6,000 troops on board. In fact, the commander circulated a letter headed, "Indiscretion Shown by the Master of a Transport" in which Hayes' misdoing was detailed.

Hayes was given his next orders to sail to Spezia for coal, and then as soon as possible to Liverpool. However, because of the disorganization at Mudros, the troops didn't fully disembark until 8 days later. It was not until the evening of October 11th that the *Olympic* was cleared to depart. The ship arrived at Spezia virtually empty of personnel except for the crew. On arrival, Hayes found that the provisions of coal and water were inadequate, which led to another 8-day layup. During the voyage home to Liverpool, it was discovered that the water was contaminated, and on the ship's

arrival on October 31, 1915, many of the crew were sick with stomach problems. The *Olympic* made two more runs to the Mediterranean with the usual stop at Spezia for coal and water. On her return to Liverpool on December 21st, she had somewhat of a reunion with the *Britannic*, commissioned 6 weeks earlier, which also was tied up. The two ships would meet again only one more time.

The *Olympic* was not ready to depart again for Mudros until January 4, 1916, as time was allowed for the crew to celebrate Christmas and New Year's at home with their families. On February 12th, the *Olympic* arrived at Southampton to embark troops, and it was here where she would meet for the last time the *Britannic*, which had arrived 3 days earlier with her second batch of wounded troops from the Mediterranean. On March 13th the *Olympic* completed her fourth and final trooping run to Mudros. The fate of the *Olympic* was unsure, as there was a debate over the cost of victualling the troops between Sanderson and the Admiralty. White Star had been spending approximately £3,000 out of pocket because of the discrepancy between the Admiralty's payment and the actual cost of feeding the troops. As of spring 1916, the *Olympic*'s continued use as a trooper was seriously in doubt.

Sir Bertram Hayes, K.C.M.G., D.S.O.
In the uniform of Captain, R.N.R.

With the massive evacuation of troops from Gallipoli in December 1915, the use for such huge liners for troop transport between England and the Mediterranean—especially the use of hospital ships—was not needed. The *Britannic*'s and *Olympic*'s use to the service was at stake, but because there was no hurry to lay up the *Olympic*, plans were made to use her as a troop ship to India. The problems that surrounded the use of the *Olympic* for the Indian run mostly concerned the ship's ability to maintain coal for the journey. In order for the *Olympic* to be able to reach Capetown, there would have to be an enlargement made to the reserve coal bunker by cutting a hole in the bulkhead between the Nos. 2 and 3 holds, and part of the double bottom would have to be filled with the extra 5,400 tons of fresh water that would be needed. Because of this, a new problem arose: With the added weight came a deeper draught of 38 ft. In order for the *Olympic* to facilitate coaling, she would have to sit some 1,200 yards out to sea from the dock entrance. At Bombay, she would have to sit about 2–3 miles out to sea. Although Trincomalee would provide a good place to anchor, the coaling facilities were inadequate, and there was a need for extra ships just to transport the troops from the liner. The whole idea was a nightmare, and the officer investigating the use of the *Olympic* for this particular service decided that it was impracticable. On February 8th, the whole idea was dropped, leaving the future of the *Olympic*'s war service again in question. She would be laid up until the Canadian government came to the rescue.

At midnight on March 22, 1916, the *Olympic* left Liverpool to travel across the Atlantic for the first time in 18 months. The Canadian government had asked for extra ships to transport soldiers from Halifax for the war cause, and the *Olympic* was perfect for the job. It would be while under this assignment that the *Olympic* would again write herself into the history books.

The ship made her maiden voyage to Canada on March 28th, but Captain Hayes was concerned about the intended use of the *Olympic* by the Canadian government. Hayes had originally thought that the *Olympic* would be part of a protected convoy, but when he heard that the speed would be reduced to around 12 knots, he was worried that they would be a sitting target for the German U-boats. Hayes had protested strongly to the Canadian authorities to allow the *Olympic* to run unescorted, using her speed as her best defense. The *Olympic* had zigzagged up and down the Mediterranean, which was supposedly more infested with U-boats than the Atlantic, and had never had a problem. Hayes succeeded in his argument, and on April 5th the *Olympic* sailed with a full complement of Canadian troops for Liverpool. The only problem that occurred during this journey was a collision with the patrol boat that pulled alongside the *Olympic* to remove the pilot. There were no casualties, but the mast of the patrol boat carried away lifeboats 24 and 26 on the port side, damaging one of the davits in the process. Nevertheless, the *Olympic* went on her way, arriving in Liverpool on April 11th.

The Olympic *in Halifax.*

The *Olympic* made 10 voyages between Halifax and Liverpool without once seeing an enemy vessel. However, she did not escape bad luck throughout the year: On October 29th, she grounded while at anchor outside of Halifax for 4½ hours. There was concern about hull damage, but after the ship floated off, she was sounded, and no damage was found. On November 5th, a fire broke out in the flue of the third-class galley, which took more than 2 hours to extinguish. The ship had sustained structural damage because of this fire, but the damage was only patched up, because she would be put up for a refit after the next scheduled voyage. The *Olympic* completed her 10th run to Halifax on December 30th. After spending the first week of the new year in her home port she departed for Belfast, arriving on January 12, 1917. For the next 3 months the *Olympic* remained at Harland & Wolff for a refit while Captain Hayes was transferred to the *Celtic*. His trip on this new assignment was cut short, because just as the ship was approaching the Isle of Man it ran into a mine. The explosion blew a hole between the Nos. 1 and 2 holds, but thankfully the damage was shored, and the *Celtic* was brought back to Liverpool. Hayes was then transferred to the *Adriatic* for a passage to New York, after which he was ordered to rejoin the *Olympic* at Glasgow.

The Olympic *leaving port in new dazzle colors.*

By the end of March, work on the *Olympic* was coming to a close, and the White Ensign on the flagstaff was officially raised on April 4, 1917. The *Olympic* was now commissioned as one of His Majesty's Transport Ships. This time she would look very different. Her gray war colors were gone, and a new type of camouflage, known as *dazzle paint*, was applied. This new scheme would incorporate a series of geometric shapes painted on her hull, matching on the superstructure and the lifeboats. The intended purpose was to confuse a U-boat captain who would try to get a bearing on the liner through the periscope. The dazzle paint was supposed to make the ship blend in with the horizon when seen through the lens of a submarine. The Admiralty would change the configuration of the dazzle paint to ward off the possibility of the enemy being able pick out bearing points on the hull by repetition. The shapes and colors of the dazzle color schemes changed on the *Olympic* at least four times throughout the war.

In addition to the contrasting colors of his ship, Captain Hayes found that the *Olympic* was fitted with six 6-in. guns while in Belfast and that his crew had been augmented by about 40 Naval ratings in charge of a mate gunner. Two days later, the United States declared war on Germany.

The *Olympic* continued her Halifax-to-Liverpool transport route until Christmas Day 1917, when she returned to her pre-war terminus in New York to embark American troops. However, the Hudson was so overwhelmed with ice that coaling could not be completed for the journey until January 11th. The American authorities, eager to get as many troops over to the war as soon as possible, tried to overcrowd the

Another one of the Olympic's *dazzle paint schemes. This one has seen better days.*

Olympic by about 2,000 men. Captain Hayes, knowing the consequence of this, convinced the Americans to reduce the number, because they would not get there any faster, and they would not be in good shape after arriving after a journey with such overcrowded conditions.

Old Reliable

The *Olympic* made her second journey to New York carrying the new British ambassador to America, Lord Reading. Lord Reading made it a point to mention how fine the food was aboard the *Olympic* and that the men were being fed better than the Prime Minister himself. Captain Hayes informed him that the food was brought on at Halifax or New York, as surplus food in England was needed for the war cause. Lord Reading went on to ask Captain Hayes his opinion of the *Olympic–Hawke* collision, because Reading had had the opportunity to appear before the Admiralty in the hearings. Being aboard the *Olympic* must have spurred Reading's memory. Hayes replied that "the Admiralty must have had the better lawyer as they certainly hadn't the better case." Reading smiled and asked Hayes if he was in command at the time. "No," said Hayes, "I only joined when she was taken for transport." The spring of 1918 arrived with the *Olympic* having more than 2½ years distinguished service under her belt, but the best was yet to come.

On April 24, 1918, the *Olympic* left Southampton on her 22nd trooping run, and a submarine was spotted. The destroyers in the area dropped depth charges, and the *Olympic's* gunners tried to hit the periscope, to no avail: A confirmed kill was not established. On May 6th, the *Olympic* took on a full load of troops at New York. After crossing the Atlantic, the *Olympic* met four American destroyers at a prearranged location to be escorted into the English Channel, where British ships would take over. At 3:55 a.m. on May 12th, the *Olympic* sailed into the pages of history as the lookout at the stem of the ship sighted a U-boat sitting off the starboard bow. The submarine was not aware of the *Olympic's* presence, because the ship was masked in darkness, but the *Olympic* could see the sitting submarine because of the sunrise across the horizon to the east. The submarine was so close that an attempt was made to fire one of the guns at it, but the angle and proximity caused the shot to be far too high. According to intelligence reports, *U103* was about to torpedo *Olympic*: they sighted her at 4.37 a.m. *U103* time (3.37 a.m. *Olympic* time) and were getting ready for firing, but the ship just came up so quickly they weren't aware of her until the *Olympic's* guns rang out. Hayes decided the best form of defense would be to attack, so he altered course straight for the U-boat. Captain Rucker of the *U-103*, seeing the danger, attempted to run right toward the *Olympic* in the hopes of hiding within her turning circle. All was in vain, as Hayes ordered the helm hard to port. The *Olympic's* bow turned to starboard, striking the *U-103* a glancing blow. As the submarine passed the bridge, Hayes noticed that the hull of the submarine was standing nearly on end. As the submarine passed the stern, the *Olympic's* guns were fired, but at that point the submarine was already out of commission. The impact had startled Hayes and the officers on the bridge as the shock jumped them off their feet. Hayes had always thought that a submarine would be more fragile than that; he even questioned whether they had actually hit the submarine or if they had struck something else. He relaxed when he observed the tower and the guns mounted on the hull of the submarine as they passed. While the *Olympic* continued her voyage, the American destroyer U.S.S. *Davis* remained to pick up the 31 survivors of the *U-103*. However, the *Olympic* did not sail away from the incident undamaged. After returning to Southampton, divers found that the hull had sustained damage: There were a number of dented plates, the starboard paravane chains were torn away, and the stem was bent about 8 ft out of alignment to port. Hayes was praised for this unique piece of seamanship by being awarded the Distinguished Service Order. The lookout who spotted the submarine was awarded a medal and received a £20 bonus from the White Star Line, which was awarded to any seaman who sighted a submarine from which his ship escaped. The lookout in the crows nest also laid a claim to the cash, stating that he had been in the process of calling the bridge after sighting the submarine when the other lookout sighted it. In the end, the two men split the reward money. There was also a reward from the Admiralty and Lloyds of London of some £1,000 to be distributed among the crew for successfully destroying an enemy submarine. The officers of one of the regiments on board collected a sum of money and gave it to the purser for the purpose of putting a plaque somewhere on the ship. Later, when the *Olympic* was being refitted after the war, the plaque was positioned in the landing of the main companionway. The inscription on it read:

> This tablet, presented by the 59th Regiment
> United States Infantry, commemorates the sinking
> of the German Submarine *U103* by the *Olympic*
> on 12th May, 1918, in lat. 49, 16 N. long. 4, 51
> on the voyage from New York to Southampton
> with American Troops.

The war was coming to an end, with the British naval blockades forcing starvation on the German mainland. The push to drive France out of the war was unsuccessful, and the German army was forced to give up nearly all of the territory they had occupied, bringing surrender in November 1918. The *Olympic* received the news of the armistice while bound for New York. Captain Hayes read the official announcement in the morning paper as he stayed at the apartment of his good friends, Mr. and Mrs. Vickers, after arriving late at night in New York. Through her years of war service, *Olympic* had carried some 200,000 troops, including thousands of civilian passengers, and Chinese military construction workers.

After the celebrations at New York, the *Olympic* returned to Southampton with only a handful of passengers, being able for the first time in 4 years to run without the lights blackened out at night. For the passengers, this signified that the war was really over, but Hayes knew that it would be some time before the ship could be returned to White Star service, because all of the troops brought to Europe had to be brought back home again. It was only natural that the first troops to be returned back home on the *Olympic* be Canadians. The first peacetime arrival at Halifax was met by a crowd that was so noisy in their cheers that the docking instructions had to be transmitted with signals. The people of Halifax so loved the

The Olympic's *twisted stem after striking the* U 103

Olympic, and treated her crew like one of the family, that they nicknamed the ship "Old Reliable." This nickname was so prevalent to the people of Halifax and the Navy that there was even a time in the past where a newly assigned checkpoint seaman became confused when Captain Hayes referred to his ship as the "*Olympic*." The checkpoint seaman had known the ship only as "Old Reliable."

Captain Hayes was awarded with plaques and a loving cup from the mayor of Halifax and the Halifax Board of Trade for all of his service to the war effort and to the people of Halifax. For the rest of the year, the *Olympic* would sail between Europe and North America.

In February 1919, the *Olympic* was finally decommissioned while in the Gladstone graving dock in Liverpool. While this routine overhaul was being undertaken, the workers noticed an 18-in. dent in the shell plating containing a 6-in. crack 14 ft below the waterline, between the second and third funnels. The corresponding space between the inner skin and outer shell plating had been flooded, but because this area was inaccessible there was no way of noticing it. This dent was not there during the last time the *Olympic* was put in the dry dock, so Captain Hayes could only assume that it must have been caused by an unexploded torpedo and that it had happened after the last refit. Hayes remembered an instance while the *Olympic* was coming up channel before the armistice, when some crewmen who were working the hold to pull up baggage came running up to the deck thinking the ship had been torpedoed but went back down in the hold after they noticed there was no excitement topside.

At noon on February 16, 1919, the *Olympic* departed Liverpool with a load of American troops bound for America. When the ship approached the dock in New York, the men became very excited and crowed onto the side of the ship closest to the pier. The accumulated weight of the troops concentrated on one side of the ship, in her lightened condition, caused a considerable list to the point that docking operations had to be suspended. The soldiers had to be persuaded to move in order to trim the ship; otherwise they would have carried away the shed while pulling into the berth. The *Olympic* made five more voyages to Halifax before returning to Belfast on August 16th for the second major refit of her career.

The Olympic *bringing troops back home. The remains of the dazzle paint is still evident at the bow.*

Throughout the winter of 1919–1920 the ship was basically gutted as the interior fittings that were stored away before the war were replaced. The á la carte restaurant was temporarily closed at this time. First-class passengers were advised in the travel brochures that they could dine in either the main dining saloon or "in a first class saloon on another deck." What was once an extra tariff restaurant for first-class passengers who did not wish to dine in the saloon was now just another dining area, an extension of the main dining saloon. This, along with the old restaurant reception room, was crammed with extra tables to accommodate an additional 200 passengers. Within a year the á la carte restaurant was restored as an extra tariff facility, but under a different name. It was now called the Parisien Café, the former Café Parisien having been renamed the Garden Café. Later, the Garden Café was renamed the Verandah Café. Both optional dining areas remained, regardless of their names, until the depression forced White Star to close them down as an economical measure.

In a move by White Star to change with the times, the boilers were converted to burn oil fuel instead of coal. The *Olympic* would be the first of the large ocean liners to undergo this conversion. The transition would require replacement of the old furnace fronts with burner units, and the coal bunkers would require considerable modification to be made suitable for the storage of liquid fuel. Although oil was more expensive than coal, it made refueling easier and faster, cutting down the time required to replenish the bunkers from a number of days to a few hours. Oil also did away with the never-ending problem of coal dust permeating the ship's decks and interiors. No longer would there be a haze of coal dust surrounding the ship while the bunkers were loaded. A further inducement was the reduction in engine room personnel from 350 to 60 men. With the "black gang" gone there would be no visible difference between a fireman and a sailor. It was at this time that the lifeboat arrangement on the *Olympic* would also change. With the installation of the Murray's nested lifeboats there would be a line of twelve 30-ft boats on each side of the ship. Nested inside the 30-ft boats were 28-ft. boats, with 26-ft. cutters stowed inside the forward sets.

Post war refit at Harland & Wolff. September 9th 1919

With the *Olympic* scheduled to return to service in the summer of 1920, Harold Sanderson was busy reconfiguring the passenger services of the other White Star ships. The *Celtic, Cedric, Baltic,* and *Adriatic* had survived the war but were not compatible to be running mates with the *Olympic* because they were not as big or fast. With the loss of the *Titanic, Britannic,* and *Oceanic,* Sanderson encountered some problems, as rebuilding the White Star fleet would take time and money.

The *Titanic* was originally supposed to be replaced with the planned *Germanic*, the name of which had been changed to the *Homeric* for obvious reasons. Construction on yard No. 470 was brought to a halt because of the war, and it seemed that the building stages would remain as merely plans even after the signing of the armistice.

In the end, it turned out that Germany bowed to an unconditional surrender. The German merchant fleet was reduced to nothing, as any ship of worth was taken by the Allies as war reparations. Britain, France, and America haggled for months over the final allocations of Germany's ships. On November 17th, the British Shipping Controller was finally able to release a list of ships allocated to England. Cunard had first choice, as it had sustained the heaviest loss: 22 ships. For the White Star Line Sanderson chose the 35,000-ton Norddeuscther-Lloyd liner *Columbus* and the Hapag (Hamburg American Line) liner *Bismarck*. Although the *Bismarck* would require another 9 months to be completed for service, these two vessels were suitable to operate out of Southampton as running mates for the *Olympic*.

People line up to view the newly refitted Olympic *on June 12th 1920*

In Belfast, the *Olympic*'s refit came to an end with a 2-day public inspection of the now 46,439-ton, oil-fired flagship of the White Star Line. On June 17th, the *Olympic* departed Belfast for Southampton with Sanderson on board heading off a banquet in celebration of the liner's return to the Atlantic service. Among the dignitaries and guests were Captain Hayes; Viscount and Lady Pirrie; Lady Pirrie's sister, Miss Carlisle; and Field Marshall Sir William Robertson. At the banquet, they opened the new ballroom in the 1st class reception room, which had been added to the *Olympic*, with music and dancing.

On June 26, 1920, the *Olympic* pulled out of the Southampton dock en route to New York for her first commercial voyage after her reconditioning. The *Olympic* was spic and span—like a new ship, according to Captain Hayes. The conversion to oil firing was pleasing to the passengers; for the first time they did not have to deal with cinders falling from the funnels and getting in their eyes. Cinders were pieces of ash that would blow out of the funnels and into the eyes of passengers on the promenade deck. Needless to say, the ship's surgeon was also pleased to see the cinders go, as he didn't have to be called at all hours of the day to remove them from the eyes of people anymore.

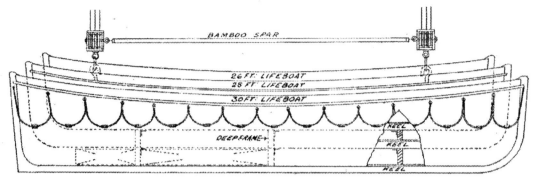

General arrangement of Captain Murray's Nested Lifeboats

On December 12, 1921, while eastbound for Cherbourg, the *Olympic* ran into heavy weather which required her to slow down. At 3:44 a.m. the ship was hit by heavy seas that smashed out five galley portholes, necessitating a further speed reduction while the damage was repaired. Five hours later the starboard portholes of the reception room also were smashed out, and the forward tackle of the starboard emergency cutter was also damaged. At 2:05 p.m. the seas had become so fierce that they caused the ship to undergo a series of quick rolls. The motion of the ship caused problems with the clasps that held some of the watertight doors, causing one of them to come loose and close on the foot of a third-class passenger. Another third-class passenger died when a door slammed shut on him, dislodging his vertebrae and compressing his spinal cord.

Captain Hayes sailed aboard the *Olympic* for another 2 years, and on January 7, 1922 he arrived at Southampton for his last time before being transferred to the new *Majestic* (ex-*Bismarck*), which was still being completed in Hamburg. During his last journey on the *Olympic* he had his successor—Captain Alec E. Hambelton of the *Adriatic*—onboard, as a pupil who was to "pick up the ropes." Hayes had written in his book that Hambelton was known throughout the company "as being the biggest liar crossing the Atlantic when recounting some of his experiences." Hambelton was noted for being plagued by foggy weather when making the Nantucket Lightship, and he himself said "he had only seen it twice in a number of years." Hayes sent down an officer to wake Hambelton to invite him to come on the bridge to see the Nantucket Lightship as the Olympic was arriving in New York, so he could recognize it if he were fortunate enough to see it again. On hearing Hayes's invitation, Hambelton rolled over in his bed and said he would take Hayes's word that it had not been altered in character since he saw it last and then went to sleep again.

With Hambelton's new command of a ship twice the size of what he was used to came a difference in clientele. In May 1921, the American government put a lid on immigration with the Dillingham Immigration Restriction Act, which limited immigration after July 1, 1921 to just 3% of the foreign-born population of the American 1903 census. This meant that only 360,000 immigrants per year would be allowed to enter the United States. Immigration was the lifeblood of many of the Atlantic passenger lines, and with this new law the White Star Line found itself with the door being slammed in its face. White Star was just starting to pull out of the slump of the war and once again becoming competitive thanks to the new glory of the refurbished *Olympic*. However, a newer and larger running mate would soon be completed in Hamburg. On February 15, 1922, the *Homeric* (ex-*Columbus*) was released to join the Southampton–New York service as the second ship taken as part of the German war reparations. The first reparation was the *Arabic* (ex-*Berlin*), which made one voyage from Southampton to New York before being put in the New York–Mediterranean service. On

April 12, 1922, the *Majestic* completed her sea trials. During her completion, she had been converted to oil fuel. At 56,551 gross registered tons, the *Majestic* was now the largest ship in the world and the fastest liner White Star would ever own.

Captain Hambelton's year in command of the *Olympic* would be uneventful. At the end of January 1923, Hambelton handed over command to Captain Hugh David, who had also been transferred from the *Adriatic*. On November 21st, command of the *Olympic* changed again as David handed over the reigns to Captain J. B. Howarth, who remained in charge until the end of the year, when the *Olympic* would return to Harland & Wolff for her annual overhaul.

On February 20, 1924, the *Olympic* left Southampton for her first scheduled voyage after her annual layup. However, 1924 would be the turning point that changed the North Atlantic ferry service forever. In this year, the American government lowered the immigration number to 2% of the foreign-born population according the American census of 1890. This meant that now only 160,000 immigrants per year would be admitted to the United States: Before the war the number was approximately 1 million. The shipping companies would have to adapt to the new law, which still was a number of months from going into effect. On March 22, 1924, the *Olympic* was backing out of Pier 59 at New York when the Bermuda-bound Furness Withy liner *Fort St. George* steamed past her stern. The *Olympic* collided with the vessel, causing major damage to the *Fort St. George*. The *Fort St. George* had a broken mainmast and damage to lifeboats, decking, and railings over a length of some 150 ft. The *Olympic* suffered the second instance of a major collision in her career (the first being with the HMS *Hawke*) with damaged plating and a cracked sternpost. The sternpost was an important structural part of the ship, because this steel casting carried the rudder and formed the aperture around the center propeller in addition to housing the center propeller's stern tube and bearing. Harland & Wolff workers undertook the repairs at the Southampton dry dock, but because of the time involved with replacing the complete sternpost it was decided to patch the affected areas temporarily. The complete sternpost would be replaced in the future during the winter of 1925–1926. It would be the first time a repair of this type had been carried out.

An era came to an end for Harland & Wolff when the *Olympic* returned to Queenstown on June 20th for the first time since the war, carrying the body of Lord Pirrie. He had died while aboard the SS *Ebro* on June 7th while returning from South America with Lady Pirrie from a business trip. The body of Lord Pirrie was transported to Belfast, where he was buried on June 23rd. An image of the *Olympic* was incorporated with his gravestone as a remembrance of his crowning achievement.

On October 25th the *Olympic* left New York with the Prince of Wales aboard. The prince's voyage on the ship was the social highlight of the year for those on board. Captain Howarth had allowed the prince up to the bridge, permitting photographs to be taken of himself and the prince outside, by the starboard bridge wing bulwark. The prince would later be photographed in different areas of the boat deck.

The *Olympic* was thought to be a hard ship to handle in piloted waters, as is evidenced by the many near misses and collisions she had with other vessels throughout the years, but she was a good ship in dirty weather at sea. One master stated that she had a corkscrew-type motion when hit with high water, enough so that people with queasy stomachs were best off staying in their rooms. When other liners were seen to be sitting stationary and rolling heavily, the *Olympic* would just plow right through the waves. In February 1925 during a storm, a huge wave 72-ft above the waterline engulfed the bridge, breaking out a window and bending a steel compass pedestal. A year later, also in February, a storm came on the *Olympic* that was so fierce that waves flooded the crows nest, tore off 30 ft of railing from the starboard bow, carried away both forward staircases from the boat deck, broke out four bridge windows, and tore up 10 ft of bridge decking.

The starboard side of Olympic's *bridge with the Prince of Wales and Captain Howarth.*

At the end of February 1925, a new captain, William Marshall, took command of the *Olympic*. With his new command came a change of policy in April 1925, handed down from the North Atlantic Conference. A new class of travel known as *tourist third cabin* came into effect. On the *Olympic*, passengers traveling in this new class were given either the less attractive second-class accommodations or the best of the third-class accommodations available and paid just slightly more than the normal third-class fare. In 1928, second class was eliminated completely, and tourist third cabin became simply *tourist class*.

The beginning of the end would occur for the *Olympic* in January 1926 after her stern frame was replaced. The *Olympic* had damaged a number of starboard shell plates after striking a fender while undocking. A further investigation of the hull revealed a number of cracks along the side of the bridge deck. The repairs were considered to be adequate, but when similar cracks were found on the port side the following year, the Board of Trade inspectors concluded that the *Olympic* should be put on their confidential list and carefully watched for any sign of further deterioration. After a five-year period, it was found that these cracks did not extend and the rivets nearby were all tight and sound.

On December 28, 1926, the *Olympic* left New York to return to England, but this time there was a change in the air for the British Mercantile Marine. The IMM had become a rare failure among J. P. Morgan's many investments. If it had not been for World War I, the IMM might have collapsed years earlier, but by the mid-1920s it was still managing to keep its head above water. After the war, there was an attempt by the IMM to sell the foreign shipping interests to a British buyer. This deal fell through but was not forgotten by the British. In the summer of 1925, Sir Frederick Lewis of Furness

Withy tried to purchase the Oceanic Steam Navigation Company, but the general strike of 1926 caused the deal to fall through. The next negotiations would be followed through with Sir Owen Phillips, better known as Lord Kylsant, chairman of the Royal Mail Steam Packet Company. Lord Kylsant purchased the Oceanic Steam Navigation Company for £7,000,000, and on January 1, 1927, the White Star Line became a part of the Royal Mail Group. Those aboard the *Olympic* heard of the sale while at sea from New York. The *Olympic* was now officially a British owned ship after 16 years of service.

The immigration restrictions brought on by America were starting to catch up with the British shipping industry in general and with the *Olympic* in particular. There was no longer a need to build ships as big as the *Majestic* or the *Olympic,* because the number of passengers had fallen in accordance with the immigration law. The shipping companies had no choice but to adapt.

A post 1927-28 refit photo of Olympic *at Southampton. The B deck windows have been changed to the Utleys pivoting type because of the extension of the staterooms.*

In the winter of 1927, just before her next refit, the *Olympic* again was caught in a storm that was so intense that it burst open a porthole in the firemen's quarters. The flooding caused the ship to hove until the damage was repaired with a plug specifically designed for this purpose. The broken porthole had caused considerable flooding in the lower decks.

When the *Olympic* was brought in for her third major refit in December 1927 a major reconditioning of a number of her first-class staterooms on A deck was carried out. (The promenade deck had formerly been known as A deck. The former B deck had been renamed A, C was now B, etc.) On A deck, most of the rooms forward of the main first-class entrance were gutted, and 16 new staterooms, extending to the sides of the ship, were created. Each of these had a private bath created from space formerly occupied by smaller inside cabins. These new staterooms were approximately the same size as the deluxe B deck staterooms, which had been located between the fore and aft first-class staircases on the *Titanic*. As of February 14, 1928, the *Olympic* was registered with a net tonnage of 21,727, which was a reduction, because in some cases two rooms had been cannibalized and made into single berths to provide for the private bathrooms, the second stateroom having been used for this purpose. This was one of the drawbacks of the *Olympic*, in that she was built back before private bathrooms became a requested perk by many passengers. It is interesting that passengers of the Edwardian era weren't very concerned about the lack of private bathrooms, even in first class. This form of cabin upgrade was continued into the 1930s with subsequent refits lowering the number of passenger accommodations. In attempting to upgrading the ship with the times, there was even a makeshift movie theater added in the first-class lounge that consisted of nothing more than moving the chairs to face a screen that was positioned over one of the big bay windows. With the reduction in passenger numbers came a change to the dining saloon. The central section amidships, where there once had been a great oval table, was covered over in parquet and converted into a dance floor, and a podium for an orchestra was added at the forward end of the room. This was one of the few instances where an orchestra played for dancing and for the mere enjoyment of the diners. The *Olympic's* Jacobean dining room would be converted into a pseudo nightclub, allowing passengers to dance between courses. Dancing had once been restricted to the reception room outside, or to what was now called the *drawing room* up on the upper promenade deck.

Olympic's *new dance floor in the center of the 1ˢᵗ Class dining saloon.*

In September of 1928 Captain Marshall was given command of the *Majestic* and was replaced by Captain Walter Parker, who had been transferred from the *Homeric*. Marshall's departure from the *Olympic* was an emotional time for him. Parker even offered to take the *Majestic* for him, but Marshall replied: "I suppose I ought to be honored. She is, after all, the largest ship in the world, you know, Parker—but I am leaving the best to you, for all that."

Captain Parker was in command of the *Olympic* when, on November 18, 1929, a most peculiar event happened. While the ship was at lat. 42°, 12', N long. 56°, 56' W, a sudden tremor of the hull was experienced that lasted for about 2 minutes. Parker was in the chart room when the ship's officers advised him that there had been no collision. The possibility of a thrown propeller was out of the question as the engines were running smoothly and there was no sign of a wreck in the wash. Except for a short loss of power in the mailroom, the ship was just fine. Captain Parker suspected an underwater earthquake; this was confirmed when messages started coming in. The 1929 Grand Banks earthquake had resulted in a massive underwater landslide that severed many submersed telegraphic cables. The earthquake happened 2½ miles below the *Olympic's* position on the sea, not affecting her in any major way, and she arrived safely at New York. At the end of the next voyage, Parker and Chief

The makeshift movie theater

147

Engineer J. H. Thearle both retired. Thearle had been with the *Olympic* since she entered service in 1911. The *Olympic* would see yet another commander with Captain E. R. White, again from the *Adriatic*.

The Great Depression was taking its toll on the shipping industry as well as on the *Olympic* with her ever-increasing number of structural problems. In 1929 the new stern frame was showing signs of pitting caused by an "obscure electrochemical reaction", and the magnetic cement applied to reinforce the pitted areas proved ineffective. In 1930 the stern frame was showing increasing signs of pitting, so Harland & Wolff applied a white metal sheath over the affected area and there was little trouble after this.

Lord Kylsant circa 1925

In 1931, the yearly inspection revealed that the cracks found in 1927 in the upper parts of the bridge deck were getting worse. This was brought on by a winter of horrific weather earlier in the season that also affected the *Aquitania* as she came away with cracked deck girders. Replacing shell plating on a ship the Olympic's age was not economically feasible. White Star compromised by using extensive welding combined with the placement of doublers to reinforce the fractured areas. The Board of Trade was concerned enough about the condition of the *Olympic's* welds that it would issue a certificate of seaworthiness only for short periods of time, in this case 6 months. The repairs were checked again at the end of this period and were found to be holding, so a certificate was given for an additional 6 months. When the hull was inspected again the next year, the repairs were found to still be holding, and the *Olympic* was given the full 12-month certificate of clearance. The *Olympic* traveled over 70,000 miles in 1932 averaging 21.8 knots. On October 14, 1932, the *Olympic* returned to Southampton for her lay-up and to perform some last minute repairs. Cracks were found in the engine bedplates, and

The Olympic *in 1933, looking like new.*

parts of the crankshafts. When the engines were raised to service the bedplates, it was noticed that the double bottom was in generally good condition apart from a few loose rivets, however the main problem was with the riveting of the thrust blocks.

On March 1, 1933, the *Olympic* returned to service after 12 hours of sea trials, "looking like new." The chief engineer was very impressed at how the engines and thrust blocks showed little sign of movement for the first time in months. However, much of her beautiful interior paneling had been painted forest green, its carved detailing picked out in gilt. Klysant had enough sense however, to leave the oak and mahogany untouched in the lounge and the smoking room.

On the management side, Lord Kylsant was buying up other lines that were stricken by the Depression, borrowing money to the point that he compromised his own investments. He became far too confident in acquiring these lines to expand his shipping empire even when he had controlling interest in some of them before he bought them. Kylsant also had control of Harland & Wolff when he placed an order for the new *Oceanic*, a 60,000-ton liner intended to be added to the White Star Line. The *Oceanic* would never be completed, because by the autumn of 1929 Kylsant's empire was already starting to crumble. The reason for the suspension on the *Oceanic's* work was said to be because of discrepancies as to the type of propelling machinery, namely new turbo electric technology, but in reality it was that Kylsant just couldn't come up with the funds. Kylsant had problems paying back the British government's loans to expand the Royal Mail fleet back in the early 1920's and his financial troubles were catching up with him. The future of the White Star Line was carved in stone.

Damage caused to Olympic's *bow from the lightship collision.*

Captain Binks shaking hands with the captain of the lightship."from a sailor to a sailor"

Rescued crewmen of the lightship. R to L: Roberts, Perry, Marshall.

In September of 1931, Lord Kylsant was charged and imprisoned for publishing misleading statements in the 1928 Royal Mail prospectus. The last straw for White Star was when the Australian government refused to extend the company's payments on the Commonwealth Line. This incident caused a loss of nearly £1,500,000 to the White Star Line. In a last attempt to save what was left of White Star, one of the managers, Col. Frank Bustard, approached none other than J. Bruce Ismay in an attempt to construct some form of a bailout. However in 1933, White Star listed another yearly loss. The treasury stepped in, and it was too late.

The shortfall in the North Atlantic trade was also hitting Cunard, the old rival of White Star, pretty hard. The British government agreed to provide a loan, but only if the two companies merged. After this had been agreed to, the British government would release an amount of up to £9,500,000 to support the new company. On December 30, 1933, the board members of both companies met to outline the terms of the merger, and on May 10, 1934, the Cunard–White Star Line was officially registered. White Star would contribute about 10 ships to the new company, but before the end of the year the *Adriatic, Albertic* and *Calgaric* would be sold for scrap, leaving the future of the *Olympic* in question.

Before the new company was even a week old, the *Olympic* experienced yet another collision that would bring back some of her 1911 style bad luck. The *Olympic* was bound for New York on May 15th, under the command of the very exhausted Captain Binks, who was suffering from lack of sleep. At 10:50 a.m. the ship was nearing the Nantucket Lightship in deplorable weather. The radio operator aboard the *Olympic* was having a hard time keeping in touch with the homing beacon of the lightship, when at 10:56 a.m. he heard the last transmission before the air went dead. The officers on the bridge of the *Olympic* heard the foghorn of the lightship but could not get the exact bearing. The only thing they knew, on the basis of the strength of the last radio signal, was that the *Olympic* was within 30 miles of the lightship. Unknown to the officers aboard the *Olympic*, the lightship was much closer. At 11:06 a.m. the red hull of the lightship appeared out of the fog—directly in the *Olympic*'s path. Binks ordered "full astern," but it was too late. The hull of the huge liner smashed into the lightship. The massive weight of the *Olympic* plowed the other vessel into pieces. Binks later stated that the speed of the *Olympic* was not more than 3 or 4 knots, but the weight of the 46,439 liner moving forward was no match for the tiny lightship. The *Olympic* released a number of her lifeboats to pick up survivors. The boats returned with 3 bodies and 4 survivors of the lightship's original 11 men. At 12:29 p.m. the *Olympic* raised her anchors and carried on to New York. Looking for the remaining crew proved to be fruitless.

On May 17th an inquiry into the accident opened in the New York Customs House. Captain Binks found himself in the hot seat, much like what Captain Smith would have faced had he survived the sinking of the *Titanic*. It was found by the inquiry that it was not uncommon for liners to pass within a close proximity of the lightship at high speeds; in fact, two close calls of the same type of incident had happened the night before. In response to this, the captain of the lightship had ordered his crew to wear their life jackets and swing the emergency boats out. The other point of discussion during the inquiry was the inability of the liners to read the codes of the Cape Cod and Pollock Rip lightships because of a code change. Clark, the radio operator, had lost contact with the Nantucket lightship, but it was not because of a failure in the *Olympic*'s radio system: He had been able to receive the transmissions of other beacons. The White Star Line once again had to take responsibility for an accident involving the *Olympic*; however, it did appeal the judgment of $500,000 in claimed damages, which was reduced to $325,000 by 1936.

The *Olympic*'s return voyage to New York on June 5th marked the last time that she would berth at the old White Star Pier 59. From that point forward she docked five blocks south, at Cunard's Pier 54.

The end of the *Olympic*'s career was less than a year away, because liners of her age were just no longer needed on the Atlantic run. When the *Olympic* struck the Nantucket lightship, she was carrying only about 200 passengers. Many of the big liners were reduced to making weekend cruises, because the Depression was causing a big reduction in the passenger industry. In October 1934 the *Mauretania* was pulled from service for these reasons. In January 1935 the *Olympic* sailed for one more spring season. On March 27, 1935, the *Olympic* left Southampton for New York on her 257th— and last—voyage, while under the command of Captain Reginald Peel. The *Olympic* returned to Southampton on April 12th, ending her White Star career with Frederick Fleet—who had served as a lookout on the *Titanic* 23 years earlier—aboard as one of the crew. For the next 6 months the *Olympic* was tied up and left deserted at Berth 108, located at the new Western Dock, in Southampton. There were rumors that she would be used by the British Admiralty, or resurrected by a sale to the Italian government as a troop ship. These rumors were dispelled when in September 1935 she was sold for £100,000 to Sir John Jarvis, who in turn sold her to Thomas Ward & Sons, the Jarrow shipbreakers. The move was nothing more than an attempt by Sir Jarvis to provide employment to his constituents, as he was a Member of Parliament.

Left: *The* Mauretania *and* Olympic *sit idle at Southampton's Western Docks.*
Right: *The vacant decks of Old Reliable.*

Another view of Olympic *at Southampton's Western Dock*

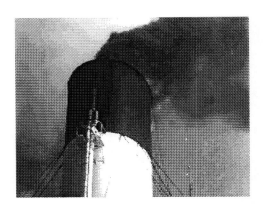

The Olympic's *final journey from Southampton.*
Top left: *Her whistles blow Farwell*
Top right: *Her funnel billowing smoke*
Middle: *Reliable to the end*
Bottom left: Olympic *arrives at Jarrow.*
Bottom right: Olympic's *whistles sound.*

The saddest of moments occurred at 4:12 p.m. on October 11, 1935, when the *Olympic*, under the command of Captain P. R. Vaughn, sailed past the Ocean Dock where the *Homeric* and *Majestic* were moored. The *Olympic*'s house flag was dipped, and the whistles let loose one last salute, as she was given an honorary escort down Southampton Water by speedboats owned by Mr. Hubert Scott Paine.

After a 2-day journey, the *Olympic* arrived at Jarrow, where she awaited the tide to make her way up the River Tyne. There was a large reception for the *Olympic* on her arrival, with tugs and boats all responding to her whistles, which consisted of three long, blasts, the liner's traditional signal of thanks and farewell. By 3:00 p.m. the *Olympic* had arrived at Palmers Yard, where she would be broken up. At 5:00 p.m. Vaughan rang down to the engine room for the final time the order "finish with engines."

In the weeks before the final dismantling began, there was an auction of many of the ship's salvageable fittings, comprising a list of some 4,456 lots. The auction company called in to do the work on Tuesday, November 5, was Knight, Frank & Rutley from London. Among the fittings that were auctioned and sold to many private parties and hotels were chairs, light fixtures, sconces, doors, windows, wooden paneling, and many other articles, some of which exist even to this day.

The final dismantling took nearly 2 years to complete. On September 19, 1937, the remaining hulk of the hull was towed to Inverkeithing for final scrapping.

Perhaps the end of the *Olympic* also brought about the end of one of the men who conceived her: J. Bruce Ismay. On October 17, 1937, Ismay died after suffering a stroke. The age of the Last Grand Lady would be gone forever, but not forgotten. She touched many people, including the mariners who had served aboard her.

The *Olympic* is perhaps best described in the words of the man who commanded her from 1915 to 1921, Captain Bertram Fox Hayes, who wrote that *Olympic* was: "The finest ship in my estimation that has ever been built or ever will be."

The Olympic's *woodwork displayed for auction in 1991. From the catalog sold by the auctioneers Anderson & Garland.*

By Direction of

Messrs. THOS. W. WARD, LTD.
SHEFFIELD.

A

CATALOGUE

of the Contents and Equipment of

THE OLYMPIC

WHICH

KNIGHT, FRANK & RUTLEY

Alfred J. Burrows, F.S.I., P.P.A.I., Arthur H. Knight, F.A.I., William Gibson, D.S.O., F.S.I.
Gordon M. Cannon,   Herbert D. Kelleway, F.S.I., F.A.I.   Charles J. Worsnam,
Alfred J. Baker, F.S.I., F.A.I.   Malcolm Mackenzie (U.S.A.)

WILL SELL BY AUCTION IN THE SHIP

AT THE WHARF OF MESSRS. THOS. W. WARD LTD.,

PALMERS WORKS, JARROW-ON-TYNE.

**On TUESDAY, NOVEMBER 5th to FRIDAY, NOVEMBER 8th,
MONDAY, NOVEMBER 11th to FRIDAY, NOVEMBER, 15th,
and MONDAY, NOVEMBER 18th, 1935.**

AT ELEVEN O'CLOCK PRECISELY EACH DAY.

Private View (admission by Catalogue only, price 5 - each) on
Thursday, October 31st, from 10 to 5 o'clock.

Public View (admission by Catalogue only, price 2/6 each) on
Friday, Saturday and Monday, November 1st, 2nd and 4th, from
10 to 5 p.m.

Catalogues from the Auctioneers, at their Offices.

20, HANOVER SQUARE, LONDON, W.1

Telephone: Mayfair 3771 (ten lines)
Telegrams: Galleries, Wesdo, London

ALSO AT
41, Bank Street, Ashford, Kent

Printed by H. Davy, Mansfield House, Strand, W.C.2, England.

Olympic – *The Ship Magnificent.*

A P P E N D I X   I I I

His Majesty's Hospital Ship *Britannic*

When Lord Pirrie and J. Bruce Ismay discussed the design for their new class of liners, they originally planned for two, the *Olympic* and *Titanic*, to be built immediately, with the third to follow at a later date. By the time the *Titanic* was launched and the *Olympic* was on her maiden voyage, Cunard was laying the keel plates for the *Aquitania*. This new Cunard ship was started in response to the size of the White Star Line's two new additions.

On June 20, 1911, before the *Olympic* arrived in New York City on her maiden voyage, the order was placed for the third ship. The keel was laid for the *Gigantic*, yard number 433, on November 30, 1911, in slip number 2, the original construction berth of her older sister, *Olympic*.

Progress on the hull slowed dramatically after the sinking of the *Titanic* on April 15, 1912, as White Star awaited the outcome of two government inquiries into the disaster. White Star had originally intended the *Gigantic* to be in service by the end of 1913; however, due to the amount of retrofitting required after the inquiries, in May of 1913 it was announced that the super liner would not be ready until the beginning of 1914.

Following the tragic loss of the *Titanic*, White Star renamed their newest liner *Britannic*. Though hotly denied by J. Bruce Ismay that there ever was any intention to name this ship *Gigantic*, an ex-employee of Harland & Wolff validated that fact years later. It is unlikely that White Star would not have made their choice of name for the new ship known to the builder early on, as it was the practice at Harland & Wolff to incise the ship's name directly into the shell plates on either side of the bow as well as those on the stern. After the *Titanic* disaster, White Star immediately returned to their former policy of using names associated with geographical locations and historical periods. Names that even hinted at a ship's strength or invulnerability to the forces of nature were immediately abandoned. Instead, the name *Britannic* was chosen to evoke nationalism and pride in Great Britain and as a memorial to a beloved White Star ship which had earlier been removed from service. It is reasonable to conclude that the original name *Gigantic* had been selected as the first two names were derived from Greek mythology (*Olympic* from the Olympians and *Titanic* from the Titans) and *Gigantic* would have come from the Giants.[*]

Like her infamous sister ship *Titanic*, the *Britannic* would never complete a commercial voyage. In fact, the *Britannic* would never even make it into company service. She was requisitioned by the British Admiralty as a hospital ship and served in this capacity during World War I, striking a mine in the Kea Channel off the coast of Greece and sinking before she was even a year old. It is an ironic twist of fate that "*Gigantic*" would rest forever in Greek waters.

On February 26, 1914, at 11:15 a.m., 27 months after the keel was laid, *Britannic* left her construction berth and slid down the ways. In a light drizzle, the massive hull took 81 seconds to launch, achieving a speed of 9½ knots, accompanied by sirens and cheering from the large crowd in attendance. Dignitaries attending the event included Lord and Lady Pirrie; Harold Sanderson who replaced J. Bruce Ismay as the chairman of the White Star Line; and Captain Charles Bartlett, White Star's Marine Superintendent at Belfast. J. P. Morgan, whose empire had played a major part in the creation of the *Olympic*-class ships, had been present at *Titanic*'s launch. Unfortunately, he passed away in Rome at the end of March 1913 prior to the launch of the third sister.

At the time of her launch, she was the largest British-built liner based on gross registered tonnage, and would remain so until the advent of the *Queen Mary* some 20 years later. *Britannic* had an overall length of 882 ft, 9 in. and a molded breadth of 93 ft, 6 in. or 94 ft, 0 in. extreme when

---

[*] There is strong debate over whether or not 433 was actually intended to be named the *Gigantic*. It is said that the name "*Gigantic*" was merely a coverall term used by the press to indicate an up and coming White Star ship of mass proportions. The "*ic*" being utilized to fit with White Star's naming scheme.

measured to the outside of the shell plates. This represented an 18 in. increase in beam over that of her sisters.

The *Britannic* was intended to compete with the new Hamburg-American and Cunard Line ships. This is most likely the reason for the many exaggerated interpretations of the *Britannic*'s length and beam. It appears that someone didn't want the actual measurement of 882 ft, 9 in. revealed to the general public. Even the much admired "Shipbuilder" magazine had the *Britannic*'s length overall listed as "about 900 feet". With the new *Aquitania* planned at "about 900 feet", it is no mystery as to why the actual numbers have been "adjusted" over time. However, builder's plans of the *Britannic* that still exist show the same number of construction frames as her older sisters and the scale drawings indicate an identical length of 882 ft, 9 in.

She would have a displacement of over 53,000 tons at a maximum load draught of 34 ft, 7 in. Her gross tonnage of 48,158 would be 1,830 tons larger than the *Titanic's* and her wider beam would add greater stability. She had accommodations for 2,579 passengers and a crew of 950. As with her sisters, there was no attempt to make the *Britannic* an ocean greyhound. She would maintain an average speed of 21 knots, unaffected by conditions at sea, maintaining her planned itinerary as was intended with the other two *Olympic* class liners.

It was incorrectly stated in the past that the *Britannic*'s beam was widened amidships as the result of the inner skin added after the loss of the *Titanic*. Records available from Harland & Wolff contradict this, showing that the decision to widen the *Britannic* was made by October of 1911, well before *Titanic* set out on her fateful journey. A table of particulars was submitted to Lord Pirrie dated October 17, 1911, giving the molded breadth of number 433 as 93 ft, 6 in. This change in beam modified the *Britannic*'s lightship GM (metacentric height) to about the same as the *Olympic*'s. The additional passenger accommodations incorporated into *Titanic*'s B deck had resulted in a lightship GM of six inches less than that of the *Olympic*. The value of 6 inches was probably calculated right after the *Olympic*'s maiden voyage. It was reported that the *Olympic* had a tendency to roll in high seas. Though not in anyway unstable, her roll approached the limit of what was considered to be comfortable for the passengers. The stiffness of a ship, and the ability to right itself after a heel brought on by outside forces, is determined by the metacentric height, or the calculated distance at which the "metacenter" is located above the ship's center of gravity. When it was decided by J. Bruce Ismay to increase *Titanic*'s first class accommodation, additional staterooms, many having an adjoining private bathroom, were added to what was formerly enclosed promenade space on each side of B deck. With the *Titanic* having the same hull dimensions as the *Olympic*, the extra weight added to her superstructure resulted in a heavier displacement and a different metacentric height. It

Publicity model of the Britannic *at Harland & Wolff.*

was too late to correct this problem on the *Titanic* as her hull was well on its way to final fitting and the additional accommodations were an afterthought. This change was made to the *Britannic* to adjust the metacentric height, thereby increasing her stability and passenger comfort. The inner skin was between 3 to 4 feet deep from the sides, port and starboard. An increase of beam of 18 in. overall would therefore do nothing to accommodate the lost space caused by the inner skin. The added weight on the upper decks of the *Britannic* and the experiences with the *Olympic* made this increase of beam a necessity.

Each successive liner launched at the Belfast works of Messers. Harland & Wolff represented a distinct advance over the preceding ship. In this case, not only was her size increased, but the strength and passenger provisions were increased over that of the *Olympic* and *Titanic*. The public was pleased with the *Olympic*, and her popularity continued even after the loss of the *Titanic*, as White Star had a keen grasp of what passengers wanted in way of comfort and luxury.

Britannic *prior to launch*

It is quite probable that the *Britannic* was originally designed to be nearly identical to the *Olympic* and *Titanic* prior to April 15, 1912. With this in mind, it seems very unlikely that the huge lifeboat davits would have been fitted to the boat deck as was done after the disaster. Aside from the added beam and the extra passenger accommodations and upgrades brought on by White Star's competitiveness in the passenger trade, the three ships would probably have been configured much the same. Certainly the internal arrangements of the hull would have been much the same. However, after the sinking of the *Titanic* there were some improvements made for safety purposes. The *Britannic* would have a double bottom over 5 feet in depth, increased to 6 feet throughout the machinery compartments, with six longitudinal girders on both sides of the centerline. This feature, with added transverse plating, divided the double bottom into a very large number of cellular spaces. An inner skin was added along the sides of the ship encompassing the machinery bulkheads and the boiler rooms, and extending up past the load water line about three and a half feet above F deck. This inner skin as fitted to the *Britannic*

was claimed to be superior to the arrangement used in the Cunard ships, with their longitudinal coal bunkers located along the sides of the hull. The theory of the design used on the *Mauretania* and *Lusitania* was to make these compartments act as an inner skin in themselves. However, Harland &

Wolff felt that coal bunkers acting as inner skins allowed the possibility of an open door through which the skin would be breached in the event of a collision. Harland & Wolff may have been correct in their theories in that if there were a breach allowing water into a coal bunker, the coal would have absorbed the water and probably caused an excessive list. This would make the lowering of lifeboats on the high side of the ship very difficult. An additional risk to cross flooding a compartment in order to correct such a list is that it is actually possible to worsen such a situation. The main drawback with Harland & Wolff's method of sealing off the inner skin was that it couldn't be accessed and, if unknowingly flooded as was the case with the *Olympic* during World War I, corrosion could occur within the cellular spaces.

In areas where there would be extra stress on the hull, namely in the doublers on the topmost plating of B deck, Harland & Wolff quadruple riveted that which was originally triple riveted on the earlier sisters. Harland & Wolff boasted about the use of extra heavy girders to reinforce the superstructure and the areas around the boilers and machinery and the addition of an extra transverse watertight bulkhead. The *Britannic* would now have 16 transverse bulkheads, creating 17 watertight compartments instead of the original 15 bulkheads. Five of these bulkheads extended 40 feet above the deepest load waterline to B deck, while the other eleven extended over 21 feet above the waterline at E deck. These improvements would give the *Britannic* the ability to stay afloat with a six compartment standard.

The propeller boss arms would once again be massive, with the weight of the forging and castings over 300 tons. The rudder weighed over 102 tons and was 78 ft, 8 in. high by 15 ft. 3in. wide. The steering gear was the Harland & Wolff design encompassing two steering motors fitted in duplicate to avoid the possibility of steering failure at sea. Provisions were also made to handle any shock caused by green water hitting the stern of the ship and rattling the rudder.

The propelling machinery and engines would be much the same as fitted on the *Olympic* and *Titanic*. The set of four cylinder, triple expansion engines generated 32,000 horsepower at their normal running speed, burning 6,000 tons of coal per voyage. A notable difference in this ship when compared to the *Olympic* and *Titanic* was that the center turbine of the *Britannic* was larger than the turbines used on the earlier ships. Built entirely by Harland & Wolff in the Belfast yard, the turbine engine could generate 18,000 horsepower and even more power at the maximum number of revolutions. Weighing about 500 tons, the *Britannic*'s exhaust steam turbine was the largest on any liner in the world. This turbine operated in the ahead direction only, a practice common to exhaust turbines. Maneuvering in port was accomplished with the reciprocating engines powering the wing shafts.

The 5 single-ended and 24 double-ended boilers (the double-ended boilers were a foot longer than those fitted on the older sisters), were once again equipped with 159 furnaces. They were distributed in the usual six boiler rooms, separated by watertight bulkheads and their corresponding coal bunkers whose bulkheads were also raised above the level of the waterline. The waste exhaust exited out the forward three funnels positioned about 166 feet above the keel. The auxiliary pumps were capable of handling each compartment independently and the valves for the pumps could be operated from a room above the waterline.[*]

The *Britannic* would see upgrades to all classes of accommodation. At this time in history private washroom facilities were becoming popular in ocean liners. Accordingly, a large number of first class staterooms on the *Britannic* were single berth rooms with a water closet and either a bath or shower. Many of the double berth rooms were also similarly equipped.

On the boat deck, there was a children's playroom and the customary first class gymnasium, both with nine and a half foot ceilings. A proposed first for any ocean liner would be an addition of a lady's hairdressing salon. The dog kennel would be located abaft the fourth funnel on the boat deck as opposed to the past practice of placing the kennels below deck.

---

[*] Many of the fittings and design features of the *Britannic* which were expounded on in marine trade journals of the era, gave the impression to the reader that they were specific upgrades for this ship. However, some of these items were also incorporated into *Olympic* and *Titanic* from the beginning.

The A deck promenade would be like the *Titanic's* in that there were windows fitted to protect strolling passengers from ocean spray while allowing for an unobstructed view of the open sea. Also included would be the usual first class smoking room, lounge, verandah cafe and palm court, and the a la carte restaurant and reception room, which now extended the whole width of the ship, eliminating the Cafe Parisian.

On the *Titanic*, most of the B deck enclosed promenade space was converted into deluxe first class staterooms. The remaining portions aft were given over to an expansion to port of the a la carte restaurant and the addition of the Café Parisian on the starboard side. On the *Britannic*, B deck was reconfigured much like the original arrangement of the *Olympic*. The promenade extended from the forward end of the deck to the forward first class entrance. The B deck Private Promenade suites were retained on the *Britannic*, but here the starboard side private promenade was reduced from 50 feet to 25 feet and renamed a "verandah". This new floor plan created more spacious sitting rooms which were furnished with a dining table with chairs and four armchairs. Instead of the usual wicker furniture, the "verandah" was furnished with three settees and tables, two armchairs and two round-back chairs. The port side Private Promenade would remain at 50 feet in length, being basically the same as what was on the *Titanic*.

For added elegance, the main forward Grand Staircase was to be fitted with a huge Aeolian organ complete with huge storage chests for music rolls. For convenience, the three first class electric elevators, located forward of the main grand staircase, now traveled up to the boat deck and a fourth elevator in the region of the aft grand staircase was added.

The barber shop and the ladies hairdressing salon were located on B deck, while the saloons for maids and valets were moved from C deck down to D deck. As with the *Olympic* and *Titanic*, the Turkish baths, racquet court, swimming pool and the first class dining saloon were also present on the *Britannic*.

Britannic *in the outfitting wharf*

The second class accommodations would be the same as the other two sisters with the exception of a second class gymnasium. The third class accommodations would also be much the same, only with an increase in companionways, drinking fountains, and an external feature that would make the *Britannic* visually different from what had been seen before: enclosed well decks for the third class promenades. When examining photos of the *Britannic*, one cannot miss the covered well decks with the cargo loading apparatus mounted on top the newly formed roof. At the stern of the ship, the third class smoking room was relocated to the area above the third class general room which changed the appearance of the poop deck.

A new sanitation feature introduced, probably for the first time in a seagoing vessel, ended the old time practices of discharging waste from lavatories and sinks via numerous waste discharge pipes located just above the load waterline on each side of the ship. Instead, waste was collected in tanks in much the same manner as in a municipal sewage system. When the level in these tanks neared capacity, a float switch activated pumps which discharged the contents into the ocean beneath the waterline.

Harland & Wolff accommodated the ventilation system of the *Britannic* by fitting 1,500 louvers around the ship and equipping public rooms and every first class room with electric fans. Main entrances around the ship were equipped with electric radiators having a capacity of 3,500 to 6,000 watts.

The Marconi apparatus had the usual antennae wires suspended between the masts. The ability to transmit over 2,000 miles was intended to communicate with the main land and, occasionally, both Europe and America while in mid ocean. Safety features resulting from the *Titanic* disaster were the installation of a pneumatic tube to transport messages from the Marconi room to the bridge and the soundproofing of the Marconi room as the escaping steam during the fateful night of April 14, 1912, made it impossible for wireless operator Jack Phillips to hear through the headphones. Included with the mass of instruments were the usual electric sounding machines and submarine indicators.

The *Britannic* had a separate Accumulator Room above the water

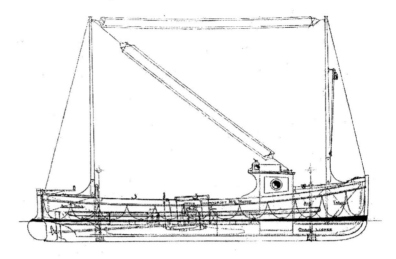

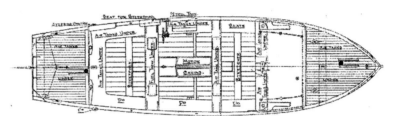

Plan of motor lifeboat similar to that fitted on Britannic. *34'-0" x 10'-0" x 4'-0" Designed and constructed by Messrs. Sir John Thornycroft & Co., Ltd.*

line. Situated in this room were not only a mass of emergency batteries, but also two electric generators used to charge the batteries while under load as well as supplying power to the emergency circuit. These two generators would also power the electric service of the ship while in port.

The navigating bridge had an assortment of instruments for the officers including the usual engine telegraphs and steering telegraph. In addition, there was an indicator to show whether the watertight doors were open or closed.

With the upgrades brought about from the new British Board of Trade requirements, *Britannic* would not compromise the open promenade space along the boat deck with rows of Welin davits as the *Olympic* had done. The *Britannic*, instead, was to be fitted with huge Harland & Wolff built "gantry" style davits that flanked the number 1, number 3 and number 4 funnels, as well as having two of the same davits mounted on a newly designed shade deck built over the existing poop deck. These electric powered davits were lit to illuminate the surrounding space and accommodated the lowering of lifeboats even if the ship were to maintain a heavy list. The wire hawsers

A model of Britannic's *davits*

were wound on drums attached to the same shaft for the level lowering of the boats, but could also be worked independently if needed. The *Britannic* was intended to carry 46 lifeboats (34 feet in length) and 2 cutters (26 feet in length). With these were two gasoline-powered motor cutters, each with its own Marconi apparatus. These full sized lifeboats eliminated the need for collapsibles.

The *Britannic's* scheduled completion date of September 1914 was pushed back for numerous reasons including almost continuous labor disputes and strikes. On July 2nd it was announced that the ship would not be completed until the spring of 1915. This latest delay was because Harland & Wolff was at full capacity completing other contracts, unlike when the *Olympic* was under construction.

The finishing touches on the *Britannic* were then delayed by the outbreak of World War I. Without government contracts, Harland & Wolff found it difficult to acquire the supplies needed. When the lack of Admiralty contracts compounded the supply shortage, Harland & Wolff laid off some 6,000 workers, most of whom promptly enlisted into the service.

The *Britannic* would enter dry-dock in September, but the tide would turn the following month for her builders. When the need to augment the Grand Fleet became apparent, Harland & Wolff received several large government contracts centered on converting small merchant ships into dummy warships. The process of converting small merchant ships to look-alike Navy cruisers was a ruse attempted at the beginning of the war to confuse the enemy as to the number of ships actually in the fleet, and to have these "warships" act as literal sitting ducks for U-boats. Harland & Wolff were to mount phony gun turrets and towers made from wood and canvass on these ships. However, to make room for these Admiralty projects, Harland & Wolff had to complete the old private orders with a shortage of employees at hand. Now Harland & Wolff had more work then they could handle and the *Britannic* would sit, silent, until November of 1915.

The *Olympic* was laid up after her last voyage from New York City under the command of Captain Haddock, arriving in Belfast on November 3, 1914. It was at this time that Harland & Wolff photographed the sisters together moored side by side. The two ships would remain together for ten months.

Britannic *in the foreground with* Olympic's *funnels behind.*

Harland & Wolff informed Harold Sanderson, Chairman of the White Star Line, in May of 1915 that the *Britannic* had passed her mooring trials when they turned over the engines while docked and that the *Britannic* could be ready for war service, if needed, in about four weeks.

With the British evacuation of Gallipoli and the huge numbers of casualties from the Dardanelles came the need to requisition passenger liners to be used as hospital ships and work on the *Britannic* resumed at a feverish pace. The still incomplete interiors were now converted to accommodate wounded soldiers and hospital staff. The lounge, smoking room, reading and writing room, gymnasium, children's playroom and restaurants were converted to wards. The dining saloon and adjoining reception room on D deck, both with unobstructed access to the main staircase and elevators leading to the boat decks, were suitable for the operating theaters and main ward. The enclosed promenades were fitted with cots and hammocks to ease evacuation to the boat deck. Other cabins were converted into berths for hospital personnel. When all was completed, the *Britannic* had the capacity to carry 3,309 wounded.

Because the *Britannic* had been incomplete when she was rushed into conversion to a hospital ship, some of the intended accommodations and features were bypassed and not installed. Among these were the davits intended for the shade deck on the poop deck and the davits intended for the forward boat deck on the port side of the No. 1 funnel. Twelve standard Welin davits would be placed along the open spaces on the boat deck amidships with their corresponding 14 lifeboats and collapsibles below. Further aft, two davit sets were installed on the poop deck where the "Gantry" davits were originally planned. The total compliment of lifeboats came to 58. There were supplemental stacks of wooden "Carley floats" stacked on the boat deck along with an abundant number of storage boxes containing life preservers. Many of the luxury fittings already installed were removed and stored.

The ship was painted in the Red Cross standard colors required under the Geneva Convention. The hull was painted white with a green horizontal line 1-1/2 meters wide circling the perimeter of the hull horizontal to the waterline. Dividing the green band were a series of red crosses. The funnels were painted a buff color while strings of green lights were added along the promenade for night illumination. Ships seen in pictures with red crosses painted on white funnels were within regulation. However, many British liners like the *Britannic* did not comply with regards to funnel color and kept plain buff painted funnels. An illuminated red cross was hung between the first and second funnels at night to further identify the ship. Two large red crosses were mounted on the bulwarks on both sides of the boat deck, each one illuminated by 125 electric light bulbs. However, the cross mounted on the starboard side bulwark created a problem with navigation on some hospital ships as its illumination overpowered the green starboard navigation lamp. The solution was a switch installed on the bridge enabling the Captain to turn the cross off at the approach of another vessel.

White Star would charter the *Britannic* to the Admiralty for approximately £24,000 a month with the Admiralty fully insuring the vessel. Unlike negotiations regarding the *Olympic*, there was no need to determine depreciation of the *Britannic* as she was, for all intents and purposes, new.

The *Britannic* left Belfast on December 11, 1915, under the guidance of five tugs. The voyage would include sea trials and war service preparations under the command of Captain J. B. Ranson. She would return from the sea trials only long enough to disembark some engine room officers. She had taken a year and a half longer than the *Olympic* to complete due to the many delays, accumulating a construction time of over four years.

Britannic *in His Majesty's Hospital Ship livery.*

Britannic arrived in Liverpool under armed escort on December 12, 1915 as the HMHS *Britannic* which indicated her protected classification of "His Majesty's Hospital Ship". She would be outfitted to accommodate a medical staff of 52 officers, 101 nurses, 336 orderlies and a crew of 675. Effective December 14, 1915, the ship was under the command of Captain Charles A. Bartlett, chosen because

Captain Haddock could not be released from his assigned command with the Admiralty. Captain Bartlett, with White Star since 1894 and at one time Commander of the White Star Line ship *Cedric*, had been White Star's Marine Superintendent at Belfast and present during the *Britannic*'s construction and launch. At the beginning of World War I, he was transferred to patrolling duties in the North Sea but was released to command the *Britannic*. There would be 2,034 berths and 1,035 cots to service injured soldiers. The medical staff on board the *Britannic* was rotated with each voyage so that the ship's staff could accompany their assigned patients back on shore. The on shore personnel would then have the opportunity to work aboard the ship in turn. This type of rotation would allow more medical staff to participate in the war effort. The head nurse on board the *Britannic*, Mrs. E. A. Dowse did not rotate, but would remain on board to oversee the Voluntary Aid Detachment (V.A.D.) nurses.

The *Britannic* left on her first voyage on December 23, 1915, bound for the Mediterranean in the "Dardanelles Service". It would be at Mudros, off the island of Lemnos, that she would serve with the *Mauretania*, *Aquitania* and her sister, the *Olympic*. Too large to dock, the ships anchored off the coast and embarked the sick and wounded from the military hospital located at Mudros via smaller ships based at the port.

The first Journey of the HMHS *Britannic* encompassed the Christmas holiday, which would be celebrated on board as she sailed for Naples to replenish her coal. On December 29th, she departed for Mudros where she would see in the New Year and receive some 3,300 wounded.

The Panama

Aboard ship, the crew and patients were to follow the schedule set forth by the Admiralty. Ambulatory patients were issued hospital suits consisting of blue trousers and jackets with brown facings. No patients were allowed on deck unless wearing these clothes to prevent the enemy from seeing a large number of men on deck in service uniforms and mistaking the ship for an armed troop transport. At 6:00 am patients were awakened so the wards and passageways could be thoroughly cleaned. The patients were served breakfast between 7:30 and 8:00 am after which the tables, benches and water closets were cleaned before Captain Bartlett and Chief Medical Officer Colonel Henry Anderson made their rounds at 11:00 am. Lunch was served at 12:30 pm, after which the wards and medical areas were cleaned and disinfected. Tea was served at 4:30 pm. The patients were put to bed at 8:30 pm, half an hour before an officer would make the final rounds. Patients' diets were regulated in accordance with the injury or sickness. The Chief Medical Officer would provide Chief Purser Claude Lancaster with a list of the provisions needed for the next day and the Chief Chef was then responsible for providing the correct menu requirements. Patients who were officers could receive a ration of wine or spirits if their medical condition allowed.

The *Britannic* returned to Southampton on January 9, 1916. As with all hospital ships, she informed Southampton upon approach with the numbers of dysentery and enteric cases on board so that appropriate preparations and routing destinations could be accomplished on the trains awaiting their arrival for transportation of the wounded to London.

The second voyage would begin from Southampton shortly after noon on January 20th and would be much shorter than anticipated. After arrival in Naples on January 25th to take on wounded, Captain Bartlett signaled ahead to Mudros that the *Britannic* would arrive around dawn on January 28th. Bartlett was ordered to remain at Naples to receive injured from five other ships that were being redirected away from Mudros and toward Naples. The *Britannic* took on 438 patients from the *Grantully Castle* and 393 from the *Formosa* on January 28th; 594 from the *Essequibo* on February 1st and 493 from the *Nevasa* on February 2nd. The last ship to disembark patients would be the *Panama* with 319 patients. After the final transfer of injured on February 4th, the *Britannic* returned to Southampton, arriving on February 9th.

The third voyage was uneventful. The *Britannic* arrived at Naples to take on water and coal, departed for the port of Augusta two days later to take on wounded, and returned to Southampton on April 4, 1916. Upon leaving port, she anchored off of the Isle of Wight for four weeks as a floating hospital. With Gallipoli evacuated, the Admiralty no longer needed as many hospital ships. The *Britannic* returned to Belfast on May 18, 1916, and was officially released from service on June 6, 1916.

Shortly after, however, on July 1, 1916, Britain participated in an offensive on the Somme in France and on the first day alone suffered 20,000 fatalities and 40,000 casualties. This, coupled with the decision by the Germans after their naval defeat at Jutland on May 31st to center their efforts not on battleships, but on submarine warfare, overwhelmed the hospital ships handling the channel.

Even after the evacuation of Gallipoli, the Allies maintained a presence at Salonika in neutral Greece. The troops in this area were attempting to block German supplies being carried into Turkey. This offensive in September of 1916, along with two other battles with the Turkish Army, revived the need for hospital ships to once again service the medical post at Mudros.

During the time *Britannic* was laid up at Belfast, Harland & Wolff began to re-fit her for commercial service. Pictures taken at that time show that some onboard apparatus was changed or updated after the first three voyages. With the huge numbers of casualties coming out of the Mediterranean, the services of the *Britannic* would be needed within a short time frame.

The *Britannic* was reinstated on August 28, 1916, and left Belfast for Southampton to be refitted as a hospital ship, once again under the command of Captain Bartlett. After provisions were loaded on board, she anchored off Cowes while a new crew was assembled. The *Britannic*'s fourth voyage began out of Southampton on September 24, 1916, with stops at Naples and Mudros before returning to Southampton on October 11th.

The fifth voyage of the *Britannic* involved transporting a contingent of R.A.M.C. personnel and stores to Egypt, Malta and Salonika. Departing as scheduled on October 20th, the *Britannic* arrived at Naples for coal and water on October 25th. After arriving at Mudros on October 28th, the passengers disembarked and were replaced by wounded both from shore facilities and from six other hospital ships. Unfortunately, this transportation of personnel to other parts of the war theatre was an abuse of the hospital ships in the eyes of the Germans and was later one reason used to justify unrestricted submarine warfare.

This particular voyage of the *Britannic* also resulted in an embarrassment for the Admiralty. While at Mudros, an Austrian invalid named Adalbert Messany was transferred to the *Britannic* from the Hospital ship *Wandilla*. Messany was a 24-year-old opera singer and Austrian National captured in Egypt at the outset of the war. Messany was to be returned to England and then repatriated to Austria. While on board the *Britannic*, Messany witnessed the transfer of supplies and personnel to the *Wandilla* and observed onboard activities of the ship. Upon returning to Austria, Messany issued a statement that the *Britannic* was carrying some 2,500 armed troops below deck and claimed 22 abuses by the allies in the operation of the hospital ships. This information supposedly came from discussions with two officers on board named Harold Hickman and Reg Taplay who were returning to England with some of their injured troops. The British Government denied the statement stating that there were no armed troops, nor had there ever been any armed troops, on board the *Britannic*. On this particular voyage, the ship was carrying 3,022 wounded soldiers. After an investigation by the Admiralty, it was revealed that Taplay was actually a private in the R.A.M.C. being transported to Southampton with a case of dysentery and Hickman was identified as a private in the Welsh Hussars being treated aboard the *Britannic* for malaria. Both Taplay and Hickman denied having any discussion with Messany on this matter. In addition, even if it were physically possible for the *Britannic* to accommodate 2,500-armed troops plus over 3,000 wounded, such an increase in passengers would hardly go unnoticed. It would have been impossible to maintain secrecy and if true, it would have left the hospital ship open for attack. Captain Rostron, captain of the *Mauretania*, formally of the

Carpathia, stated in his autobiography that "no troops were ever transported aboard the large hospital liners".

At the end of October 1916, an order that would eventually determine the fate of the *Britannic* was issued. The German submarine *U-73* left Cuxhaven, Germany, with instructions to lay mines in the Mediterranean shipping paths.

It should be stated that this practice was unusual for the German submarines. Normally the submarines left Germany without mines and received them at a predetermined location at sea. Reportedly the *U-73* left Germany with the mines already in her possession.

As the *Britannic* arrived at Mudros on October 28th on her fifth voyage, she was unaware that enemy submarines were keeping close watch. The log of the *U-73*, commanded by Kapitanleutnant Gustav Siess, reported that hospital ships had been sighted at 8:15 pm on the evening of October 27th and again at 3:25 am on October 28th. Supposedly it was because he observed the hospital ships traveling along the same route that he decided to lay the mines in the Kea Channel off the coast of Greece. As another point of interest, it is also reported that there was intent by the *U-73* to torpedo a liner, but this idea was abandoned.

On the return leg of the fifth voyage, the *Britannic* encountered heavy seas from a storm that so severely damaged the *Aquitania* that the *Aquitania* had to be laid up at Southampton for repairs. With the completion of her fifth voyage, the *Britannic* had returned some 15,000 injured and sick soldiers to England. With the *Aquitania* laid up, the *Britannic* departed on her sixth voyage and final voyage on November 12, 1916, after only four days in port.

This sixth voyage differed from previous voyages as there was no medical staff or personnel to be transferred to other duty ships. With no passengers on board, Mrs. Dowse removed the ropes that sectioned off the decks so that the nurses could walk about the ship, play deck games and use the swimming bath. The *Britannic* arrived at Naples on Friday, November 17th, took on coal and water, and prepared to leave port. However, weather conditions delayed her departure.

During the morning of November 21, 1916, the *Britannic* sailed from Naples in good weather bound for Mudros. By the next morning the ship had made it safely through the Straits of Messina. One of the passengers, Reverend Fleming, would write later that he was so overtaken by the beauty of the morning and the islands they were passing, that they didn't even notice the 8:00 am breakfast gong being sounded. It was shortly after the breakfast gong that an explosion was heard.

Reverend Fleming would write: -

"I was just leaving my cabin late for breakfast, when there was a great crash, as if a score of plate glass windows had been smashed together; and the great ship shuddered for a moment from end to end."

The Britannic struck one of the mines laid on October 28th by *U-73* and was mortally wounded in nearly the same area of the hull that had proved disastrous for the *Titanic* some four years prior. To avoid a panic, Major Harold Priestly assumed control of the situation and advised everyone to return to their meal as the Captain had not sounded the alarm. Further aft, crewman Percy Tyler would state that he "felt a violent bump which sent him forward a few paces then back again". Some of the other men assumed that the *Britannic* had hit another ship. After about five minutes a man ran in and instructed everyone to get their belts and head to the boat deck.

Some of the survivors later stated that they saw torpedoes hit the ship. Though there are surviving logs from the *U-73* that indicate she was laying mines, the theory that the *Britannic* actually hit a mine has never been proven. As of this writing, the seabed anchor that would have secured the mine from floating away has not been found. Given the German declaration of unrestricted submarine warfare, the possibility certainly exists that she was hit by a torpedo and did not strike a mine.

It was standard procedure, at 8:00 am each morning, to open the watertight doors during the change of watch. It is ironic that the Britannic would sustain damage at the precise moment she would be most vulnerable. She was designed to allow six watertight compartments to flood without foundering. If the explosion had happened just moments later, the doors would have been closed per regulations and the flooding contained.

The damage was near the bulkhead joining holds No. 2 and No. 3, approximately 150 feet aft of the bow on the starboard side. These forces probably opened about 250 feet of the Britannic's hull to the sea. It is believed that the doors at the aft end of the firemen's passage and the door between boiler room number 5 and 6 were damaged and did not close, allowing water to run further aft. The bulkhead between holds number 1 and number 2 was apparently also damaged and it is suspected that the bulkhead between the number 1 hold and the forepeak was also breached. With additional flooding by open portholes aft of the bulkhead between boiler room numbers 5 and 6 admitting water once the ship took on a list, the *Britannic's* fate was sealed.

In a desperate attempt to save the *Britannic*, Captain Bartlett turned toward land to beach the ship. The emergency alarm sounded and distress signals were sent while the lifeboats were prepared. The nurses were advised to retrieve their belongings and report to their lifeboat stations. From her position on the boat deck, head nurse Mrs. Dowse recorded each nurse as she passed en route to her assigned lifeboat. She refused to leave until all of her nurses were accounted for.

Because Captain Bartlett was attempting to beach the ship, he delayed issuing the final orders to lower the lifeboats all the way to the water. During that delay, Fifth Officer G. Fielding allowed two of the port lifeboats to be lowered within six feet of the water, but halted them at that height until the propellers stopped and awaited the order to proceed.

The port propeller was still turning as it broke the surface of the water. Because of this, two of the lifeboats, launched without direction from the Third Officer, were drawn into the blades. These boats were heavily loaded and would result in the only casualties during the sinking. Captain Bartlett would not give the official order to lower the boats until it became apparent the ship could not be saved and after the propellers stopped.

One of the few to survive the smashing of the lifeboats would be none other than a V.A.D. nurse named Violet Jessop. Violet became infamous for surviving incidents on all three of the sisters. She was aboard the *Olympic* during the *Hawke* collision and the sinkings of both the *Titanic* and the *Britannic*. She wrote in her memoirs that she craved for a toothbrush when she was aboard the *Carpathia* after the *Titanic* disaster and was determined not to leave this ship without her toothbrush. She sustained an injury to her head from the lifeboat incident while evacuating the *Britannic* that she left untreated for many years. Years later, through X-rays, it was discovered that she had actually suffered a skull fracture. She would later blame this injury for losing her hair in old age.

Among the last crewmen to leave the *Britannic* were a handful of engineers who escaped up through the stairwell in the number 4 funnel casing. The last on board was the Captain. Assured that no one remained on board, he simply stepped into the water from the bridge sinking beneath him. He had witnessed the *Britannic* being born and now witnessed the *Britannic* die.

The *Britannic* sank beneath the waves at 9:07 am, leaving 35 lifeboats and hundreds of survivors scattered in the water. From sea trials to sinking, the *Britannic* would live only 351 days -- not quite one year. The 1,106 survivors included all the women on board (approximately seventy-six nurses and four stewardesses); only 28 men were listed as missing or dead. The Britannic would claim 30 lives, after two later succumbed to injuries incurred from the sinking.

The final resting place of His Majesty's Hospital Ship *Britannic* is five miles from the area originally indicated on the Admiralty charts, off the coast of the island of Kea. The wreck of the *Britannic* was found on December 3, 1975, at a depth of 390 feet by world-renowned Oceanographer Jacques Cousteau after significant encouragement from the late William H. Tantum IV and Ed Kamuda of the *Titanic* Historical Society. Her bow is bent and twisted on the ocean floor from striking the bottom before the stern was awash due to the shallowness of the water. She lies on her starboard side, hiding the damage caused by the explosion, with her stem buried in the sediment.

HMHS Britannic

GLOSSARY OF SHIP AND SHIPBUILDING TERMS

Abaft. Towards the stern; aft, relative to.

Abeam. At right angles to the vessel's longitudinal axis and in her plane of flotation.

Aft. In the direction of or toward the stern.

Aground. The situation of a ship in which its bottom touches or rests on the ground; stranded.

Ahead. Forward; in front of.

Amidships. In the vicinity of the middle portion of a vessel as distinguished from her ends. The term is used to convey the idea of general locality but not that of definite extent.

Anchor. A heavy iron or cast steel implement attached to a vessel by a rope or chain cable. When the anchor is thrown overboard it lays hold of the ground and holds the vessel in its place. The earlier anchors were made of wood, with one arm and later with two. Stones were attached to give weight to sink and to increase holding power. An iron anchor, having a wood stock, followed the wood anchor. This in turn was replaced by an all-metal anchor. The *solid* or old-fashioned anchor consisted of the shank, the ring (shackle or Jew's harp), the arms, and the stock. The shank is the main body of the anchor, having the ring bolted to one end and the arms welded to the other, the crown being the heavy end of the shank from which the arms branch out, The stock is the beam attached to the shank opposite the arms. Various patent anchors exist, most of which are stockless and have their arms pivoted upon the shank and the palms in the plane of the arms.

Anchors, Bowers. The principal anchors carried by a vessel. They are so named because they are carried on the bows. In earlier times they were of different weights, the larger being known as the *best* bower and the smaller as the *small* bower.

Anchor, Kedge. A term applied to a light anchor used for warping or kedging.

Anchor, Stream. An anchor used for anchoring in a narrow roadway or channel to prevent the stern swinging with the tide. The weight of this anchor is equal to about one-fourth that of the bower anchor.

Astern. Signifying position, in the rear of or abaft the stern; as regards motion, the opposite of going ahead; backwards.

Athwart, Athwartship. In a transverse direction; from side to side at right angles to the fore and aft centerline of a vessel.

Backstays. Stays which extend from all mast levels, except the lower, to the ship's side some distance abaft the mast. They serve as additional supports to prevent the mast from going forward and at the same time contribute to the lateral support, thereby assisting the shrouds.

Ballast. Any weight carried solely for the purpose of making the vessel more sea-worthy. Ballast may be either portable or fixed, depending upon the condition of the ship. Permanent ballast in the form of sand, concrete, scrap or pig iron is usually fitted to overcome an inherent defect in stability or trim due to faulty design or changed character of service. Portable ballast, usually in the form of water pumped into or out of bottom, peak or wing ballast tanks, is utilized to overcome a temporary defect in stability or trim due to faulty loading, damage, etc.

Batten (noun). A thin strip of wood, usually tapered, used in laying down lines. A strip of wood or steel used in securing tarpaulins in place. (Verb) To secure by means of battens, as to "batten down a hatch."

Battening Down. Making the hatches watertight by means of tarpaulins firmly secured to the hatch coamings with battens, wedges, etc.

Becalmed. (Applied only to sailing vessels.) That condition in which there is insufficient wind to give steerage wary even though all sail is set.

Belay. To secure a rope or line about a cleat or belaying pin by winding it back and forth in the manner of the figure eight.

Belaying Pin. A small iron or tough wood pin consisting of a head, shoulder and shank. The pin, being securely fitted in a rail, is used for belaying the hauling parts of light running gear, signal halyards, etc.

Berth. A term applied to a bed or a place to sleep. Berths, as a rule, are permanently built into the structure of the staterooms or compartments. They are constructed singly and also in tiers of two or three, one above the other. When single, drawers for stowing clothing are often built-in underneath. Tiers of berths constructed of pipe are commonly installed in the crew space. The term berth is also used to designate a stateroom or cabin, and also to specify a position; for example, he has the berth of captain. Still another use of the term is to designate the place where a ship is docked or tied up.

Bilge and Ballast System. A system of piping generally located in the hold of a vessel and connected to pumps. This system is used for pumping overboard accumulations of water in holds and compartments, and also for filling ballast and peak tanks.

Boatswain (Bo's'n). One of the lower officers on shipboard who has immediate charge of the deck force, deck gear, boats, rigging, cordage, etc.

Boatswain's Call. A small silver whistle or pipe used by a boatswain or his mates to summon men to their stations and direct them in their duties.

Boatswain's Chair. A piece of plank forming a seat hung in two straps on which a man may be hoisted aloft or lowered over the ship's side.

Boiler. Any vessel, container or receptacle that is capable of generating steam by the internal or external application of heat. There are two general classes of boilers, i. e., fire tube and water tube.

Boiler, Scotch. This type consists of a cylindrical shell with internal circular furnaces which are generally corrugated to enable them to withstand external pressure. Grate bars subdivide the furnaces into two parts, the upper part for the fire and gases and the lower part for the ash pit. The hot gases pass to a combustion chamber in the back of the boiler and from there return through tubes to the front end and uptake. The water should be kept to a level above the top of the tubes and combustion chamber and occupies all the space not taken up by the furnaces, combustion chamber, tubes, stay rods, stay bolts and steam space. Large Scotch boilers have as many as four furnaces.

Bollards. A term applied to short metal columns extending up from a base plate which is attacked to a wharf or dock and used for securing the lines from a ship. Also, applied to timber posts extending above the level of a wharf for the same purpose. The bitts on a ship are frequently called bollards.

Boss, Propeller-Post. That portion of the propeller post that is swelled out to receive the stern tube.

Bow. The sides of a vessel at and for some distance abaft the stem, designated as the right hand, or starboard bow, and the left hand, or port bow.

Breadth (extreme). The maximum breadth measure over plating or planking, including beading or fenders.

Breadth, Molded. The greatest breadth of a vessel, measured from the heel of frame on one side to the heel of frame on the other side.

Breadth, Register. The breadth of the broadest part on the outside of the vessel shall be accounted the vessel's breadth of beam, and should be taken either by plumb lines let full so as to touch the sides of the vessel or by other practical means.

Breakwater. A term applied to plates or timbers fitted on a forward weather deck to form a V-shaped shield against water that is shipped over the bow.

Bridge. A high transverse platform, often forming the top of a bridge house, extending from side to side of the ship, and from which a good view of the weather deck may be had. An enclosed space called the pilot house is erected on the bridge in which are installed the navigating instruments, such as the compass and binnacle, the control for the steering apparatus and the signals to the engine room. While the pilot house is generally extended to include a chartroom and sometimes staterooms, a clear passageway should be left around it. As the operation of the ship is directed from the bridge or flying bridge above it, there should also be clear open passage from one side of the vessel to the other.

Bridge, Navigating or Flying. The uppermost platform erected at the level of the top of pilot house. It generally consists of a narrow walkway supported by stanchions, running from one side of the ship to the other and the space over the top of the pilot house. A duplicate set of navigating instruments and controls for the steering gear and engine room signals are installed on the flying bridge so that the ship may be navigated in good weather from this platform. Awnings erected on stanchions and weather clothes fitted to the railing give protection against sun and wind.

Bulkhead. A term applied to any of the partition walls used for subdividing the interior of a ship into the various compartments. The main partition walls also serve as strength members of the ship's structure and as a protection against water passing from one compartment to another.

Bulkhead, Coal Bunker. A term applied to a coal bunker partition wall. These bulkheads, when they serve no other purpose than enclosing coal bunkers, need not be made watertight.

Bulkhead, Collision. The foremost transverse watertight partition in a ship that extends from the bottom of the hold to the freeboard deck. The principal object of this bulkhead is to keep the water out of the forward hold in case of a collision or damage to the bow.

Bulkhead, Deck. The uppermost continuous deck to which all transverse watertight bulkheads are carried. The term is used in connection with the method of subdividing merchant ships described in the Report of the Committee appointed by the president of the British Board of Trade.

Bulkhead, Engine Room. A term applied to a bulkhead bounding the machinery space.

Bulkhead, Longitudinal. A partition wall of planking or plating running in a fore and aft direction. Fore and aft bulkheads are very common on warships.

Bulkhead, Partial. A term applied to a bulkhead that only extends to a portion of the way across a compartment. They are generally erected as strength members of the structure.

Bulkhead Stiffeners. A term applied to the beams or girders attached to a bulkhead for the purpose of supporting it under pressure and holding it in shape. These steering beams are usually spaced from about two to four feet apart and are attached to the shell, tank top and decks by brackets or lugs. Vertical stiffeners are most common on bulkheads, but horizontal stiffeners or a combination of both may be used.

Bulkhead, Transverse. A partition wall of planking or plating running in an athwartship direction across a portion or the whole breadth of a ship. The principal function of transverse bulkheads is to divide the ship into a series of watertight compartments so that any rupture of the shell will not cause the loss of the vessel. The best practice is to fit transverse bulkheads near enough together so that the admission of the sea to any two adjacent compartments will still leave the ship enough reserve buoyancy to float. Transverse bulkheads also serve as efficient strength members and are important in preserving the transverse shape of a vessel. These bulkheads also serve the purpose of subdividing the cargo space and quarters into compartments of desirable length.

Bulkhead, Trunk. A term applied to the casings or partition that forms an enclosure running from deck to deck and surrounding hatch openings.

Bulkhead, Watertight. A partition of planking or plating reinforced where necessary with stiffening bars and capable of preventing the flow of water under pressure from one compartment to another. To do this all seams, butts or connections of the plating or planking must be efficiently calked and the strength of the structure must be sufficient to stand up under pressure.

Bulwark. A term applied to the strake of shell plating or the side planking above a weather deck. It helps to keep the deck dry and also serves as a guard against losing deck cargo or men overboard. Where bulwarks are fitted it is customary to provide openings in them which are called freeing ports, to allow the water that breaks over to clear itself. Bulwarks interfere with the rapid handling of cargo as care must always be taken to hoist everything clear of its top.

Bunkers, Coal. The spaces or compartments of a ship in which is stowed the coal used as fuel for the boilers.

Buoyancy. The supporting effort exerted by a liquid (usually water) upon the surface of a body, wholly or partially immersed in it.

Cabin. The interior of a deck house, usually the space set aside for the use of officers and passengers.

Cable Length. A rough measure of distance equal to about six hundred feet.

Camber. Round of Beam. The weather decks of ships are rounded up or arched in an athwartship direction for the purpose of draining any water that may fall on them to the sides of the ship where it can be led overboard through scuppers. This arching or rounding up is called the camber or round of beam and is expressed in inches in connection with the greatest molded breadth of the ship in feet.

Capstan. A device made of iron and wood for hauling up anchors and cables, taking down the foresail tack, aboard ship, or for drawing light boats above high watermark.

Casing, Engine Room. The partitions or walls enclosing the space above the engine room in the way of the engine room skylight and hatchway. The casing forms a trunk suitable for access, light and ventilation. At the top of the casing a skylight with hinged covers is fitted through which the heat from the engine room escapes. Doors are fitted in the casing at the deck levels which give access to gratings and ladders leading down into the engine room. Care should be taken that the engine room casing encloses a space sufficiently large to provide for installing the engines and for lifting the cylinder covers where reciprocating engines are used. Portable strong beams are fitted in the casing trunk to compensate for the opening and for convenience in lifting covers, etc. The top of the casing should project well above the weather deck where there is no superstructure and should be carried up through the superstructure where one is erected.

Chock. A term applied to oval shaped castings, either open or closed on top, and fitted with or without rollers, through which hawsers and lines are passed. Also applied to blocks of wood used as connecting or reinforcing pieces, to blocks of wood used as filling pieces, and to supports for life boats.

Chock, Roller. A term applied to an oval shaped casting fitted with one or more rollers and used for the purpose of passing hawsers and lines through.

Chronometer, Marine. A timepiece mounted on gymbals in a glass-covered case to keep it horizontal and to preserve it from vibration, dust, drafts, and fluxuations of temperature. The mechanism is of a superior construction, having adjustments and compensations for temperature. While generally designed to run 56 hours, it is wound daily at a stated hour and is not regulated. The instrument is set as accurately as possible and its accuracy observed in an observatory. A certificate of rating is issued, showing its rate of gain or loss and this cumulative error must be considered when observing the time.

Compass, Magnetic. The compass is the most important instrument of navigation in use on board ship, the path of a ship through the waters depending upon the efficient working and use of this instrument. There are two kinds of compasses, the Dry Card Compass and the Liquid Compass. The Dry Compass consists essentially of a number of magnetic needles suspended parallel to each other and fastened to the rim of a circular disc that has a paper cover upon which are marked the points of the compass and the degrees. This card rests upon a pivot centered in the compass bowl, which in its turn is suspended by gimbals in the binnacle or stand, the latter having means of lighting the card at night and for the adjustment of compass errors due to the magnetism of the ship. In the Liquid Compass, the bowl is filled with alcohol and water, or oil. The needles are sealed in parallel tubes and form a framework which connects the central boss with the outer rim, the whole resting upon a pivot in the compass bowl. Upon the rim are printed the points and degrees. As regards the relative uses of these compasses, it may be said that the dry compass is the standard in the world's Merchant Marine, while the liquid compass is the standard in Navies, because of its freedom of vibration from the shock of gunfire, etc. The compass has been used for purposes of navigation since the third or fourth century, and the points of the compass were a natural development of subdivision of the card and have been in use since the fourteenth century. Capt. Flinders, R.N., was the first to investigate the laws of the deviation of the compass, and was the first to introduce the method of swinging ships for obtaining the deviation, in 1814. The construction of iron vessels and the consequent errors of the compass caused investigation, and in 1838-39 Sir George B. Airy, then Astronomer Royal for Great Britain, at the instigation of the Admiralty, conducted a series of experiments for "the purpose of discovering a correction for the deviation of the compass produced by the iron in the ship." The result of this investigation was immediately given to the world, and the principles then discovered form the basis of our compass knowledge of today. To the late Lord Kelvin, navigators the world over are indebted for his untiring work in the interests of practical navigation, and through his researches we have accurate knowledge of how a compass, its binnacle and accessories should be made, based upon scientific and mathematical formulae, and compasses so made are "Standard" for that instrument.

Condenser. A chamber of rectangular or cylindrical shape whose function is to convert the exhaust steam from the engine, turbines, and auxiliary machinery into water.

Counter. That part of a ship's after body extending aft from the after perpendicular (usually above the water line).

Countersink. A term applied to the operation of cutting the sides of a drilled or punched hole into to shape of a frustum of a cone. This shape provides a shoulder for a rivet or a bolt and allows a flush surface to be maintained. Also applied to the tool doing the work.

Course. The path over which a vessel proceeds. Some courses used habitually are known by name. This applies especially to measured mile courses, where trial trips are conducted and to racing courses. In the open sea the course is designated by the point of the compass toward which the vessel is headed.

Cover, Boat. A Piece of canvas used as a cover for a small boat when it is not in use.

Crane, Jib. A boom or arm fitted to swing in sockets attached to a wall or column. The boom in this type of crane is generally fixed in a vertical direction but free to move horizontally.

Crank Shaft. That portion of a reciprocating engine in which rotary as distinguished from rectilinear motion first appears. The term is applied to the portion of the shaft which (depending upon the number of cylinders) is composed of one or more cranks rigidly attached to one another and arranged to work about a common axis viz.: that of the propeller shaft. Crank shafting may be either built up or forged. Built up crank shafts are composed of a series of crank pins, crank axles, and crank webs formed separately and shrunk and keyed together. This type is common in merchant practice where might is not of first importance. It lends itself readily to fabrication and repair. Forged crank shafting is cut and machined from a single forging. It effects a saving in weight over the built-up type and is becoming more popular. It is at the present time universally used in naval practice and in high grade work outside naval practice.

Cutter. A boat carried by war vessels, and on Merchant vessels they are generally employed as emergency boats.

Davit. A crane used to lower and raise lifeboats and sometimes anchors.

Dead Light. A term applied to a port lid or cover. A metal shutter fitted to protect the glass in a fixed or port light,

Deck. A deck in a ship corresponds to the floor in a building. It is the plating, planking, or reinforced concrete covering or any tier of beams above the inner bottom, forming a floor, either in the hull or superstructure of a ship.

Deck, Canvas Covered. To secure water tightness wood decks that are not calked and also wood decks within the quarters are often covered with canvas. After the canvas is laid it is given a coat of paint.

Deck Chair. An item of furniture still found on beaches and in parks, but originally designed for the use of passengers and for easy stowing on liners. Developed from the hammock, and consisting of canvas stretched on a collapsible wooden frame. Luxury liners eventually had cane-seated, mahogany or teak chairs, which, however, could similarly be collapsed.

Deck Covering, Decking. Various compositions and materials have been used for covering decks. The light upper weather decks are commonly covered with canvas and then given a coat of paint. The heavy steel weather decks, when not planked over, are often covered with a composition which serves as a protection to the steel and makes a better surface for working. The decks in the living quarters are usually covered with linoleum or some composition with the object of protecting the steel and of providing a surface that is easily kept clean and sanitary. In addition to the above some of the compositions are insulating and fireproof as well as elastic and neat appearing.

Deck, Forecastle (Fo´c'sle). A term applied to a deck worked from the stem aft over a forecastle erection.

Deck House. A term applied to a partial superstructure that does not extend from side to side of a vessel like a bridge, poop or forecastle.

Deck Planks or Planking. A term applied to the wood sheathing or covering on a deck. Oregon, yellow pine or teak are used for this purpose. The seams between the planking should be thoroughly caulked.

Deck, Poop. A term applied to a deck worked from the stern forward over a poop erection.

Deck, Promenade. An upper superstructure deck on a passenger ship designed as a promenade for the passengers.

Deck Scuppers, Upper. Scuppers for draining water from the upper deck, gutters or waterways.

Deck, Tongue and Groove. A deck covered with thin machined planks and generally used on the upper light decks of vessels. Tongue and groove decks are usually covered with canvas after which a coat of paint is applied.

Deep Tank. A tank extending from the bottom of a vessel or from the top of the inner bottom up to or higher than the lower deck.

Deep Water Line. The water line at which a vessel floats even carrying the maximum allowable load.

Depth Molded. The vertical distance from top of beam of uppermost strength deck at side of vessel amidship to top of keel.

Depth, Register. The register depth should be taken from the underside of the tonnage deck plank, midship, to the ceiling in the hold, average thickness, at the side of the keelson, in a direction perpendicular to the keel, which may be done by a square placed upon the upper side of the keelson. If the vessel has a third deck, then the height from the top of the tonnage deck plank to the under side of the upper deck plank shall be accounted as the height under the spar deck.

Derrick. An apparatus designed to hoist heavy weights. The general design of a derrick is similar to that of a post crane except that the boom is hinged at the heel which allows it to be set at any angle with the post. The post of a derrick usually rotates with the boom.

Derrick, on a Ship. A spar or a boom, one end of which is stepped in a pivot bearing on the lower portion of a vertical post erected on the deck of a ship or on a pedestal fitted to the deck at the foot of the vertical post. A hinged connection fitted to the pivot bearing allows the boom to be inclined at any angle with the post while the pivot permits it to be revolved. The derrick is fitted with ropes, guys and tackles and is used for transferring cargo from and into the hulls. Unlike most derricks on land the derrick post itself does not revolve.

Displacement. The amount or quantity of water displaced by a floating vessel. It exactly equals the weight of the vessel itself with whatever is on board at the time at which the displacement is recorded. Displacement may be expressed either in cubic feet or tons; a cubic foot of sea water weighs 64 pounds and one of fresh water 62.5 pounds, consequently one ton is equal to 35 cubic feet of sea water of 35.9 cubic feet of fresh water. The designed displacement of a vessel is her displacement when floating at her designed draft. In merchant vessels this is generally taken with full cargo, fuel, stores and water on board. In the case of naval vessels it corresponds to the vessel complete with full supply of ammunition, and two-thirds full supply of fuel, stores and water.

Displacement, Volume of. The volume of water displaced by a vessel. In the English system of units the volume of displacement is given in cubic feet and equals thirty-five times the displacement in salt water or thirty-six times the displacement in fresh water.

Dock. A basin for the reception of vessels. Wet docks are utilized for the loading and unloading of ships. Dry docks are utilized for the construction or repair of ships.

Dog. A short metal rod or bar fashioned to form a clamp or clip and used for holding watertight doors, manholes, or pieces of work in place.

Door, Cargo. A door, usually composed of two or more parts, fitted in the side or an upper bulkhead of a vessel for the purpose of providing access through which cargo may be trucked.

Door, Dutch. A term applied to a door built in two independent sections, one above the other, so that the upper half may be open while the lower half is closed. These doors are commonly used for access to galleys.

Door Gangway. A door fitted in the side of a vessel to provide access for a gangway.

Door, Horizontal or Vertical, Sliding. A door so constructed and operated that it can be slid, horizontally into position in the case of horizontal doors and vertically into position in the case of vertical doors. Such doors are usually watertight and so fitted with shafting and bevel gears or other means that they can be closed from the weather or upper deck.

Door, Watertight. A door so constructed that when closed it will prevent water under pressure from passing through. A common type consists of a steel plate, around the edges of which a frame of angle bar is fitted, having a strip of rubber attached to the flange that is parallel to the door plate. The strip of rubber is compressed against the toe of the flange of an angle iron door frame by dogs or clamps.

Double Bottom. A term applied to the space between the inner and outer skins of a vessel. Also applied to indicate that a ship has a complete inner or extra envelope of watertight plating. A double bottom is usually fitted in large ships extending from bilge to bilge and nearly the whole length fore and aft.

Double Bottom Cellular. A term applied where the double bottom is divided into numerous rectangular compartments by the floors and longitudinals.

Draft, Draught (of a vessel). The depth of a vessel below the waterline measured vertically to the lowest part of the hull, propellers or other reference points.

Draft Marks. The numbers which are placed at the bow and stern of a vessel to indicate how much water she draws. These numbers should be as near the stem and stern as possible and should be six inches high and spaced twelve inches apart vertically.

Draft, Mean. The mean of the drafts measured at the bow and the stern, or in the case of vessels with straight keels the draft measured at the middle of the waterline length.

Dry Dock, Graving. A basin excavated at a waterway and connected thereto by gates or a caisson which may be opened to let a vessel in or out and then closed and the water pumped out. Graving docks are constructed by making a large excavation, driving pile or building concrete foundations in the bottom and by constructing wood, concrete or stone retaining walls around the sides. The sides are usually built in the form of steps.

Dunnage. Loose wood or waste material placed in the hold of a vessel for the protection of the cargo from dampness. Also used as descriptive of a sailor's kit or personal belongings.

Engine, Reciprocating. An engine designed to convert the pressure of live steam into work. This is accomplished by means of the backward and forward motion of a piston from end to end of a cylinder as the result of steam being alternately admitted to each end of the cylinder and the expanded steam exhausted from the other end. The straight line motion of the piston is communicated to the piston rod to which it is directly attached and is then transformed into rotary or circular motion by means of suitable mechanism.

Expansion Joint. A term applied to a joint which permits. linear movement to take up the expansion and contraction due to changes in temperature.

Fairleads. A term applied to fittings that are used to change or preserve the direction of a rope or chain so that it is delivered fairly to a sheave or drum. Large fairleads in the shape of a drum on a vertical shaft are used to deliver a hawser coming through a chock or mooring pipe to a gypsy our a winch or windlass. Fairleads are also used with the steering leads in which case they may be fittings with small sheaves or annular rings. With steering leads the fairleaders are generally more for preserving than changing the line of the ropes.

Fairwater. A term applied to plating fitted in the shape of a frustum of a cone, around the ends of shaft tubes and struts to prevent an abrupt change in the stream lines. Also applied at any casting or plating fitted to the hull for the purpose of preserving a smooth flow of water.

Fall. By common usage the entire length of rope used in a tackle, though a strict adherence to the term would limit its application to the end to which the power is applied. The end secured to the block is called the standing part, the opposite end, the hauling part.

Fathom. A unit of length used in measuring cordage, depths, etc. The length varies in different countries, being six feet in Great Britain and the United States. This is roughly obtained by extending both arms.

Fidley. Also spelled "Fiddley" A term applied to the top of a boiler casing. Through it pass the smoke stack and boiler room ventilators. The top around the stack and cowls is fitted with gratings made of bar steel with metal covers that can be closed when the weather is very bad.

Fidley Gratings. A term applied to gratings made of bar steel and fitted over the top of the boiler hatch.

Fore. A term used in indicating portions or that part of a ship at or adjacent to the bow. Applied to that portion of the ship lying between the midship section and stem as fore body. Also to portions or parts of the ship lying between the midship section and stem as fore hold and foremast.

Fore Peak. The extreme forward end of the vessel below decks. The forward trimming tank.

Fore and Aft. Parallel to the ship's centerline.

Forebody. That portion of the ship's body forward of the midship section.

Forecastle (Fo'c' sel). A short structure at the onward end of a vessel formed by carrying up the ship's shell plating a deck height above the level of her uppermost complete deck and fitting a deck over the length of this structure. The after end of the forecastle may or may not be closed by a transverse bulkhead. The name given to the crew's quarters on a merchant ship when they are in the fore part of the vessel.

Forecastle Deck. See Deck, Forecastle.

Forecastle Sheerstrake. The strake of outside plating adjacent to the forecastle deck.

Forward. In the direction of the stem.

Forward Part. The portion of the vessel in the vicinity of the stem, the bows.

Forward Perpendicular. A line perpendicular to the base line and intersecting the forward side of the stem at the designed waterline.

Frame. A term generally used to designate one of transverse ribs that make up the skeleton of a ship. Where the structure is built up of a relatively small number of strong transverse webs or belt frames and a relatively large number of smaller fore and aft bars, the fore and aft bars are called the frames. The frames act as stiffeners, holding the outside plating in shape and maintaining the transverse form of the ship.

Galley. The space on shipboard where the food is prepared; a ship's kitchen.

Galley Smoke Pipe or Funnel. A smoke pipe fitted to the galley range. It is constructed of sheet iron and led up through the deck above or through the galley skylight to the open air.

Gang board, Gangplank. A term applied to boards or a movable platform used in transferring passengers or cargo from vessel to wharf or dock or vice-versa.

Gangway. A term applied to a place of exit from a vessel. Gangways are fitted in the shape of ports, which may be closed, in the sides of a vessel and in the shape of movable portions of bulwarks or railings on the weather decks.

Gooseneck. A fitting used to attach and support a cargo boom. A short piece of pipe, used as a ventilator, one end of which is given a 180° bend and the other end attached to a deck over an opening equal to the diameter of the pipe. Also applied to pipes and fittings in which a large bend or curve is worked.

Gratings, Fidley. See Fidley Gratings.

Gratings, Hatch. Gratings usually constructed of wood, fitted over hatch openings. They are particularly desirable where hatch covers are removed or opened.

Gripes, Boat. An arrangement for holding small boats securely in their stowage chocks. They are made up of lashings or chains fitted on one end with a turnbuckle or pelican hook and a shackle for attachment to a pad eye on the deck and on the other end with a flat bar hook for attachment to the gunwale of the boat.

Gunwale. A term applied to the line where an upper deck stringer intersects the shell.

Guys. Wire or hemp ropes, or chains to support booms, davits, etc., laterally. They may consist of single lines or purchases, leading from the davit head or boom end to the deck. In the case of single lines they are either lashed to eyes or rings or else fitted with turnbuckles and hooked or shackled to deck connections. Guys are employed in pairs. Where a span is fitted between two booms or davits one pair only is required for the two. Guys to booms that carry sails are sometimes known as backropes.

Halyards. Light lines used in hoisting signals, flags, etc. Also applied to the ropes by which gaffs, sail or yards are hoisted.

Hand Wheels. Wheels for operating machinery, valves, doors, etc., by hand.

Hatch or Hatchway. An opening in a deck through which cargo may be handled, machinery or boilers installed or removed, and access obtained to the decks and holds below.

Hatch Battens. A term applied to the flat bars used to fasten and make tight the edges of the tarpaulins that are placed over hatches. The batten and edge of the tarpaulin are wedged tightly in closely spaced cleats.

Hatch Beams. A term applied to the portable beams fitted to the coamings for the purpose of supporting the hatch covers.

Hatch, Cargo. A term applied to the deck openings leading to the cargo holds.

Hatch Cleats. A term applied to the clips attached to the outside of the hatch coamings for the purpose of holding the hatch battens and edges of the tarpaulin covers.

Hatch, Coaling. An opening in the deck provided for the purpose of filling the coal bunkers. A trunk or casing is fitted from the upper opening to the top of the coal bunker.

Hatch Covers. Covers for closing up the top of hatchways, usually made of wood planks and in sections that can be handled by the crew. When made of wood one or more tarpaulins are stretched over them to keep out the rain and sea. Watertight covers made of steel plates are also in use, but they are more or less in the way when the cargo is being handled.

Hawse Pipes. Tubes leading the anchor chain from the deck on which the windlass is located down and forward through the vessel's bow plating. Hawse pipes are generally of cast iron or cast steel. They are of heavy scantling and sometimes made in two or more parts to facilitate construction.

Hawser. A large rope, either fiber or wire, used for warping, towing, mooring, etc.

Hawser Reel. A heavy reel for the stowage of hawsers when not in use. In its simplest form it consists of a cylindrical body on which the hawser is wound. At each end a disc shaped guard is fitted to keep the hawser in place. Hawser reels are sometimes mounted on frames and fitted with friction brakes with which to control the paying out of the rope.

Head of a Ship. The fore end formerly fitted up for the accommodation of the crew. A vessel is trimmed by the head when drawing more water forward and less aft than contemplated in her design.

Heave. To haul; to cast or hurl; as, to heave the lead, to heave a line, The alternate rising and falling of a vessel in a seaway.

Helm. A term applied to the tiller, wheel or steering gear, and also to the rudder. It indicates the control of the maneuvering or steering gear as in the term "Port the helm," and again the position of the rudder in the expression "Lee helm."

Holds. Spaces or compartments between the lower-most decks and the bottom of the ship, or top of the inner bottom if one is fitted. The spaces below decks allotted for the stowage of cargo.

Holystone. A soft sandstone used in scrubbing wood decks. The origin of the name is probably due to the kneeling posture of the men while using the stone, or else to the fact that they were formerly most frequently used on Sunday; to clean a deck by the application of a holy-stone.

Horsepower. The unit of power is a "horse-power," which is taken as "33,000 ft. lbs. of work performed in one minute" or its equivalent.

Horsepower, Effective. The actual power available for propulsion which is equivalent to the indicated or shaft horsepower less all losses due to friction of machinery, line shafting, stern bearings, etc.

Horsepower, Indicated. A term applied to the horsepower actually developed in the cylinder or cylinders of an engine.

Horsepower, Shaft or Brake. A term applied to the power of turbines where it is not possible to use an indicator. It is measured from the shaft by an instrument called a torsion meter, and corresponds to brake horsepower.

Hulk. The body of an old, wrecked, or dismantled vessel unfit for sea service, but sometimes used for other purposes, as a coal depot, prison, etc.

Hull. The framework of a vessel, together with all decks, deck houses, the inside and outside plating or planking, but exclusive of masts, yards, rigging and all outfit or equipment.

Hydrant. An outlet in a pipe line suitable for a hose

Inboard. Towards the center; within the vessel's shell and below the weather decks.

Jackstay. A rope, rod or pipe rove through eyebolts fitted on a yard or mast for the purpose of attaching sails to the yard or mast. The term is also applied to the outer or boundary rope of a netting or awning.

Jacob's Ladder. A ladder having either wire or fiber rope sides with wood or metal rungs attached at regular intervals. One end is usually fitted with sister hooks or shackles for hooking on.

Keel. A center line strength member running fore and aft along the bottom of a ship and often referred to as the back bone. In wood ships, it is composed of as long pieces of timber as can be obtained, which are scarped together at their ends. In steel vessels it is composed either of long bars scarped at their ends or by flat plates connected together by butt straps.

Keel, Bilge. A fin fitted on the bottom of a ship at the turn of the bilge to reduce rolling. It commonly consists of a plate running fore and aft and attached to the shell plating by angle bars. It materially helps in steadying a ship and does not add much to the resistance to propulsion.

Keel, Flat Plate. A plate of extra thickness riveted to the bottom angles of the keelson. The flat plate keel has been substituted for the bar keel in most steel ships because it saves draft and is sufficient for docking purposes. Grounding on a rocky or uneven bottom is a rare occurrence, and when this does happen a bar keel is usually not strong enough to prevent disaster. Where extra strength is required the flat plate keel consists of two plates riveted together and having their butts staggered.

Knot. A unit of speed equaling one nautical mile per hour; a division of the log line which serve to measure a vessel's rate of speed; a term applied to a connection made with a piece of cordage to another piece or to another object.

Ladder. A framework consisting of two parallel sides connected by bars or steps which are spaced at intervals suitable for ascending or descending. On shipboard the term ladder is also applied to staircases and to other contrivances used in ascending or descending to or from a higher or lower level.

Ladder, Accommodation. A term applied to a staircase suspended over the side of a vessel from a gangway to a point near the water, to provide an easy means of access from a small boat to the deck of a vessel.

Lamp, Arc. An electric lamp in which the light is produced by an electric arc drawn between two electrodes. The arc lamp is arranged to separate the electrodes automatically when the current begins to flow and to feed them toward each other as they burn away at the tip.

Lanyard. A length of rope or cord used in numerous dissimilar ways, i. e., as a fall rove through the dead eyes in setting up the shrouds or other standing rigging; as a knife-lanyard to prevent a knife falling from aloft. In this case it consists of a small cord attached to the ring in the end of the knife, the other end being worn around the neck; a port lanyard is a light line used to haul a port into the closed position or to support it when open. The term is also applied to the rope handle of a bucket. The present tendency seems to limit the application of the term to any line having a loose end the other being attached to any object for the purpose of either near or remote control.

Lead. An apparatus used for determining the depth of water under a vessel. It is generally made of lead of nearly prismatic shape tapering slightly to the upper end through which is made a hole for bending a strap to which a marked line is attached.

Lead Line. A fine line marked in fathoms or feet to which the lead is attached and from which the depth of water is read off.

Lee Side. The opposite side to that which is exposed to the wind; the opposite of windward side.

Length Over All. The total Length over all, i. e., the length measured from the foremost to the aftermost points of a vessel's hull.

Length, Register. The length from the fore part of the outer plating or planking on the side of the stem to the after part of the main sternpost of screw steamers, i. e., the one to which the rudder is attached, and to the after part of the rudderpost of all other vessels measured on top of the tonnage deck. The register length of scows and barges with a square bow and stern sloping up from the bottom to the deck and with neither stem, sternpost or rudder-post is to be taken on the deck from the extreme point of the hull at the bow to the extreme point of the hull at the stern, i. e., the overall length of the hull is to be considered the register length of such vessels.

Lengthening (of a Ship). The act of increasing a vessel's length by inserting a section amidships. The vessel is placed in a dry dock or on a marine railway, the longitudinal members are cut through in a staggered direction at about amidships, the two resulting parts separated the desired distance, and the intervening space fitted up with frames, stringers, plating, etc., so as to unite the forward and after portions in a new and longer hull.

Life Buoy, Ring. A ring made of solid cork or equivalent buoyant material having an outside diameter of not less than thirty inches and an inside diameter of not less than seventeen inches. The number of buoys a vessel should carry depends on her length. They should not be permanently fastened to a vessel, but should be so placed as to be readily accessible in case of emergency. One of the buoys on each side of the vessel should have a life line attached of at least fifteen fathoms in length. Life ring buoys are also placed on wharves and along water fronts, and as on a ship they are thrown to persons in the water for the purpose of sustaining them until they can be reached.

Life Preserver, Life Jacket. A wide belt of good cork blocks, or other suitable buoyant material, made to wrap around the body under the armpits, and having shoulder straps so fitted that the device may be put on like a vest. The object of a life preserver is to keep a person from sinking in case a vessel has to be abandoned.

Lifeboat. A small boat carried on davits or on one of the upper decks of a vessel where it can be easily lowered into the water in case of an emergency.

Limber-Boards. Removable boards serving as covers for water-courses.

Line. A general term for a rope of any size used for various purposes; small cords such as log line, lead line and small stuff as marline, ratline, houseline, etc.

Liner, Atlantic. A merchant vessel engaged in regular transatlantic service, usually having high speed, comfortable passenger accommodations, moderate freight capacity, and large size, The term probably originated with the first efforts to place in service ships which should maintain a regular schedule across the Atlantic Ocean.

Longitudinal. A general term meaning fore and aft, as longitudinal bulkhead, longitudinal strength, etc. A fore and aft girder in the bottom of a ship or a side keelson.

Louver. An opening partially closed with slats, which are fitted diagonally so that they overlap, shutting out the view but allowing the free passage of air. They are frequently constructed in the sides of skylights and fidleys.

Margin Plank. A term applied to the plank forming the boundary of the deck planking.

Mast. A long pole of steel or wood, usually circular in section, one or more of which are erected vertically on the center line of a ship. The mast may be in one piece or it may be a series of pieces banded together to form one continuous pole. The masts were originally erected for the sails but they are now used more as supports for the rigging, cargo handling gear and wireless.

Mast, Main. The principal mast in a vessel. It is generally the second mast from the bow.

Molded Breadth. The ship's maximum breadth measured to the outside or heel of frame bar and occurring generally, though not always, at the midship section.

Molded Depth. The vertical distance from the base line to the molded line of main deck at side measured at the midship section.

Molding, Knuckle. A batten or strip of wood or steel usually cut to a half round cross-section and used to cover the knuckle line.

Mooring. To make a vessel fast to a buoy, quay or wharf or by anchoring. Technically, a vessel is moored when she has two anchors down at a suitable distance apart with such a length of chain on each that she is held with her bow approximately stationary on a line between them, although allowing the stern of the vessel to swing with the tide and wind.

Mooring Pipe. A round or oval casting or frame inserted in the apron plate or bulwark plating of a ship through which the mooring chains, hawsers or warps are passed.

Movable Propeller Blades. Propeller blades cast separate from the boss and attached thereto by bolts. These bolts are sometimes worked in such a manner as to permit of a slight adjustment of the pitch of the blade.

Mushroom Ventilator. A ventilator shaped like a mushroom, and designed so that the air will be drawn up under the overhanging umbrella of the mushroom and thence into openings into the vertical pipe leading down into the vessel. The object of the mushroom is to permit access of air but prevent access of water.

Nautical Mile. A distance approximately equal to 6,080 feet, or exactly one-sixtieth of a degree on the equator.

On Board. Aboard; in or on a ship, but having a different significance from "on deck" in that "on board" applies to any location in or on the ship as any of its parts, while the term "on deck" is generally limited to a location on the weather deck.

On Deck. On the weather deck; frequently used to imply "on duty."

Open Bridge House. A bridge house open to the weather at each end.

Outboard. Away from the center toward the outside; without the hull.

Pad Eye. A fitting having an eye integral with a plate or base in order to distribute the strain over a greater area and to provide ample means of securing. The pad may have either a "worked" or a "shackle" eye or more than one of either or both. The principal uses of such a fitting is that it affords means for attaching rigging, stoppers, blocks, and other movable or portable objects. Pad eyes are also known as lug pads, the two terms being practically synonymous.

Paint. A viscous or plastic mixture of solids and liquid applied in thin coats for protection or decoration or both. Paint may be defined as a close union of solids or pigments and liquids or binder.

Anti-Corrosive Ship's Bottom Paint

This paint is generally made of metallic zinc, zinc oxide, shellac, alcohol, pine tar and turpentine and is designed to insulate the metal in the anti-fouling coat from the steel plating, preventing corrosion and pitting. Anti-corrosive and anti-fouling ship's bottom paints differ radically from oil paints in that the vehicle portion consists of shellac, alcohol, and pine tar solution. This produces a very rapid drying paint which can be submerged a few hours after application. Anti-corrosive ship's bottom paint is designed to prevent corrosion from electrolysis. This coat does not offer resistance to the flow of electric current but contains a metal which is electropositive to iron. Electrolysis decomposes this metal and deposits it on the steel hull. Insulation or protection from electrolysis is not obtained by

178

paint which offers resistance to the flow of electric current since abrasion and movement of the plates will prevent the maintenance of a continuous film necessary to prevent the passage of current.

Anti-Fouling Ship's Bottom Paint

This paint is intended to prevent marine growth from adhering to the underwater surface of the hull. This is effected by the presence of a poisonous compound in the film, usually mercuric oxide, copper oxide, copper cyanide, etc. An efficient antifouling paint is so designed that it will exfoliate, thereby presenting new surfaces at regular intervals, In this class falls the so-called copper paint for wooden hulls. This paint usually contains a substantial percentage of copper oxide ground in a special vehicle.

Priming Paint

Red lead, free from coarse vitrified particles mixed with pure linseed oil makes the best priming coat for iron and steel. When pure dry red lead (containing a substantial amount of litharge as a natural constituent) is mixed with pure raw linseed oil within 18 hours before application it can be applied to iron and steel without the addition of a thinner or drier. This practice is not recommended, however, since the drying conditions usually encountered in marine painting are not very favorable and the addition of a thinner and drier will enable the operator to apply a thin uniform coat which will dry rapidly, forming a very tenacious, hard, elastic weather resisting film. Rust resisting or preservative coatings are usually dark in color, since the white pigments (basic carbonate, basic sulphate white lead and zinc oxide) have certain physical and chemical characteristics which make them unsatisfactory for priming paints for iron and steel.

Smoke Stack Paint

Smoke Stack Paint is usually made of zinc oxide, white lead, litharge and Damar varnish thinned with kerosene and a substantial amount of dryer added. This paint is very resistant to high temperatures. Another type of smoke stack paint is made as follows: white lead, silica, litharge, boiled linseed oil and mineral spirits. This mixture is tinted to the desired shade and applied in the usual manner.

Red Lead

This pigment is prepared by heating litharge to approximately 700 degrees Fahr. in contact with the air. It then takes up more oxygen and turns red. The composition of red lead varies from 65 per cent practically pure red lead, little or no litharge being present. The latter type is more expensive to make and is therefore sold at a higher price. Red lead is used extensively for the protection of metal and is usually applied as a priming coat.

Peak. A term applied to the outer and upper end of a gaff.

Peak, Fore or After. The space at the extreme bow or stern below the decks.

Peak Tank. A tank or tank space built into or formed in the extreme forward or after lower portion of a vessel's hull.

Pelorus. A navigational instrument similar to a binnacle and mariner's compass but without a magnetic needle. The instrument is used for taking bearings, especially when the object to be sighted is not visible from the ship's compass. Also known as a Dumb Compass.

Pilot House. A house designed for navigational purposes. It is usually located forward of the midship section and so constructed as to command an unobstructed view in all directions except directly aft along the center line of the vessel where the smoke stack usually interferes.

Piping, Steam. Piping designed to carry live steam from the boilers to the main engines and to the various steam driven auxiliaries.

Pitch. A term applied to the distance a propeller will advance during one revolution, the distance between centers of the teeth of a gear wheel, the spacing of rivets, etc.

Plank, Margin or Nibbing. The extreme out plank of wood deck generally fitted just inboard of the waterways and sometimes notched out to revive the ends of the deck planks. Also placed around the outside of coaming of hatches, and around manhole frames where wood decks are fitted.

Planking. A term applied to wood decks and to the outside planking in wood or composite ships.

Plate. Steel of other metal rolled or cast into form such that it has in general a consistent thickness which is small relative to its length and breadth. In ship work mild steel plates cut to proper form are used for the shell, decks and bulkheads. Plate is generally referred to by thickness only.

Plating, Clinker System. Where the edges of outside plating form lap joints so that one edge of a plate is inside while the other is outside. In this case tapered frame liners are used.

Plating, In and Out System. Where the edges of the outside plating form lap joints so that both edges of the plates are alternately inside and outside. In order to do this, the frames have to be joggled in the way of the outside strakes or frame liners of the thickness of the plating have to be fitted between the frames and outside strakes.

Plating, Shell. The plating forming the outer skin of a vessel. In addition to keeping the water out of the hold, it contributes largely to the strength of the vessel.

Port. An opening in the plating or planking of a vessel for the purpose of providing access for passengers, loading and discharging cargo, taking on coal, discharging ashes and water, etc.

Port, Air. An opening in the side or deck house of a vessel, usually round in shape, and fitted with a hinged frame in which a thick glass light is secured. The purpose of the air port is to provide light and ventilation to the interior.

Port, Bow. An opening cut in the bow plating or planking to provide means of loading long timbers, piles, rails, etc. This opening must have a watertight cover as it is constantly under the pressure of head seas.

Port, Bulwark, Clearing or Freeing. A rectangular or oval opening in the bulwark just above the deck. These ports are necessary when seas break over the deck so that the ship can clear itself quickly. As these openings are about the size of a manhole, rods or bars are generally fitted across them. Flap doors are sometimes fitted on the outside hinging outboard.

Port, Cargo. An opening in the side plating or planking provided with a watertight cover or door and used for loading and unloading cargo.

Port, Coaling. An opening in the side of a vessel provided with a watertight cover used for loading coal aboard a vessel.

Port Side. That side of a vessel to the left hand when looking from the stern toward the bow.

Port the Helm. A term originally applied to the operation of putting the tiller over to the left or port side, causing the rudder and ship to turn to the right or starboard. The operation of turning a steering wheel to port may cause the vessel to turn to either the right or left according to whether the leads are open or crossed or otherwise mechanically arranged. Different localities and countries and also different branches of the marine in the same locality have their own rules as to whether the ship turns with or against the wheel. Thus an order to port the helm on a vessel plying the inland waters or harbors or on the ship of a foreign country might he interpreted in the opposite direction from the same orders issued on board some deep sea and naval vessels.

Propeller. A propulsive device consisting of a boss or hub carrying radial blades, from two to four in number, the rear or driving faces of which form portions of an approximately helical surface, the axis of which is the center-line of the propeller shaft. The propeller is ordinarily located at the after end of the propeller shaft. The rotary motion imparted to this shaft by the engine turns the propeller, thereby exerting a rearward thrust upon the water which reacts to force the ship ahead. The selection of proper characteristics, such as diameter, revolutions, pitch, etc., the accurate determination of blade thickness, shape, etc., and the great care in construction and finish are essential to the securing of the best results from the propeller in service.

Propeller Blades, Screw. The radial arms, attached to the propeller hub, the faces of which form portions of an approximately helical surface the axis of which coincides with that of the propeller shaft. Blades are either cast in one piece with the hub or cast separately and designed to be attached to the hub with bolts. In this latter case provision is usually made for a slight adjustment in pitch by means of the shape of the bolt holes.

Propeller Boss. The central portion of the screw propeller which carries the blades and forms the medium of attachment to the propeller shaft. It is taper bored for the reception of the propeller shaft and slotted for the key. When properly placed upon the shaft it is forced home and secured in its final position by means of the propeller lock nut.

Propeller Diameter. The diameter of the circle tangent to the tips of the propeller blades.

Propeller Shaft. That length of shafting in a screw steamship which carries the propeller. It is the after-most piece of shafting and at its outermost end is coned, slotted and threaded for the attachment and proper securing of the propeller itself. This piece of shafting is carried directly by the propeller strut or stern bearing and is made slightly larger than the line shafting as a precaution against corrosion and shock. It is generally encased in a brass sleeve to provide proper bearing surface and to protect the shaft from corrosion.

Pump, Ballast. A pump used for filling and emptying the ballast tanks. It has by-passes so that it can work the bilges and fire system either alone or in conjunction with the other pumps.

Pump, Bilge. A pump used aboard ship to remove accumulations of water in the vessel's bottom tanks, hold and other compartments and discharge it overboard.

Pump, Fresh Water. This pump delivers fresh water that moves back and forth or up and down in the from of the culinary or supply tanks to a gravity tank, which is called the daily supply tank. The gravity tank feeds the fresh water supply lines to the quarters, galleys, pantries, lavatories, etc.

Pump, Sanitary. The function of this pump is to supply salt water to the flushing system and for baths. It may deliver directly but commonly discharges into a gravity tank, the overflow of which is carried to the water closets and troughs. It also supplies a tank in which a steam coil is installed for the purpose of providing for hot sea water baths.

Quarter. The part of a yard just outside the slings; the upper part of a vessel's sides near the stern; portions of a vessel's sides about midway between the stem and the middle and between the middle and the stern.

Quarters. Living spaces for passengers or personnel. It includes state rooms, dining saloons, mess rooms, lounging places, passages connected with the fore-going, etc.; individual stations for personnel for fire or boat drill, etc.

Quarter Master. An under officer of a ship's crew who steers the ship and has charge of the navigating instruments.

Ram. A forward, strongly constructed, underwater projection of the stem post. They were fitted on most warships. However, on account of the severity of the stresses set up by the shocks of a collision and also on account of the fact that action between warships is generally conducted at long range, the ram as a means of offence became outdated. A name given to a vessel that is designed for the purpose of sinking vessels by head on collision or for icebreaking.

Range, Galley. The stove, situated in the galley, which is used to cook meals.

Releasing Gear. This gear is composed of specially constructed hooks attached to the davit heads and rods, chains or fittings installed in lifeboats. By the use of this gear both ends of a lifeboat may be released or picked up quickly and simultaneously.

Rigging. A term used collectively for all the ropes and chains employed to support and work the masts, yards, booms and sails of a vessel.

Rivet. A pin used for connecting two or more pieces of material by the means of passing it through a hole drilled or punched for the purpose and hammering down one or both ends. Rivets were made from high grade iron or mild steel, except that in cases where high tensile steel parts were to be connected high tensile steel rivets were generally used.

Rivet Counter. Men who count rivets in ship construction. A person so engrossed in a particular ocean liner or vessel, that he researches the structure of his subject down to the number of rivets. In some cases, Rivet Counter's are thought, by friends or mates, to have a compulsive disorder.

Riveter, Hydraulic. Usually a large C-shaped cast steel, frame with a hydraulic ram fitted at the open end which carries the rivet set.

Riveters. Workmen who drive rivets by hammering the points into the required shape either by means of hand or power tools. Riveters usually work in gangs, a gang including one or two riveters, a holder on, a heater, and perhaps one or more passers. Riveters should be responsible for the fairness of the surfaces riveted and should see that there are no lateral bends, bumps or irregularities in the plating,: because when once riveted the structure is permanent. They should also see that the surfaces are rigidly and firmly united when they perform the operation of swaging down the points of the rivets.

Rudder. A device used in steering or maneuvering a vessel. The most common type consists of a flat slab of metal or wood, hinged at the forward end to the stern or rudder post and rounded at the after end to make a fair ending to the lines of the vessel. When made of metal it may either be built up from plates, shapes and castings, with or without wood filling or it may be a casting. The rudder is attached to a vertical shaft called the rudder stock, by which it is actuated or turned.

Rudder Area. The area of the effective rudder blade. Usually referred to as a percentage of the area of the immersed middle line or lateral plane of the ship.

Rules of the Road. Regulations for preventing collisions and for promoting safety to navigation.

Scupper Holes. Drain holes cut through the gunwale of deck stringer angle bar and adjoining shell plate to allow water to drain directly from the gutter or waterway overboard. Where from strength considerations the holes cannot be cut in angle bar plating, the usual scupper pipe is fitted, leading down through decks and the ship's side.

Scupper pipes. The pipes leading from the scupper to the fitting in the ship's side, for carrying accumulations of water from the deck overboard.

Scuppers. Drains from decks to carry off accumulations of rain water or sea water. The scuppers are placed in the gutters or waterways on open decks and in corners of enclosed decks, and connect to pipes leading overboard. The flap valve at the bottom of the scupper pipe is also often called a scupper.

Scuttle. A small opening, usually circular in shape, and generally fitted in decks to provide access as a manhole or for stowing fuel, water and small stores. A cover or lid is fitted so that the scuttle may be closed when not in use. Also applied to the operation of opening a sea valve or otherwise allowing the sea to enter a ship for the purpose of sinking her.

Shafting. Cylindrical rod or tubing used, in general, for the transmission of rotary motion from the source of power, the engine, to the propelling device, the propeller, or paddle wheel.

Sheave. A wood or metal disc having a groove around its cylindrical surface to allow a rope or chain to run over it without slipping off.

Sheer. The longitudinal curve of a vessel's rails, deck, etc., the usual reference being to the ship's side; however, in the case of a deck having a camber, its centerline may also have a sheer. The amount by which the height of the weather deck at the after or forward perpendicular exceeds that at the mid perpendicular. Mean sheer is the average of the sheers forward and aft as just defined.

Sheerstrake. The strake of shell plating that runs along the level of the main or upper decks. The sheerstrake in wood ships is the strake of outside or shell plating that runs along the sides of the main or upper decks.

Shipyard Plate. This is not a utensil, but a bronze or brass plate inscribed with the name of the shipyard where a vessel was built.

Shroud. A principal member of the standing rigging, consisting of hemp or wire ropes which extend from or near a mast head to a vessel's side or to the rim of a top to afford lateral support for the mast.

Side Plating. A term applied to the plating above the bilge in the main body of a vessel. Also to the sides of deck houses, erections, etc.

Side Scuttle. A term applied to an opening in the side of a ship provided for the discharge of garbage, etc.

Skin. This term is usually applied to the outside planking or plating forming the watertight envelope over the framework. It is also applied to the inner bottom plating where it is called the inner skin.

Skin, Inner. A term applied to the inner bottom plating. This usually extends only across the bottom, but sometimes is carried up the sides.

Skin, Outer. A term applied to the outside plating, shell or planking of a ship.

Skylight. A built up frame of metal or wood having glass lights fitted in the top and installed over a deck opening for the purpose of furnishing light and, where the top covers are hinged; ventilation to the spaces below.

Skylight Coaming. The vertical sides of a skylight frame whether of steel or wood.

Skylight Cover. The top of a skylight, having glass lights fitted in it and often hinged and operated from below. Brass rods are generally fitted over the glass for protection.

Slop Chute. A chute hung over the ship's side or built into the ship with discharge through the ship's side, for discharging garbage overboard.

Sounding. Measuring the depth of water or other liquid.

Sounding Line. The fine piano wire or wire rope used with a sounding machine.

Sounding Machine. A machine which has almost wholly superseded the antiquated and clumsy deep-sea lead, being designed to ascertain, accurately and quickly, the depth of water at rather high speeds, say up to 16 or 17 knots, in depths not exceeding 100 fathoms.

Spanner. A form of open head wrench for use with special fittings whose character is such as to preclude the use of the ordinary type of wrench.

Stability. The tendency which a vessel has to return to the upright when inclined away from that position.

Stanchions. Short columns or support for decks, handrails, etc. Stanchions are made of pipe, steel shapes or rods according to the location and purpose they serve.

Standing Rigging. Rigging that is permanently secured and is not hauled upon such as shrouds, stays, bob-stays, martingales, mast pendants, etc.

Starboard Side. That side of a vessel to the right hand when looking from the stern toward the bow.

Starboard the Helm. See Port the Helm. A term originally applied to the operation of putting the tiller over to right or starboard side causing the rudder and ship to turn to the left or port. Different countries and different branches of the marine have their own rules as to whether this order means to turn the ship to the right or left.

Stateroom. A private room or cabin for the accommodation of passengers or officers.

Stays. The ropes, whether hemp or wire, that support the lower masts, topmasts, top-gallant masts, etc., in a fore and aft direction. They extend from the heads of the masts they support to the next lower mast head of the adjacent forward mast except the lower mast stays which extend to the deck. Any rope used as a tension member, as an awning stanchion stay, a canopy frame stay, etc. A bar, pipe, or plate used as a support against racking, bending, etc.

Steerage. The least desirable portions of a vessel as to accommodations for passengers and occupied by those paying the very lowest fare.

Stem, Stem Post. The bow frame forming the apex of the triangular intersection of the forward sides of a ship. It is rigidly connected at the lower end to the keel. In wood ships the main piece of the bow frame is called the stem.

Stern Frame. A heavy casting or forging for the purpose of supporting the rudder and the propeller shaft in single screw vessels. It also serves as a frame for rigidly connecting the converging sides of the ship at the stern.

Stokehold. That portion of the ship's boiler room from which the fires are fed and cleaned.

Strake. A term applied to a continuous row or range of plates. The strakes of shell plating are usually lettered, starting with A at the bottom.

Strake, Bilge. A term applied to a strake of outside plating running in the way of the bilge.

Strake, Bottom. Any strake of plating on the bottom of a ship that lays between the garboard and bilge strakes.

Strake, Doubling. A term applied to a strake made up of two thicknesses of plates. Also to the extra range of plates fitted in conjunction with the regular strake. The sheer strake and topside plate are often doubled amidship for extra strength.

Strake, Drop. A term applied to a strake that is terminated before it reaches the bow or stern. The number of strakes dropped depends on the reduction of girth between the midship section and the ends.

Strake, Garboard. The strake of shell plating adjacent to the keel. This row of plates act in conjunction with the keel and are made heavier than the other bottom plates.

Strake, Inner. A term applied to the inner strake of an in and out system of shell plating. The strakes adjacent to the molded frame line.

Strake, Outside. A term applied to the outer strake of an in and out system of shell plating. The strakes which lap on the inner strakes and which are the thickness of the plating outside of the molded frame line.

Strake, Topside. The strake next below the upper or strength deck sheerstrake. The second range of shell plating down from the upper of strength deck.

Stringer. A term applied to a fore and aft girder running along the side of a ship and also to the outboard strake of plating on any deck. There are three sets of fore and aft girders in the framing of a ship, viz.: Longitudinals or keelsons, which are the approximately vertical strength members in the bottom; Stringers, which are the approximately horizontal strength members on the sides; and Girders, which are the approximately vertical members under the decks. The word stringer is sometimes used to apply to all three groups but it should only be used for the side girders. Also applied to the side pieces of a ladder or stair case into which the treads and risers are fastened.

Tank, Ballast. A space or compartment which may be filled with water to add weight when it is necessary to produce a change in trim or in the stability of the ship.

Tank, Peak. All classification societies require that transverse bulkheads be built near each end of a ship to prevent water from flowing into the larger compartments should the ends of the ship become damaged. The observation of this rule leaves narrow "V" shaped compartments in which no cargo is stored, but they may be filled with water to alter the longitudinal inclination of the ship.

Telegraph. An apparatus, either mechanical or electrical, for transmitting orders from a ship's bridge to the engine room, steering gear room, or elsewhere, or between fire rooms, and from engine room to fire rooms. The transmitting apparatus, operated by the sender, is termed the transmitter, and the receiving apparatus, the indicator. A gong is usually fitted in order to call attention to the movement of the indicator.

Telemotor. A device for operating the valves of the steering engine from the pilot house either by fluid pressure or by electricity. When fluid pressure is utilized, two leads of pipe are necessary so that the fluid may move aft in one pipe and forward in the other, or vice-versa. The movement is provided for by a small pump or ram actuated by the steering wheel.

Thrust Block. Thrust Stools are to be of ample size and strength in proportion to the power transmitted to the thrust bearing; they are to extend well beyond the thrust block and are to be stiffened and supported by extra intercostals, double reverse angles, etc. All shaft stools are to be of ample strength and stiffness, in proportion to the weight of shaft and height of stool.

Thrust Block Foundation. A term applied to the seating to which the thrust block is attached. As the whole push or pull exerted on the ship by the propeller is taken through the thrust block it is necessary to construct a strong foundation that will distribute the pressure to the hull of the ship without undue local strain. This foundation should be built as high up to the center line of the shaft as possible to decrease the overturning moment on the bolts holding the thrust block in place.

Tongue and Groove. A term applied to a plank one of the edges of which is cut away to form a tongue and the other recessed to form a groove. The tongue on one plank is matched with the groove on the other.

Tonnage, Gross. The entire internal cubic capacity of a vessel expressed in tons of one hundred cubic feet each.

Tonnage, Gross Registered. The gross tonnage as entered on the register or other official certificate of the tonnage of the vessel.

Tonnage, Net. The internal cubic capacity of a vessel which remains after the capacities of certain specified spaces have been deducted from the gross tonnage. These deductible spaces include principally crew's quarters, working spaces and machinery compartments.

Tonnage, Net Registered. The net tonnage as entered on the register or other official certificate of the tonnage of a vessel.

Transverse. At right angles to the ship's fore and after center line.

Trim. The longitudinal deviation of a vessel from her designed waterline at a given draft. When expressed in feet and inches it is equal to the sum of the distances that points on the waterline at the bow and stern are above or below the designed waterline at the mean draft at which the vessel is floating. The variation in a vertical direction of the fore and aft extremities of the actual position of a vessel's plane of floatation from its designed position.

Trim by Head. That condition of trim in which a vessel inclines forward so that her actual plane of flotation is not coincident with or parallel to her designed plane of flotation.

Trim by Stern. That condition of trim in which a vessel inclines aft so that her actual plane of flotation is not coincident with or parallel to her designed plane of flotation.

Trunk. A vertical or inclined shaft formed by bulkheads or casings extending one or more deck heights, around openings in the decks, through which access can be obtained, cargo stores, etc., handled or ventilation provided without distributing or interfering with the contents or arrangements of the adjoining spaces.

Trunk, Ventilating. Trunks through which air is led for supplying fans and blowers, or through which heated air is allowed to escape.

Tubes, Sounding. Small pipes leading vertically up from a tank and arranged with the lower end opening into the tank so that the liquid rises in the pipe so its height can be measured by lowering a sounding rod into the pipe.

Turbine. A machine in which the kinetic energy of the steam is transformed into direct rotary motion. A reciprocating engine produces work by the relatively slow overcoming of resistance by the pressure of the steam up to the cut off and by the hyperbolic expansion of the steam up to the release while a turbine does its work through the impulse reaction of steam or steam jets at high velocity on rotary vanes.

Turning Circle. The approximate circle described by a vessel in turning when the helm is hard over.

Under-Deck Tonnage. The enclosed volume of a vessel below the tonnage deck expressed in tons of one hundred cubic feet.

Under Way. A vessel is under way according to the navigating laws, "when she is not at anchor, made fast to the shore or aground." Generally speaking, it means that she is proceeding on a course.

Union Jack. A mall flag flown from a jack staff forward. It is set out on Sundays and when dressing ship. The design embodies that of the upper inner corner of the national ensign. In the United States the design is stars on a blue field. In Great Britain the design is composed of the crosses of St. George, St. Andrew -and St. Steven, on a blue field.

Unship. To remove anything from its accustomed or stowage place; to take apart.

Ventilating System. A system consisting of light metal pipes, blowers, special intakes, etc., for supply of fresh air to and removing foul air from the various compartments in a vessel.

Ventilation. The process of providing fresh air to the various spaces and replacing foul or heated air by fresh air.

Ventilation, Mechanical. Ventilation supplied by fans or blowers and sometimes by compressed air, the fans being operated by electric motors, steam engines or other mechanical means. The ventilation in this case is forced or induced by the fan through a pipe or pipes to one or more compartments whereas natural ventilation would require a separate pipe and cowl for each compartment.

Ventilation, Natural. Ventilation depending on the wind blowing into the cowls and down the ventilators, and also on the natural tendency of heated air to rise and escape through the pipes and trunks provided.

Ventilation, "Thermotank" System. A ventilation system in which the air is heated by passing over or around tubes through which steam or hot water is circulated. The box or tank containing the steam coils is called the Thermotank.

Warping. A term applied to the: operation of moving a vessel from one place to another about a dock or harbor by means of hawsers. The operation of changing a vessel's berth when it is not performed by tugs or its own propelling machinery.

Watches. Nautical divisions of time usually four hours each for standing watch or being on deck ready for duty. The first watch extends from 8 p. m. to mid-night, the mid watch from midnight to 4 a.m., the morning watch from 4 a.m. to 8 a.m., the forenoon watch from 8 a.m. to noon, the afternoon watch from noon to 4 p.m.; the watch from 4 p.m. to 8 p.m. is usually divided into two equal parts known as the first and second "dog watches"; division, usually one-half, of the officers and crew who together attend to the working of a vessel during the same watch. These are designated as the starboard and port watches, each of which is alternately on duty.

Waterline (Loaded). The waterline to which a vessel sinks when fully loaded.

Waterway. On wood ships the margin plank running along the edges of the decks adjacent to the inside faces of the frames. This timber is always thicker than the regular deck planking. On steel ships with planked decks the gutter formed along the sides of a deck by the waterway and stringer angle bars.

Ways. A term applied to the tracks and sliding timbers used in launching a vessel. Also applied in a general sense to the building slip or space upon which a vessel is constructed.

Ways, Ground. The stationary timbers or tracks laid upon the ground or foundation cribbing upon which the sliding timbers or ways, supporting a vessel to be launched, travel.

Ways, Launching. Two sets of long heavy timbers arranged longitudinally under the bottom of a ship with one set on each side, and sloping towards the water. Each set is composed of two separate members with the adjoining surfaces well lubricated with oil and tallow. The lower members are called the ground ways and remain stationary while the upper members are called the sliding ways and support the weight of the ship upon the removal of the shores and keel blocks and slide overboard with the ship at its launching.

Ways, Sliding. Timbers supporting a vessel to be launched which slide with the vessel along the stationary track or ground ways.

Wet Dock, Wet Slip. Wet docks are basins into which vessels are admitted at high tide through gates which when closed retain the water at a constant level, not being affected by change in tides without. A wet slip is an opening between two wharves or piers where dock trials are usually conducted and the final fitting out is done.

Wharf. A structure built on the shore of a harbor, river, canal or the like and extending out into deep water so that vessels may lie close alongside to receive or discharge cargo or passengers.

Wheelhouse. A shelter built over the steering wheel. The term is generally used relative to the house in which a hand steering wheel is located.

Windlass. A device for hoisting or hauling by means of a rope or wire wound on to a horizontal drum or barrel.

BIBLIOGRAPHY

BALLARD, Dr. R D., *The Discovery Of The Titanic*, London: Hodder & Stoughton, 1987

BEESLEY, L., *The Loss of the S.S. Titanic*, London: William Heinemann, 1912

BISSET, Sir J., *Ladies & Tramps,* Angus & Robertson Ltd, 1959

BONSALL, T E., *Titanic,* Gallery Books, 1987

BOYDE-SMITH, P., *Titanic - From Rare Historical Reports*, Southampton: Brooks Books,1992

DODGE, W., *The Loss Of The Titanic*, Connecticut: 7C's Press

DUNN, L., *Merchant Ships of the World 1910-1929*, New York: Macmillan Publishing Co, 1973

HAAS, C. and Eaton, J.P., *Destination Disaster,* Sparkford: Patrick Stephens Ltd, 1996

HAAS, C. and Eaton, J.P., *Titanic Triumph and Tragedy,* Somerset: Patrick Stephens Ltd, 1986

GARDINER, R., *Titanic-The Ship That Never Sank?,* Ian Allan Publishing 1998

GARDINER, R. and VAN DER VAT, D., *The Riddle Of The Titanic*, London: Orion Pub. , 1995

GRACIE, A., *The Truth about the Titanic, New York:* Mitchell Kennerley, 1913

HAYES, B., *Hull Down* , London: Cassell & Co., 1925

HOOD A.G., ed, *"The White Star Liners Olympic and Titanic." Souvenir No. of The Shipbuilder No. 21,* summer 1911

HUTCHINGS, D., *RMS Titanic. A Modern Legend*, Dorset: Waterfront Publications, 1993

JESSOP, V., *Titanic Survivor,* New York: Sheridan House Inc., 1997

KLUDAS, A., *Great Passenger Ships Of The World,* New York: Patrick Stephens Ltd, 1975

KUNTZ, T., *The Titanic Disaster Hearings, The Official Transcripts Of The 1912 Senate Investigation*, New York: Pocket Books, 1998

LIGHTOLLER, C.H., *Titanic and other ships,* London: Nicholson & Watson, 1935

LORD, W., *The Night Lives On - New Thoughts & Revelations about the Titanic,* London: Allen Lane, Penguin Books, 1987

LORD, W., *A Night To Remember*, London: Longmans, Green, 1956

McAULEY, R., *The Liners,* Macmillan Publishers Ltd, 1997

MILLS, S., *RMS Olympic-The Old Reliable,* Waterfront Publications, 1995

MILLS, S , *HMHS Britannic – The Last Titan*, Shipping Books Press, 1996

MOWBRAY, J. H , (edited by) , *Sinking Of The Titanic – Eyewitness Accounts.* Dover Publications, INC. 1998

MOSS, M. and HUME, J. R., *Shipbuilders to the World: 125 Years of Harland and Wolff,* Ireland: Black Staff Press, 1986

ROSTRON, A. H., *The Loss of The Titanic,* Riverside Connecticut: 7 C's Press, 1975

THAYER, J.B., *The Sinking Of The SS Titanic,* Riverside Connecticut: 7C's Press, 1974

TIBBALLS, G., *Titanic-The Extraordinary Story Of The Unsinkable Ship*, Carlton Books Ltd, 1997

WELS, S., *Titanic, Legacy Of World's Greatest Ocean Liner*, Time Life Books, 1997

The Authors would like to acknowledge these wonderful people:
Ray Lepien for allowing the reproductions from many of his pictures and newspapers in his collection,
R. Terrell Wright for allowing the use of his rare photographs,
Josha Inglis, Stewart Kelly for his interior woodwork photos,
Peter Davies-Garner for his photos,
Bernhard Funk for his dive footage, Mark Warren for his *Shipbuilder* photos,
Mark Darrah for his support and the use of his *Engineering* and *The Engineer* photos,
Simon Mills for his great reference books on the Olympic and Britannic,
Mark Chirnside for his editing on the Olympic appendix,
The Ulster Folk and Transport Museum- County Down-Ireland who provided the photographs from the Harland & Wolff archives,
Alastair Arnott of the Southampton City Archives who also assisted with photographs,
Charlie Haas and Jack Eaton for the use of photographic material from their book
Titanic, A Journey Through Time,
The Titanic Historical Society Indian Orchard Massachusetts,
The trustees of the Titanic Research and Modeling Association -
Scott Andrews, David Cotgreave, Jerry Davidson, Peter Davies-Garner, Robert Hahn, Larry Jibson, Ray Lepien, Doug May, Roy Mengot, Jonathan Smith and Sean Winterberg,

Frank & Dennis Finch and the Kyogle Maritime Museum, Robin Gardiner, R. J. Thomson-Manager Marine Crews at the Australian Maritime Authority (1997), Tom McCluskie of Harland & Wolff, Bob Read, Steve Rigby, the British Titanic Society,
Ralph White, Peter Quinn, Remco Hillen, George Behe, Brian Hawley,
Daniel Klistorner, The folks at the Bridgeview Public Library
and anyone we may have missed.

Illustrations in the end pages of this book courtesy of Robert Hahn.
The Hahn Titanic Plans can be obtained from:
www.titanic-plan.de

The Titanic Research and Modeling Association is an excellent source for technical & progressive research of the Olympic class vessels. The association also offers a professional consultation and advisory service upon request.

" The TRMA - Changing the Way the World Looks at Titanic."
www.titanic-model.com

PHOTOGRAPHIC CREDITS

Every attempt has been made to credit pictures to their proper source. Many of these rare images have been kindly contributed from private collections and others have been taken from actual period picture postcards.

B. Beveridge: 6 *left* (PC), 8 *left and right* (PC), 9 *upper left*, 11 *right*, 17, 23 *top* (PC), 35 *top*/National Archives, 37/National Archives, 48, 54 *upper left and right*, 57 (PC), 58, 59 *upper*, 66 (PC), 84 *all*, 85, 86, 87 *upper right, middle left and bottom left*, 90, 94 *upper*, 96 *left*, 97, 98, 99, 100, 101 *bottom*, 102 *top*, 104 - 107, 110, 111, 115 *top*/Cork Examiner, 116 – 119, 126/Southampton City Archives, 130, 135, 136 (PC), 137, 139, 147 *bottom* (PC), 148 *bottom*, 153, 154, 158 (PC), 164 (PC), 168

S. Hall: 51 *bottom left and right* (PC), 56, 59 *bottom*, 120 *bottom* (PC)

R. Terrell-Wright: Preface, 6 *right* (PC), 7 *left and right* (PC), 9 *bottom right* (PC), 18 *both* (PC), 50 (PC), 51 *upper*, 128

R. Lepien: 9 *upper right* (PC), 11 *left* (PC), 29/Daily sketch, 34 *bottom*/The Sphere, 35 *bottom*/The Sphere, 38, 39/The Sphere, 40/Daily Sketch, 44 *upper* (PC), 47/, 52, 54 *bottom*, 67 *right*, 68, 89/Hampshire Advertiser, 94 *bottom*, 95 *bottom*/Daily Sketch, 101 *top*, 115 *bottom*/Hampshire Advertiser, 127/Daily Sketch, 129/Daily Sketch, 134 (PC), 138 (PC), 147 *top*, 151, 155, 163

J. Hamilton: 10 *right*, 12 *right* (PC), 25, 26, 44 *bottom* (PC)

J. Inglis: 9 *bottom left*, 10 *left*, 12 *left*, 23 *bottom left and right*

P. Davies-Garner: 46 *top and bottom*, 88, 114, 145

S. Kelly: 80, 81, 82

B. Hawley: 108

Harland & Wolff: 19, 24, 49, 53 *top*, 87 *top left*, 91, 121, 122, 131, 141, 142, 148 *top*, 160, 162

B. Funk: 87 *bottom right*,

D. Klistorner: 95 *top*/Harper's Weekly, 123, 124, 146 (PC)

Eaton and Hass: 96 *right*

Private Collection: 67 *left* (PC), 53 *middle*, 67 *left*, 103, 140

R.Hahn: 149, 152, 157, 161 *bottom*

Ulster Folk and Transport Museum: 42 *top and bottom*, 45 *bottom*, 102 *bottom*, 120 *top*

Illustrations

B. Beveridge: 16, 33/Engineering, 34 *top*, 87 *middle*, 93 *top*/Engineering *and bottom*, 143, 154, 161 *top*
Harland & Wolff: 21

PC designates period picture postcard.

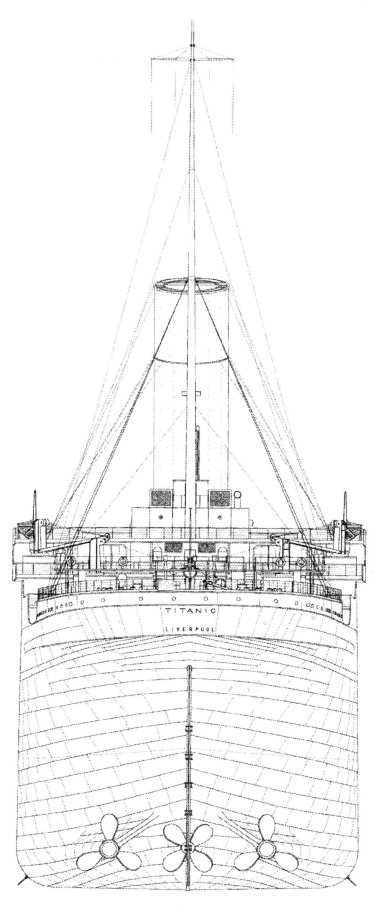

CPSIA information can be obtained at www.ICGtesting.com
Printed in the USA
LVOW09s1635150913

352534LV00003B/485/A

9 780741 419491